THE NATIONAL ACADEMIES

Advisers to the Nation on Science, Engineering, and Medicine

The **National Academy of Sciences** is a private, nonprofit, self-perpetuating society of distinguished scholars engaged in scientific and engineering research, dedicated to the furtherance of science and technology and to their use for the general welfare. Upon the authority of the charter granted to it by the Congress in 1863, the Academy has a mandate that requires it to advise the federal government on scientific and technical matters. Dr. Bruce M. Alberts is president of the National Academy of Sciences.

The **National Academy of Engineering** was established in 1964, under the charter of the National Academy of Sciences, as a parallel organization of outstanding engineers. It is autonomous in its administration and in the selection of its members, sharing with the National Academy of Sciences the responsibility for advising the federal government. The National Academy of Engineering also sponsors engineering programs aimed at meeting national needs, encourages education and research, and recognizes the superior achievements of engineers. Dr. Wm. A. Wulf is president of the National Academy of Engineering.

The **Institute of Medicine** was established in 1970 by the National Academy of Sciences to secure the services of eminent members of appropriate professions in the examination of policy matters pertaining to the health of the public. The Institute acts under the responsibility given to the National Academy of Sciences by its congressional charter to be an adviser to the federal government and, upon its own initiative, to identify issues of medical care, research, and education. Dr. Harvey V. Fineberg is president of the Institute of Medicine.

The **National Research Council** was organized by the National Academy of Sciences in 1916 to associate the broad community of science and technology with the Academy's purposes of furthering knowledge and advising the federal government. Functioning in accordance with general policies determined by the Academy, the Council has become the principal operating agency of both the National Academy of Sciences and the National Academy of Engineering in providing services to the government, the public, and the scientific and engineering communities. The Council is administered jointly by both Academies and the Institute of Medicine. Dr. Bruce M. Alberts and Dr. Wm. A. Wulf are chair and vice chair, respectively, of the National Research Council.

www.national-academies.org

COMMITTEE ON *HOW PEOPLE LEARN*: A TARGETED REPORT FOR TEACHERS

JOHN D. BRANSFORD (*Chair*), College of Education, University of Washington
SUSAN CAREY, Department of Psychology, Harvard University
KIERAN EGAN, Department of Education, Simon Fraser University, Burnaby, Canada
SUZANNE WILSON, School of Education, Michigan State University
SAMUEL S. WINEBURG, Department of Education, Stanford University

M. SUZANNE DONOVAN, *Study Director*
SUSAN R. MCCUTCHEN, *Research Associate*
ALLISON E. SHOUP, *Senior Project Assistant*
ELIZABETH B. TOWNSEND, *Senior Project Assistant*

Preface

This book has its roots in the report of the Committee on Developments in the Science of Learning, *How People Learn: Brain, Mind, Experience and School* (National Research Council, 1999, National Academy Press). That report presented an illuminating review of research in a variety of fields that has advanced understanding of human learning. The report also made an important attempt to draw from that body of knowledge implications for teaching. A follow-on study by a second committee explored what research and development would need to be done, and how it would need to be communicated, to be especially useful to teachers, principals, superintendents, and policy makers: *How People Learn: Bridging Research and Practice* (National Research Council, 1999). These two individual reports were combined to produce an expanded edition of *How People Learn* (National Research Council, 2000). We refer to this volume as *HPL*.

The next step in the work on how people learn was to provide examples of how the principles and findings on learning can be used to guide the teaching of a set of topics that commonly appear in the K-12 curriculum. The work focused on three subject areas—history, mathematics, and science—and resulted in the book *How Students Learn: History, Mathematics, and Science in the Classroom*. Each area was treated at three levels: elementary, middle, and high school.

This volume includes the subset of chapters from that book focused on history, along with the introduction and concluding chapter of the larger volume. The full set of chapters can be found on the enclosed CD. In this volume, unlike those for mathematics and science, Ashby, Lee, and Shemilt treated both elementary and middle school students in a single chapter (Chapter 3) in order to highlight the range of thinking one could expect across those years on a single topic area.

Distinguished researchers who have extensive experience in teaching or in partnering with teachers were invited to contribute the chapters. The committee shaped the goals for the volume, and commented—sometimes extensively—on the draft chapters as they were written and revised. The principles of *HPL* are embedded in each chapter, though there are differences from one chapter to the next in how explicitly they are discussed.

Taking this next step to elaborate the *HPL* principles in context poses a potential problem that we wish to address at the outset. The meaning and relevance of the principles for classroom teaching can be made clearer with specific examples. At the same time, however, many of the specifics of a particular example could be replaced with others that are also consistent with the *HPL* principles. In looking at a single example, it can be difficult to distinguish what is necessary to effective teaching from what is effective but easily replaced. With this in mind, it is critical that the teaching and learning examples in each chapter be seen as illustrative, not as blueprints for the "right" way to teach.

We can imagine, by analogy, that engineering students will better grasp the relationship between the laws of physics and the construction of effective supports for a bridge if they see some examples of well-designed bridges, accompanied by explanations for the choices of the critical design features. The challenging engineering task of crossing the entrance of the San Francisco Bay, for example, may bring the relationship between physical laws, physical constraints, and engineering solutions into clear and meaningful focus. But there are some design elements of the Golden Gate Bridge that could be replaced with others that serve the same end, and people may well differ on which among a set of good designs creates the most appealing bridge.

To say that the Golden Gate Bridge is a good example of a suspension bridge does not mean it is the only, or the best possible, design for a suspension bridge. If one has many successful suspension bridges to compare, the design features that are required for success, and those that are replaceable, become more apparent. And the requirements that are uniform across contexts, and the requirements that change with context, are more easily revealed.

The chapters in this volume highlight different approaches to addressing the same fundamental principles of learning. It would be ideal to be able to provide two or more "*HPL* compatible" approaches to teaching the same topic. However, we cannot provide that level of specific variability in this volume. We encourage readers to look at chapters in other disciplines as well in order to see more clearly the common features across chapters, and the variation in approach among the chapters.

This volume could not have come to life without the help and dedication of many people, and we are grateful to them. The financial support of our sponsors, the U.S. Department of Education and the members of the President's Circle of the National Academy of Sciences, was essential. We appreciate both their support and their patience during the unexpectedly long period required to shape and produce so extensive a volume with so many different contributors. Our thanks to C. Kent McGuire, former assistant secretary of education research and improvement for providing the initial grant for this project, and to his successor and now director of the National Institute for Education Sciences, Grover J. Whitehurst; thanks are due as well to Patricia O'Connell Ross, Jill Edwards Staton, Michael Kestner, and Linda Jones at the Department of Education for working with us throughout, and providing the time required to produce a quality product.

This report is a somewhat unusual undertaking for the National Research Council in that the committee members did not author the report chapters, but served as advisers to the chapter authors. The contributions of committee members were extraordinary. In a first meeting the committee and chapter authors worked together to plan the volume. The committee then read each draft chapter, and provided extensive, and remarkably productive, feedback to chapter authors. As drafts were revised, committee members reviewed them again, pointing out concerns and proposing potential solutions. Their generosity and their commitment to the goal of this project are noteworthy.

Alexandra Wigdor, director of the Division on Education, Labor, and Human Performance when this project was begun, provided ongoing guidance and experienced assistance with revisions. Rona Brière brought her special skills in editing the entire volume. Our thanks go to Allison E. Shoup, who was senior project assistant, supporting the project through much of its life; to Susan R. McCutchen, who prepared the manuscript for review; to Claudia Sauls and Candice Crawford, who prepared the final manuscript; and to Deborah Johnson, Sandra Smotherman, and Elizabeth B. Townsend, who willingly provided additional support when needed. Kirsten Sampson Snyder handled the report review process, and Yvonne Wise handled report production—both challenging tasks for a report of this size and complexity. We are grateful for their help.

This report has been reviewed in draft form by individuals chosen for their diverse perspectives and technical expertise, in accordance with procedures approved by the National Research Council's Report Review Committee. The purpose of this independent review is to provide candid and critical comments that will assist the institution in making its published report as sound as possible and to ensure that the report meets institutional standards for objectivity, evidence, and responsiveness to the study charge. The review comments and draft manuscript remain confidential to protect the integrity of the deliberative process. We thank the following individuals for their review of this report: Jo Boaler, Mathematics Education, School of Education, Stanford University; Miriam L. Clifford, Mathematics Department, Carroll College, Waukesha, Wisconsin; O.L. Davis, Curriculum and Instruction, The University of Texas at Austin; Patricia B. Dodge, Science Teacher, Essex Middle School, Essex Junction, Vermont; Carol T. Hines, History Teacher, Darrel C. Swope Middle School, Reno, Nevada; Janis Lariviere, UTeach—Science and Mathematics Teacher Preparation, The University of Texas at Austin; Gaea Leinhardt, Learning Research and Development Center and School of Education, University of Pittsburgh; Alan M. Lesgold, Office of the Provost, University of Pittsburgh; Marcia C. Linn, Education in Mathematics, Science, and Technology, University of California, Berkeley; Kathleen Metz, Cognition and Development, Graduate School of Education, University of California, Berkeley; Thomas Romberg, National Center for Research in Mathematics and Science Education, University of Wisconsin–Madison; and Peter Seixas, Centre for the Study of Historical Consciousness, University of British Columbia.

Although the reviewers listed above have provided many constructive comments and suggestions, they did not see the final draft of the report before its release. The review of this report was overseen by Alan M. Lesgold, University of Pittsburgh. Appointed by the National Research Council, he was responsible for making certain that an independent examination of this report was carried out in accordance with institutional procedures and that all review comments were carefully considered. Responsibility for the final content of this report rests entirely with the authors, the committee, and the institution.

John D. Bransford, *Chair*
M. Suzanne Donovan, *Study Director*

Contents

Part II: Mathematics

(on enclosed CD; not printed in this volume)

A Final Synthesis: Revisiting the Three Learning Principles

How Students Learn

HISTORY IN THE CLASSROOM

1

Introduction

M. Suzanne Donovan and John D. Bransford

More than any other species, people are designed to be flexible learners and, from infancy, are active agents in acquiring knowledge and skills. People can invent, record, accumulate, and pass on organized bodies of knowledge that help them understand, shape, exploit, and ornament their environment. Much that each human being knows about the world is acquired informally, but mastery of the accumulated knowledge of generations requires intentional learning, often accomplished in a formal educational setting.

Decades of work in the cognitive and developmental sciences has provided the foundation for an emerging science of learning. This foundation offers conceptions of learning processes and the development of competent performance that can help teachers support their students in the acquisition of knowledge that is the province of formal education. The research literature was synthesized in the National Research Council report *How People Learn: Brain, Mind, Experience, and School.*[1] In this volume, we focus on three fundamental and well-established principles of learning that are highlighted in *How People Learn* and are particularly important for teachers to understand and be able to incorporate in their teaching:

1. Students come to the classroom with preconceptions about how the world works. If their initial understanding is not engaged, they may fail to grasp the new concepts and information, or they may learn them for purposes of a test but revert to their preconceptions outside the classroom.
2. To develop competence in an area of inquiry, students must (a) have a deep foundation of factual knowledge, (b) understand facts and ideas in the context of a conceptual framework, and (c) organize knowledge in ways that facilitate retrieval and application.

3. A "metacognitive" approach to instruction can help students learn to take control of their own learning by defining learning goals and monitoring their progress in achieving them.

A FISH STORY

The images from a children's story, *Fish Is Fish*,[2] help convey the essence of the above principles. In the story, a young fish is very curious about the world outside the water. His good friend the frog, on returning from the land, tells the fish about it excitedly:

> *"I have been about the world—hopping here and there," said the frog, "and I have seen extraordinary things."*
> *"Like what?" asked the fish.*
> *"Birds," said the frog mysteriously. "Birds!" And he told the fish about the birds, who had wings, and two legs, and many, many colors. As the frog talked, his friend saw the birds fly through his mind like large feathered fish.*

The frog continues with descriptions of cows, which the fish imagines as black-and-white spotted fish with horns and udders, and humans, which the fish imagines as fish walking upright and dressed in clothing. Illustrations below from Leo Lionni's *Fish Is Fish* © 1970. Copyright renewed 1998 by Leo Lionni. Used by permission of Random House Children's Books, a division of Random House, Inc.

Principle #1: Engaging Prior Understandings

What Lionni's story captures so effectively is a fundamental insight about learning: *new understandings are constructed on a foundation of existing understandings and experiences.* With research techniques that permit the study of learning in infancy and tools that allow for observation of activity in the brain, we understand as never before how actively humans engage in learning from the earliest days of life (see Box 1-1). The understandings children carry with them into the classroom, even before the start of formal schooling, will shape significantly how they make sense of what they are

BOX 1-1 The Development of Physical Concepts in Infancy

Research studies have demonstrated that infants as young as 3 to 4 months of age develop understandings and expectations about the physical world. For example, they understand that objects need support to prevent them from falling to the ground, that stationary objects may be displaced when they come into contact with moving objects, and that objects at rest must be propelled into motion.[3]

In research by Needham and Baillargeon,[4] infants were shown a table on which a box rested. A gloved hand reached out from a window beside the table and placed another box in one of two locations: on top of the first box (the possible event), and beyond the box—creating the impression that the box was suspended in midair. In this and similar studies, infants look reliably longer at the impossible events, suggesting an awareness and a set of expectations regarding what is and is not physically possible.

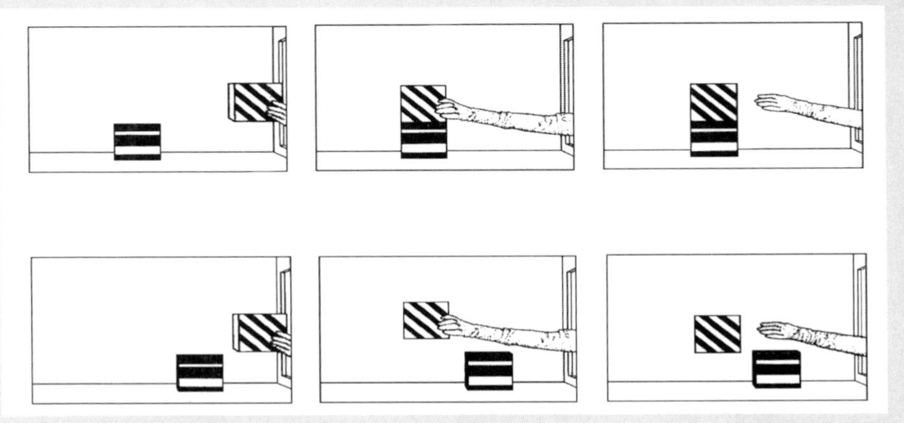

SOURCE: Needham and Baillargeon (1993). Reprinted with permission from Elsevier.

BOX 1-2 Misconceptions About Momentum

Andrea DiSessa[5] conducted a study in which he compared the performance of college physics students at a top technological university with that of elementary schoolchildren on a task involving momentum. He instructed both sets of students to play a computerized game that required them to direct a simulated object (a dynaturtle) so that it would hit a target, and to do so with minimum speed at impact. Participants were introduced to the game and given a hands-on trial that allowed them to apply a few taps with a wooden mallet to a ball on a table before they began.

DiSessa found that both groups of students failed miserably at the task. Despite their training, college physics majors—just like the elementary school children—applied the force when the object was just below the target, failing to take momentum into account. Further investigation with one college student revealed that she knew the relevant physical properties and formulas and would have performed well on a written exam. Yet in the context of the game, she fell back on her untrained conceptions of how the physical world works.

taught. Just as the fish constructed an image of a human as a modified fish, children use what they know to shape their new understandings.

While prior learning is a powerful support for further learning, it can also lead to the development of conceptions that can act as barriers to learning. For example, when told that the earth is round, children may look to reconcile this information with their experience with balls. It seems obvious that one would fall off a round object. Researchers have found that some children solve the paradox by envisioning the earth as a pancake, a "round" shape with a surface on which people could walk without falling off.[6]

How People Learn summarizes a number of studies demonstrating the active, preconception-driven learning that is evident in humans from infancy through adulthood.[7] Preconceptions developed from everyday experiences are often difficult for teachers to change because they generally work well enough in day-to-day contexts. But they can impose serious constraints on understanding formal disciplines. College physics students who do well on classroom exams on the laws of motion, for example, often revert to their untrained, erroneous models outside the classroom. When they are confronted with tasks that require putting their knowledge to use, they fail to take momentum into account, just as do elementary students who have had no physics training (see Box 1-2). If students' preconceptions are not addressed directly, they often memorize content (e.g., formulas in physics), yet still use their experience-based preconceptions to act in the world.

Principle #2: The Essential Role of Factual Knowledge and Conceptual Frameworks in Understanding

The *Fish Is Fish* story also draws attention to the kinds of knowledge, factual and conceptual, needed to support learning with understanding. The frog in the story provides information to the fish about humans, birds, and cows that is accurate and relevant, yet clearly insufficient. Feathers, legs, udders, and sport coats are surface features that distinguish each species. But if the fish (endowed now with human thinking capacity) is to understand how the land species are different from fish and different from each other, these surface features will not be of much help. Some additional, critical concepts are needed—for example, the concept of adaptation. Species that move through the medium of air rather than water have a different mobility challenge. And species that are warm-blooded, unlike those that are cold-blooded, must maintain their body temperature. It will take more explaining of course, but if the fish is to see a bird as something other than a fish with feathers and wings and a human as something other than an upright fish with clothing, then feathers and clothing must be seen as adaptations that help solve the problem of maintaining body temperature, and upright posture and wings must be seen as different solutions to the problem of mobility outside water.

Conceptual information such as a theory of adaptation represents a kind of knowledge that is unlikely to be induced from everyday experiences. It typically takes generations of inquiry to develop this sort of knowledge, and people usually need some help (e.g., interactions with "knowledgeable others") to grasp such organizing concepts.[8]

Lionni's fish, not understanding the described features of the land animals as adaptations to a terrestrial environment, leaps from the water to experience life on land for himself. Since he can neither breathe nor maneuver on land, the fish must be saved by the amphibious frog. The point is well illustrated: learning with understanding affects our ability to apply what is learned (see Box 1-3).

This concept of learning with understanding has two parts: (1) factual knowledge (e.g., about characteristics of different species) must be placed in a conceptual framework (about adaptation) to be well understood; and (2) concepts are given meaning by multiple representations that are rich in factual detail. Competent performance is built on neither factual nor conceptual understanding alone; the concepts take on meaning in the knowledge-rich contexts in which they are applied. In the context of Lionni's story, the general concept of adaptation can be clarified when placed in the context of the specific features of humans, cows, and birds that make the abstract concept of adaptation meaningful.

BOX 1-3 Learning with Understanding Supports Knowledge Use in New Situations

In one of the most famous early studies comparing the effects of "learning a procedure" with "learning with understanding," two groups of children practiced throwing darts at a target underwater.[9] One group received an explanation of refraction of light, which causes the apparent location of the target to be deceptive. The other group only practiced dart throwing, without the explanation. Both groups did equally well on the practice task, which involved a target 12 inches under water. But the group that had been instructed about the abstract principle did much better when they had to transfer to a situation in which the target was under only 4 inches of water. Because they understood what they were doing, the group that had received instruction about the refraction of light could adjust their behavior to the new task.

This essential link between the factual knowledge base and a conceptual framework can help illuminate a persistent debate in education: whether we need to emphasize "big ideas" more and facts less, or are producing graduates with a factual knowledge base that is unacceptably thin. While these concerns appear to be at odds, knowledge of facts and knowledge of important organizing ideas are mutually supportive. Studies of experts and novices—in chess, engineering, and many other domains—demonstrate that experts know considerably more relevant detail than novices in tasks within their domain and have better memory for these details (see Box 1-4). But the reason they remember more is that what novices see as separate pieces of information, experts see as organized sets of ideas.

Engineering experts, for example, can look briefly at a complex mass of circuitry and recognize it as an amplifier, and so can reproduce many of its circuits from memory using that one idea. Novices see each circuit separately, and thus remember far fewer in total. Important concepts, such as that of an amplifier, structure both what experts notice and what they are able to store in memory. Using concepts to organize information stored in memory allows for much more effective retrieval and application. Thus, the issue is not whether to emphasize facts or "big ideas" (conceptual knowledge); both are needed. Memory of factual knowledge is enhanced by conceptual knowledge, and conceptual knowledge is clarified as it is used to help organize constellations of important details. Teaching for understanding, then, requires that the core concepts such as adaptation that organize the knowledge of experts also organize instruction. This does not mean that that factual knowledge now typically taught, such as the characteristics of fish, birds, and mammals, must be replaced. Rather, that factual information is given new meaning and a new organization in memory because those features are seen as adaptive characteristics.

BOX 1-4 Experts Remember Considerably More Relevant Detail Than Novices in Tasks Within Their Domain

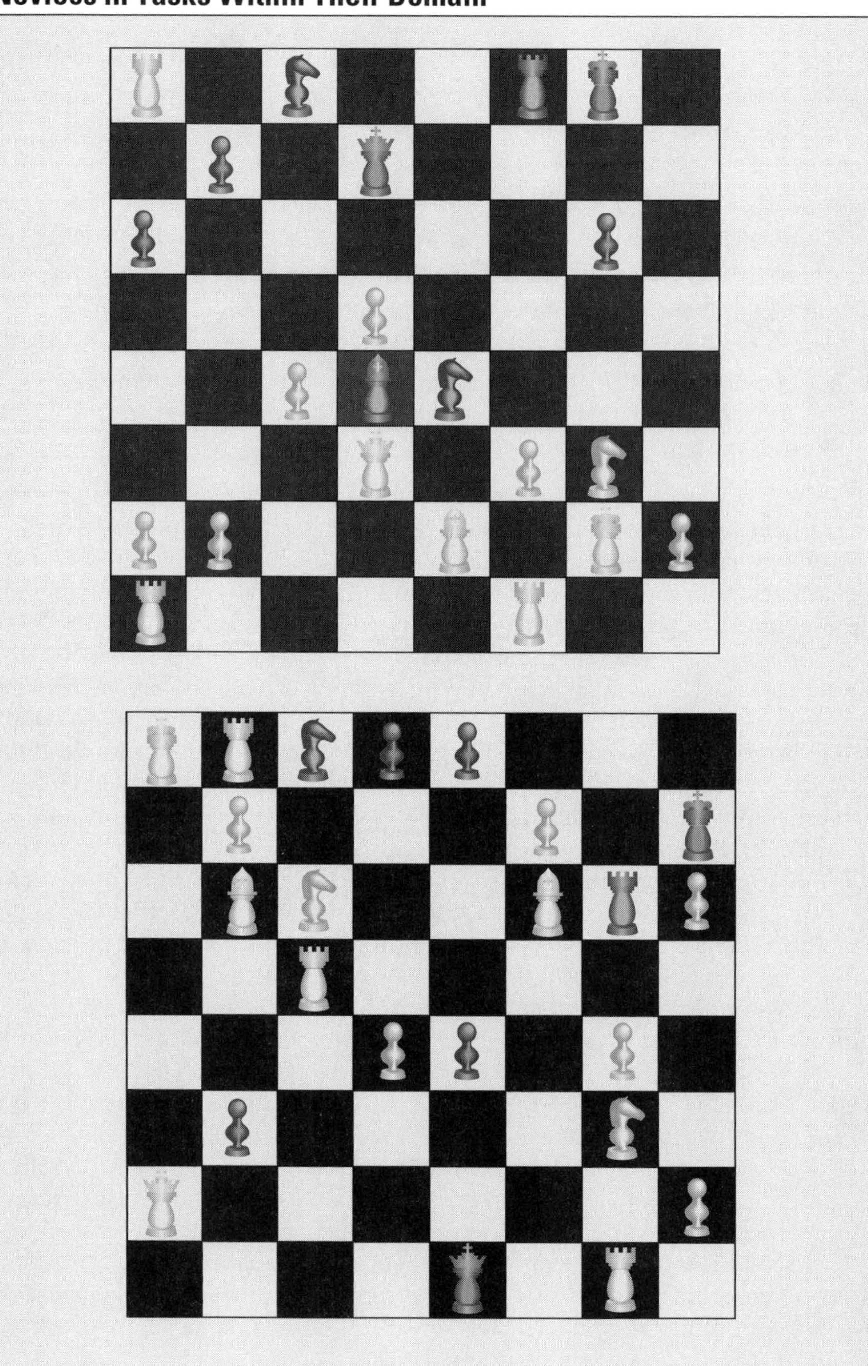

In one study, a chess master, a Class A player (good but not a master), and a novice were given 5 seconds to view a chess board position from the middle of a chess game (see below).

After 5 seconds the board was covered, and each participant attempted to reconstruct the board position on another board. This procedure was repeated for multiple trials until everyone received a perfect score. On the first trial, the master player correctly placed many more pieces than the Class A player, who in turn placed more than the novice: 16, 8, and 4, respectively. (See data graphed below.)

However, these results occurred only when the chess pieces were arranged in configurations that conformed to meaningful games of chess. When chess pieces were randomized and presented for 5 seconds, the recall of the chess master and Class A player was the same as that of the novice—they all placed 2 to 3 positions correctly. The apparent difference in memory capacity is due to a difference in pattern recognition. What the expert can remember as a single meaningful pattern, novices must remember as separate, unrelated items.

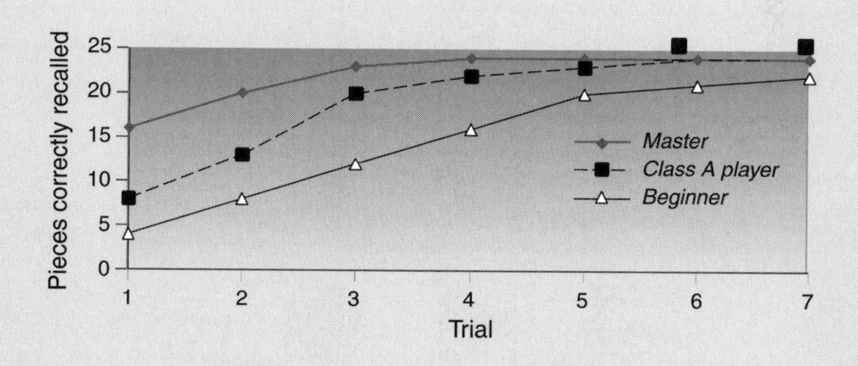

SOURCE: Chase and Simon (1973). Reprinted with permission from Elsevier.

Principle #3: The Importance of Self-Monitoring

Hero though he is for saving the fish's life, the frog in Lionni's story gets poor marks as a teacher. But the burden of learning does not fall on the teacher alone. Even the best instructional efforts can be successful only if the student can make use of the opportunity to learn. Helping students become effective learners is at the heart of the third key principle: a "metacognitive" or self-monitoring approach can help students develop the ability to take control of their own learning, consciously define learning goals, and monitor their progress in achieving them. Some teachers introduce the idea of metacognition to their students by saying, "You are the owners and operators of your own brain, but it came without an instruction book. We need to learn how we learn."

"Meta" is a prefix that can mean after, along with, or beyond. In the psychological literature, "metacognition" is used to refer to people's knowledge about themselves as information processors. This includes knowledge about what we need to do in order to learn and remember information (e.g., most adults know that they need to rehearse an unfamiliar phone number to keep it active in short-term memory while they walk across the room to dial the phone). And it includes the ability to monitor our current understanding to make sure we understand (see Box 1-5). Other examples include monitoring the degree to which we have been helpful to a group working on a project.[10]

BOX 1-5 Metacognitive Monitoring: An Example

Read the following passage from a literary critic, and pay attention to the strategies you use to comprehend:

> If a serious literary critic were to write a favorable, full-length review of How Could I Tell Mother She Frightened My Boyfriends Away, Grace Plumbuster's new story, his startled readers would assume that he had gone mad, or that Grace Plumbuster was his editor's wife.

Most good readers have to back up several times in order to grasp the meaning of this passage. In contrast, poor readers tend to simply read it all the way through without pausing and asking if the passage makes sense. Needless to say, when asked to paraphrase the passage they fall short.

SOURCE: Whimbey and Whimbey (1975, p. 42).

In Lionni's story, the fish accepted the information about life on land rather passively. Had he been monitoring his understanding and actively comparing it with what he already knew, he might have noted that putting on a hat and jacket would be rather uncomfortable for a fish and would slow his swimming in the worst way. Had he been more engaged in figuring out what the frog meant, he might have asked why humans would make themselves uncomfortable and compromise their mobility. A good answer to his questions might have set the stage for learning about differences between humans and fish, and ultimately about the notion of adaptation. The concept of metacognition includes an awareness of the need to ask how new knowledge relates to or challenges what one already knows—questions that stimulate additional inquiry that helps guide further learning.[11]

The early work on metacognition was conducted with young children in laboratory contexts.[12] In studies of "metamemory," for example, young children might be shown a series of pictures (e.g., drum, tree, cup) and asked to remember them after 15 seconds of delay (with the pictures no longer visible). Adults who receive this task spontaneously rehearse during the 15-second interval. Many of the children did not. When they were explicitly told to rehearse, they would do so, and their memory was very good. But when the children took part in subsequent trials and were not reminded to rehearse, many failed to rehearse even though they were highly motivated to perform well in the memory test. These findings suggest that the children had not made the "metamemory" connection between their rehearsal strategies and their short-term memory abilities.[13]

Over time, research on metacognition (of which metamemory is considered a subset) moved from laboratory settings to the classroom. One of the most striking applications of a metacognitive approach to instruction was pioneered by Palincsar and Brown in the context of "reciprocal teaching."[14] Middle school students worked in groups (guided by a teacher) to help one another learn to read with understanding. A key to achieving this goal involves the ability to monitor one's ongoing comprehension and to initiate strategies such as rereading or asking questions when one's comprehension falters. (Box 1-5 illustrates this point.) When implemented appropriately, reciprocal teaching has been shown to have strong effects on improving students' abilities to read with understanding in order to learn.

Appropriate kinds of self-monitoring and reflection have been demonstrated to support learning with understanding in a variety of areas. In one study,[15] for example, students who were directed to engage in self-explanation as they solved mathematics problems developed deeper conceptual understanding than did students who solved those same problems but did not engage in self-explanation. This was true even though the common time limitation on both groups meant that the self-explaining students solved fewer problems in total.

Helping students become more metacognitive about their own thinking and learning is closely tied to teaching practices that emphasize self-assessment. The early work of Thorndike[16] demonstrated that feedback is important for learning. However, there is a difference between responding to feedback that someone else provides and actively seeking feedback in order to assess one's current levels of thinking and understanding. Providing support for self-assessment is an important component of effective teaching. This can include giving students opportunities to test their ideas by building things and seeing whether they work, performing experiments that seek to falsify hypotheses, and so forth. Support for self-assessment is also provided by opportunities for discussion where teachers and students can express different views and explore which ones appear to make the most sense. Such questioning models the kind of dialogue that effective learners internalize. Helping students explicitly understand that a major purpose of these activities is to support metacognitive learning is an important component of successful teaching strategies.[17]

Supporting students to become aware of and engaged in their own learning will serve them well in all learning endeavors. To be optimally effective, however, some metacognitive strategies need to be taught in the context of individual subject areas. For example, guiding one's learning in a particular subject area requires awareness of the disciplinary standards for knowing. To illustrate, asking the question "What is the evidence for this claim?" is relevant whether one is studying history, science, or mathematics. However, what counts as evidence often differs. In mathematics, for example, formal proof is very important. In science, formal proofs are used when possible, but empirical observations and experimental data also play a major role. In history, multiple sources of evidence are sought and attention to the perspective from which an author writes and to the purpose of the writing is particularly important. Overall, knowledge of the discipline one is studying affects people's abilities to monitor their own understanding and evaluate others' claims effectively.

LEARNING ENVIRONMENTS AND THE DESIGN OF INSTRUCTION

The key principles of learning discussed above can be organized into a framework for thinking about teaching, learning, and the design of classroom and school environments. In *How People Learn*, four design characteristics are described that can be used as lenses to evaluate the effectiveness of teaching and learning environments. These lenses are not themselves research findings; rather, they are implications drawn from the research base:

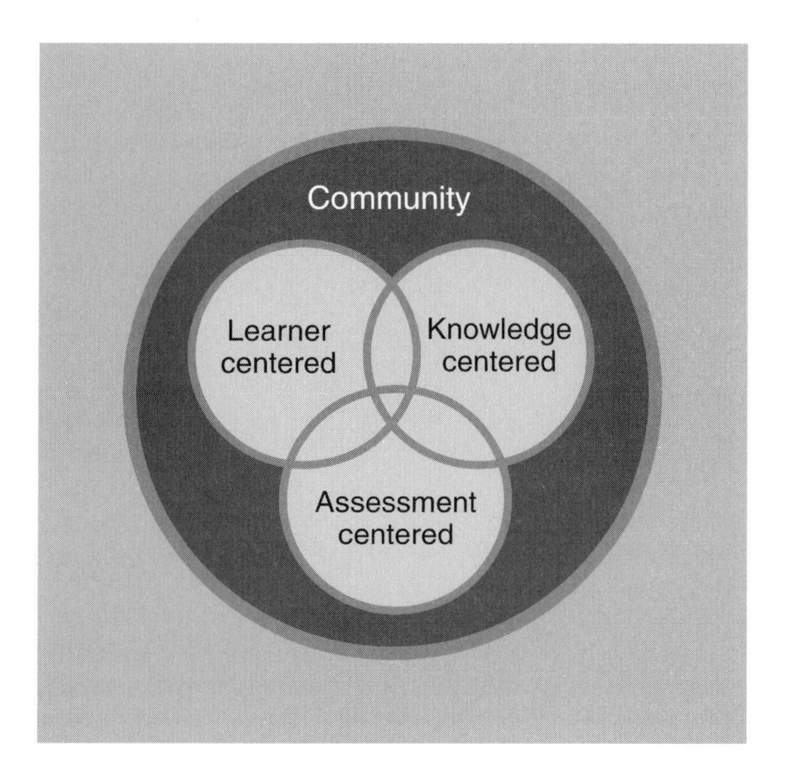

FIGURE 1-1 Perspectives on learning environments.

- The *learner-centered lens* encourages attention to preconceptions, and begins instruction with what students think and know.
- The *knowledge-centered lens* focuses on what is to be taught, why it is taught, and what mastery looks like.
- The *assessment-centered lens* emphasizes the need to provide frequent opportunities to make students' thinking and learning visible as a guide for both the teacher and the student in learning and instruction.
- The *community-centered lens* encourages a culture of questioning, respect, and risk taking.

These aspects of the classroom environment are illustrated in Figure 1-1 and are discussed below.

Learner-Centered Classroom Environments

Instruction must begin with close attention to students' ideas, knowledge, skills, and attitudes, which provide the foundation on which new learning builds. Sometimes, as in the case of Lionni's fish, learners' existing ideas lead to misconceptions. More important, however, those existing conceptions can also provide a path to new understandings. Lionni's fish mistakenly projects the model of a fish onto humans, birds, and cows. But the fish does know a lot about being a fish, and that experience can provide a starting point for understanding adaptation. How do the scales and fins of a fish help it survive? How would clothing and feathers affect a fish? The fish's existing knowledge and experience provide a route to understanding adaptation in other species. Similarly, the ideas and experiences of students provide a route to new understandings both about and beyond their experience.

Sometimes the experiences relevant to teaching would appear to be similar for all students: the ways in which forces act on a falling ball or feather, for example. But students in any classroom are likely to differ in how much they have been encouraged to observe, think about, or talk about a falling ball or feather. Differences may be larger still when the subject is a social rather than a natural phenomenon because the experiences themselves, as well as norms regarding reflection, expression, and interaction, differ for children from different families, communities, and cultures. Finally, students' expectations regarding their own performances, including what it means to be intelligent, can differ in ways that affect their persistence in and engagement with learning.

Being learner-centered, then, involves paying attention to students' backgrounds and cultural values, as well as to their abilities. To build effectively on what learners bring to the classroom, teachers must pay close attention to individual students' starting points and to their progress on learning tasks. They must present students with "just-manageable difficulties"—challenging enough to maintain engagement and yet not so challenging as to lead to discouragement. They must find the strengths that will help students connect with the information being taught. Unless these connections are made explicitly, they often remain inert and so do not support subsequent learning.

Knowledge-Centered Classroom Environments

While the learner-centered aspects of the classroom environment focus on the student as the starting point, the knowledge-centered aspects focus on what is taught (subject matter), why it is taught (understanding), how the knowledge should be organized to support the development of expertise (curriculum), and what competence or mastery looks like (learning goals). Several important questions arise when one adopts the knowledge-centered lens:

- What is it important for students to know and be able to do?
- What are the core concepts that organize our understanding of this subject matter, and what concrete cases and detailed knowledge will allow students to master those concepts effectively?
- [The knowledge-centered lens overlaps with the assessment-centered lens (discussed below) when we ask], How will we know when students achieve mastery?[18] This question overlaps the knowledge-centered and assessment-centered lenses.

An important point that emerges from the expert–novice literature is the need to emphasize *connected* knowledge that is organized around the foundational ideas of a discipline. Research on expertise shows that it is the organization of knowledge that underlies experts' abilities to understand and solve problems.[19] Bruner, one of the founding fathers of the new science of learning, has long argued the importance of this insight to education:[20]

> The curriculum of a subject should be determined by the most fundamental understanding that can be achieved of the underlying principles that give structure to a subject. Teaching specific topics or skills without making clear their context in the broader fundamental structure of a field of knowledge is uneconomical. . . . An understanding of fundamental principles and ideas appears to be the main road to adequate transfer of training. To understand something as a specific instance of a more general case—which is what understanding a more fundamental structure means—is to have learned not only a specific thing but also a model for understanding other things like it that one may encounter.

Knowledge-centered and learner-centered environments intersect when educators take seriously the idea that students must be supported to develop expertise over time; it is not sufficient to simply provide them with expert models and expect them to learn. For example, intentionally organizing subject matter to allow students to follow a path of "progressive differentiation" (e.g., from qualitative understanding to more precise quantitative understanding of a particular phenomenon) involves a simultaneous focus on the structure of the knowledge to be mastered and the learning process of students.[21]

In a comparative study of the teaching of mathematics in China and the United States, Ma sought to understand why Chinese students outperform students from the United States in elementary mathematics, even though teachers in China often have less formal education. What she documents is that Chinese teachers are far more likely to identify core mathematical concepts (such as decomposing a number in subtraction with regrouping), to plan instruction to support mastery of the skills and knowledge required for conceptual understanding, and to use those concepts to develop clear connections across topics (see Box 1-6).

If identifying a set of "enduring connected ideas" is critical to effective educational design, it is a task not just for teachers, but also for the developers of curricula, text books, and other instructional materials; universities and other teacher preparation institutions; and the public and private groups involved in developing subject matter standards for students and their teachers. There is some good work already in place, but much more needs to be done. Indeed, an American Association for the Advancement of Science review of middle school and high school science textbooks found that although a great deal of detailed and sophisticated material was presented, very little attention was given to the concepts that support an understanding of the discipline.[22]

The three history chapters in this volume describe core ideas in teaching about exploration and discovery that support conceptual understanding and that connect that particular topic to the larger discipline: the concepts of historical evidence and perspective in history. Because textbooks sometimes focus primarily on facts and details and neglect organizing principles, creating a knowledge-centered classroom will often require that a teacher go beyond the textbook to help students see a structure to the knowledge, mainly by introducing them to essential concepts. These chapters provide examples of how this might be done.

Assessment-Centered Classroom Environments

Formative assessments—ongoing assessments designed to make students' thinking visible to both teachers and students—are essential. Assessments are a central feature of both a learner-centered and a knowledge-centered classroom. They permit the teacher to grasp students' preconceptions, which is critical to working with and building on those notions. Once the knowledge to be learned is well defined, assessment is required to monitor student progress (in mastering concepts as well as factual information), to understand where students are in the developmental path from informal to formal thinking, and to design instruction that is responsive to student progress.

An important feature of the assessment-centered classroom is assessment that supports learning by providing students with opportunities to revise and improve their thinking.[23] Such assessments help students see their own progress over time and point to problems that need to be addressed in instruction. They may be quite informal. A physics teacher, for example, reports showing students who are about to study structure a video clip of a bridge collapsing. He asks his students why they think the bridge collapsed. In giving their answers, the students reveal their preconceptions about structure. Differences in their answers provide puzzles that engage the students in self-questioning. As the students study structure, they can mark their changing understanding against their initial beliefs. Assessment in this sense provides a starting point for additional instruction rather than a summative ending. Formative assessments are often referred to as "classroom-based assessments" because, as compared with standardized assessments, they are most likely to occur in the context of the classrooms. However, many classroom-based assessments are summative rather than formative (they are used to provide grades at the end of a unit with no opportunities to revise). In addition, one can use standardized assessments in a formative manner (e.g., to help teachers identify areas where students need special help).

Ultimately, students need to develop metacognitive abilities—the habits of mind necessary to assess their own progress—rather than relying solely on external indicators. A number of studies show that achievement improves when students are encouraged to assess their own contributions and work.[24] It is also important to help students assess the kinds of strategies they are using to learn and solve problems. For example, in quantitative courses such as physics, many students simply focus on formulas and fail to think first about the problem to be solved and its relation to key ideas in the discipline (e.g., Newton's second law). When students are helped to do the latter, their performance on new problems greatly improves.[25]

The classroom interactions described in the following chapters provide many examples of formative assessment in action, though these interactions are often not referred to as assessments. Early activities or problems given to students are designed to make student thinking public and, therefore, observable by teachers. Work in groups and class discussions provide students with the opportunity to ask each other questions and revise their own thinking. In some cases, the formative assessments are formal, but even when informal the teaching described in the chapters involves frequent opportunities for both teachers and students to assess understanding and its progress over time.

Community-Centered Classroom Environments

A community-centered approach requires the development of norms for the classroom and school, as well as connections to the outside world, that support core learning values. Learning is influenced in fundamental ways by the context in which it takes place. Every community, including classrooms and schools, operates with a set of norms, a culture—explicit or implicit—that influences interactions among individuals. This culture, in turn,

BOX 1-6 Organizing Knowledge Around Core Concepts: Subtraction with Regrouping[26]

A study by Ma[27] compares the knowledge of elementary mathematics of teachers in the United States and in China. She gives the teachers the following scenario (p. 1):

> ***Look at these questions (52 – 25; 91 – 79 etc.). How would you approach these problems if you were teaching second grade? What would you say pupils would need to understand or be able to do before they could start learning subtraction with regrouping?***

The responses of teachers were wide-ranging, reflecting very different levels of understanding of the core mathematical concepts. Some teachers focused on the need for students to learn the *procedure* for subtraction with regrouping (p. 2):

> ***Whereas there is a number like 21 – 9, they would need to know that you cannot subtract 9 from 1, then in turn you have to borrow a 10 from the tens space, and when you borrow that 1, it equals 10, you cross out the 2 that you had, you turn it into a 10, you now have 11 – 9, you do that subtraction problem then you have the 1 left and you bring it down.***

Some teachers in both the United States and China saw the knowledge to be mastered as procedural, though the proportion who held this view was considerably higher in the United States. Many teachers in both countries believed students needed a conceptual understanding, but within this group there were considerable differences. Some teachers wanted children to think through what they were doing, while others wanted them to understand core mathematical concepts. The difference can be seen in the two explanations below.

> ***They have to understand what the number 64 means. . . . I would show that the number 64, and the number 5 tens and 14 ones, equal the 64. I would try to draw the comparison between that because when you are doing regrouping it is not so much knowing the facts, it is the regrouping part that has to be understood. The regrouping right from the beginning.***

This explanation is more conceptual than the first and helps students think more deeply about the subtraction problem. But it does not make clear to students the more fundamental concept of the place value system that allows the subtraction problems to be connected to other areas of mathematics. In the place value system, numbers are "composed" of tens. Students already have been taught to compose tens as 10 ones, and hundreds as 10 tens. A Chinese teacher explains as follows (p. 11):

> ***What is the rate for composing a higher value unit? The answer is simple: 10. Ask students how many ones there are in a 10, or ask them what the rate for composing a higher value unit is, their answers will be the same: 10. However, the effect of the two questions on their learning is not the***

same. When you remind students that 1 ten equals 10 ones, you tell them the fact that is used in the procedure. And, this somehow confines them to the fact. When you require them to think about the rate for composing a higher value unit, you lead them to a theory that explains the fact as well as the procedure. Such an understanding is more powerful than a specific fact. It can be applied to more situations. Once they realize that the rate of composing a higher value unit, 10 is the reason why we decompose a ten into 10 ones, they will apply it to other situations. You don't need to remind them again that 1 hundred equals 10 tens when in the future they learn subtraction with three-digit numbers. They will be able to figure it out on their own.

Emphasizing core concepts does not imply less of an emphasis on mastery of procedures or algorithms. Rather, it suggests that procedural knowledge and skills be *organized around core concepts.* Ma describes those Chinese teachers who emphasize core concepts as seeing the knowledge in "packages" in which the concepts and skills are related. While the packages differed somewhat from teacher to teacher, the knowledge "pieces" to be included were the same. She illustrates a knowledge package for subtraction with regrouping, which is reproduced below (p. 19).

The two shaded elements in the knowledge package are considered critical. "Addition and subtraction within 20" is seen as the ability that anchors more complex problem solving with larger numbers. That ability is viewed as both conceptual and procedural. "Composing and decomposing a higher value unit" is the core concept that ties this set of problems to the mathematics students have done in the past and to all other areas of mathematics they will learn in the future.

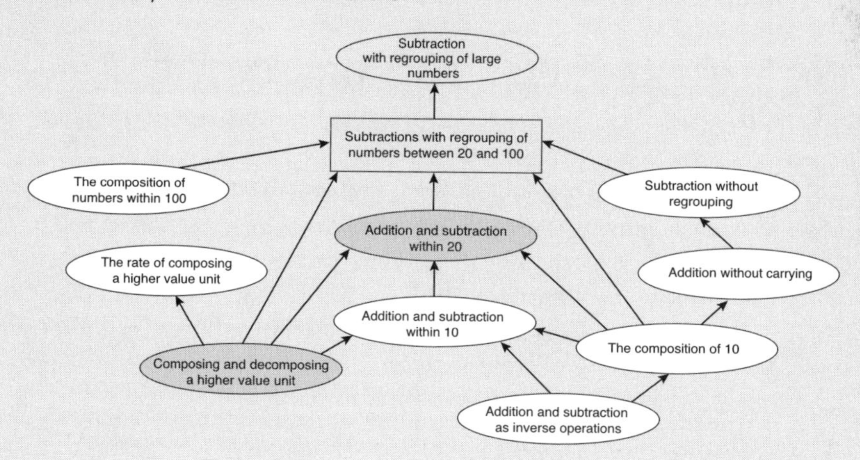

SOURCE: Ma (1999). Illustration reprinted with permission of Lawrence Erlbaum Associates.

mediates learning. The principles of *How People Learn* have important implications for classroom culture. Consider the finding that new learning builds on existing conceptions, for example. If classroom norms encourage and reward students only for being "right," we would expect students to hesitate when asked to reveal their unschooled thinking. And yet revealing preconceptions and changing ideas in the course of instruction is a critical component of effective learning and responsive teaching. A focus on student thinking requires classroom norms that encourage the expression of ideas (tentative and certain, partially and fully formed), as well as risk taking. It requires that mistakes be viewed not as revelations of inadequacy, but as helpful contributions in the search for understanding.[28]

Similarly, effective approaches to teaching metacognitive strategies rely on initial teacher modeling of the monitoring process, with a gradual shift to students. Through asking questions of other students, skills at monitoring understanding are honed, and through answering the questions of fellow students, understanding of what one has communicated effectively is strengthened. To those ends, classroom norms that encourage questioning and allow students to try the role of the questioner (sometimes reserved for teachers) are important.

While the chapters in this volume make few direct references to learning communities, they are filled with descriptions of interactions revealing classroom cultures that support learning with understanding. In these classrooms, students are encouraged to question; there is much discussion among students who work to solve problems in groups. Teachers ask many probing questions, and incorrect or naïve answers to questions are explored with interest, as are different strategies for analyzing a problem and reaching a solution.

PUTTING THE PRINCIPLES TO WORK IN THE CLASSROOM

Although the key findings from the research literature reviewed above have clear implications for practice, they are not at a level of specificity that would allow them to be immediately useful to teachers. While teachers may fully grasp the importance of working with students' prior conceptions, they need to know the typical conceptions of students with respect to the topic about to be taught. For example, it may help history teachers to know that students harbor misconceptions that can be problematic, but those teachers will be in a much better position to teach a unit on exploration and discovery if they know specifically what misconceptions students typically exhibit and how these typically change with age.

Moreover, while teachers may be fully convinced that knowledge should be organized around important concepts, the concepts that help organize their particular topic may not be at all clear. History teachers may know that they are to teach certain eras, for example, but they often have little support in identifying core concepts that will allow students to understand the era more deeply than would be required to reproduce a set of facts. To make this observation is in no way to fault teachers. Indeed, as the group involved in this project engaged in the discussion, drafting, and review of various chapters of this volume, it became clear that the relevant core concepts in specific areas are not always obvious, transparent, or uncontested.

Finally, approaches to supporting metacognition can be quite difficult to carry out in classroom contexts. Some approaches to instruction reduce metacognition to its simplest form, such as making note of the subtitles in a text and what they signal about what is to come, or rereading for meaning. The more challenging tasks of metacognition are difficult to reduce to an instructional recipe: to help students develop the habits of mind to reflect spontaneously on their own thinking and problem solving, to encourage them to activate relevant background knowledge and monitor their understanding, and to support them in trying the lens through which those in a particular discipline view the world. The teacher–student interactions described in the chapters of this volume and the discipline-specific examples of supporting students in monitoring their thinking give texture to the instructional challenge that a list of metacognitive strategies could not.

INTENT AND ORGANIZATION OF THIS VOLUME

In the preface, we note that this volume is intended to take the work of *How People Learn* a next step in specificity: to provide examples of how its principles and findings might be incorporated in the teaching of a set of topics that frequently appear in the K–12 curriculum. The goal is to provide for teachers what we have argued above is critical to effective learning—the application of concepts (about learning) in enough different, concrete contexts to give them deeper meaning.

To this end, we invited contributions from researchers with extensive experience in teaching or partnering with teachers, whose work incorporates the ideas highlighted in *How People Learn.* The chapter authors were given leeway in the extent to which the three learning principles and the four classroom characteristics described above were treated explicitly or implicitly. The authors chose to emphasize the three learning principles explicitly as they described their lessons and findings. The four design characteristics of the *How People Learn* framework (Figure 1-2) are implicitly represented in the activities sketched in each of the chapters but often not discussed explicitly. Interested readers can map these discussions to the *How People Learn* framework if they desire.

While we began with a common description of our goal, we had no common model from which to work. One can point to excellent research papers on principles of learning, but the chapters in this volume are far more focused on teaching a particular topic. There are also examples of excellent curricula, but the goal of these chapters is to give far more attention to the principles of learning and their incorporation into teaching than is typical of curriculum materials. Thus the authors were charting new territory as they undertook this task, and each found a somewhat different path.

History is treated in three chapters. The introductory Chapter 2 treats the principles of learning as they apply to the discipline of history in impressive depth. Elementary and middle school history are treated together at length in Chapter 3, a decision that permits the authors to demonstrate progression in the sophistication with which the same concept can be discussed at different grade levels. Chapter 4 on high school history then follows, also focused on the treatment of particular concepts that fall under the general topic of exploration and discovery. Because there is no agreed-upon sequence of topics in history during the K–12 years, using a single broad topic allows for a clearer focus on the nature of the investigations in which students might engage at different grade levels.

The major focus of the volume is student learning. It is clear that successful and sustainable changes in educational practice also require learning by others, including teachers, principals, superintendents, parents, and community members. For the present volume, however, student learning is the focus, and issues of adult learning are left for others to take up.

The willingness of the chapter authors to accept this task represents an outstanding contribution to the field. First, all the authors devoted considerable time to this effort—more than any of them had anticipated initially. Second, they did so knowing that some readers will disagree with virtually every teaching decision discussed in these chapters. But by making their thinking visible and inviting discussion, they are helping the field progress as a whole. The examples discussed in this volume are not offered as "the" way to teach, but as approaches to instruction that in some important respects are designed to incorporate the principles of learning highlighted in *How People Learn* and that can serve as valuable examples for further discussion.

In 1960, Nobel laureate Richard Feynman, who was well known as an extraordinary teacher, delivered a series of lectures in introductory physics that were recorded and preserved. Feynman's focus was on the fundamental principles of physics, not the fundamental principles of learning. But his lessons apply nonetheless. He emphasized how little the fundamental principles of physics "as we now understand them" tell us about the complexity of the world despite the enormous importance of the insights they offer.

Feynman offered an effective analogy for the relationship between understanding general principles identified through scientific efforts and understanding the far more complex set of behaviors for which those principles provide only a broad set of constraints:[29]

> We can imagine that this complicated array of moving things which constitutes "the world" is something like a great chess game being played by the gods, and we are observers of the game. We do not know what the rules of the game are; all we are allowed to do is to *watch* the playing. Of course, if we watch long enough, we may eventually catch on to a few of the rules. *The rules of the game* are what we mean by *fundamental physics*. Even if we knew every rule, however, we might not be able to understand why a particular move is made in the game, merely because it is too complicated and our minds are limited. If you play chess you must know that it is easy to learn all the rules, and yet it is often very hard to select the best move or to understand why a player moves as he does. . . . Aside from not knowing all of the rules, what we really can explain in terms of those rules is very limited, because almost all situations are so enormously complicated that we cannot follow the plays of the game using the rules, much less tell what is going to happen next. (p. 24)

The individual chapters in this volume might be viewed as presentations of the strategies taken by individuals (or teams) who understand the rules of the teaching and learning "game" *as we now understand them*. Feynman's metaphor is helpful in two respects. First, what each chapter offers goes well beyond the science of learning and relies on creativity in strategy development. And yet what we know from research thus far is critical in defining the constraints on strategy development. Second, what we expect to learn from a well-played game (in this case, what we expect to learn from well-conceptualized instruction) is not how to reproduce it. Rather, we look for insights about playing/teaching well that can be brought to one's own game. Even if we could replicate every move, this would be of little help. In an actual game, the best move must be identified in response to another party's move. In just such a fashion, a teacher's "game" must respond to the rather unpredictable "moves" of the students in the classroom whose learning is the target.

This, then, is not a "how to" book, but a discussion of strategies that incorporate the rules of the game as we currently understand them. The science of learning is a young, emerging one. We expect our understanding to evolve as we design new learning opportunities and observe the outcomes, as we study learning among children in different contexts and from different backgrounds, and as emerging research techniques and opportunities provide new insights. These chapters, then, might best be viewed as part of a conversation begun some years ago with the first *How People Learn* volume. By clarifying ideas through a set of rich examples, we hope to encourage the continuation of a productive dialogue well into the future.

NOTES

1. National Research Council, 2000.
2. Lionni, 1970.
3. National Research Council, 2000, p. 84.
4. Needham and Baillargeon, 1993.
5. diSessa, 1982.
6. Vosniadou and Brewer, 1989.
7. Carey and Gelman, 1991; Driver et al., 1994.
8. Hanson, 1970.
9. Judd, 1908; see a conceptual replication by Hendrickson and Schroeder, 1941.
10. White and Fredrickson, 1998.
11. Bransford and Schwartz, 1999.
12. Brown, 1975; Flavell, 1973.
13. Keeney et al., 1967.
14. Palincsar and Brown, 1984.
15. Aleven and Koedinger, 2002.
16. Thorndike, 1913.
17. Brown et al., 1983.
18. Wood and Sellers, 1997.
19. National Research Council, 2000, Chapter 2.
20. Bruner, 1960, pp. 6, 25, 31.
21. National Research Council, 2000.
22. American Association for the Advancement of Science Project 2061 Website. http://www.project2061.org/curriculum.html.
23. Barron et al., 1998; Black and William, 1989; Hunt and Minstrell, 1994; Vye et al., 1998.
24. Lin and Lehman, 1999; National Research Council, 2000; White and Fredrickson, 1998.
25. Leonard et al., 1996.
26. National Research Council, 2003, pp. 78-79.
27. Ma, 1999.
28. Brown and Campione, 1994; Cobb et al., 1992.
29. Feynman, 1995, p. 24.

REFERENCES

Aleven, V., and Koedinger, K. (2002). An effective metacognitive strategy—Learning by doing and explaining with a computer-based cognitive tutor. *Cognitive Science, 26*, 147-179.

American Association for the Advancement of Science. (2004). About *Project 2061*. Available: http://www.project2061.org/about/default/htm. [August 11, 2004].

Barron, B.J., Schwartz, D.L., Vye, N.J., Moore, A., Petrosino, A., Zech, L., Bransford, J.D., and Cognition and Technology Group at Vanderbilt. (1998). Doing with understanding: Lessons from research on problem and project-based learning. *Journal of Learning Sciences, 7*(3 and 4), 271-312.

Black, P., and William, D. (1989). Assessment and classroom learning. *Special Issue of Assessment in Education: Principles, Policy and Practice, 5*(1), 7-75.

Bransford, J.D., and Schwartz, D.L. (1999). Rethinking transfer: A simple proposal with multiple implications. *Review of Research in Education, 24*(40), 61-100.

Brown, A.L. (1975). The development of memory: Knowing about knowing and knowing how to know. In H.W. Reese (Ed.), *Advances in child development and behavior* (p. 10). New York: Academic Press.

Brown, A.L., and Campione, J.C. (1994). Guided discovery in a community of learners. In K. McGilly (Ed.), *Classroom lessons: Integrating cognitive theory and classroom practices.* Cambridge, MA: MIT Press.

Brown, A.L., Bransford, J.D., Ferrara, R.A., and Campione J.C. (1983). Learning, remembering, and understanding. In J.H. Flavell and E.M Markman (Eds.), *Handbook of child psychology: Cognitive development volume 3* (pp. 78-166). New York: Wiley.

Bruner, J. (1960). *The process of education.* Cambridge, MA: Harvard University Press.

Carey, S., and Gelman, R. (1991). *The epigenesis of mind: Essays on biology and cognition.* Mahwah, NJ: Lawrence Erlbaum Associates.

Chase, W.G., and Simon, H.A. (1973). Perception in chess. *Cognitive Psychology, 4*(1), 55-81.

Cobb P., Yackel, E., and Wood, T. (1992). A constructivist alternative to the representational view of mind in mathematics education. *Journal for Research in Mathematics Education, 19,* 99-114.

Cognition and Technology Group at Vanderbilt. (1996). Looking at technology in context: A framework for understanding technology and education research. In D.C. Berliner and R.C. Calfee (Eds.), *The handbook of educational psychology* (pp. 807-840). New York: Simon and Schuster-MacMillan.

diSessa, A. (1982). Unlearning Aristotelian physics: A study of knowledge-based learning. *Cognitive Science, 6*(2), 37-75.

Driver, R., Squires, A., Rushworth, P., and Wood-Robinson, V. (1994). *Making sense out of secondary science.* London, England: Routledge Press.

Feynman, R.P. (1995). *Six easy pieces: Essentials of physics explained by its most brilliant teacher.* Reading, MA: Perseus Books.

Flavell, J.H. (1973). Metacognitive aspects of problem-solving. In L.B. Resnick (Ed.), *The nature of intelligence.* Mahwah, NJ: Lawrence Erlbaum Associates.

Hanson, N.R. (1970). A picture theory of theory meaning. In R.G. Colodny (Ed.), *The nature and function of scientific theories* (pp. 233-274). Pittsburgh, PA: University of Pittsburgh Press.

Hendrickson, G., and Schroeder, W.H. (1941). Transfer training in learning to hit a submerged target. *Journal of Educational Psychology, 32,* 205-213.

Hunt, E., and Minstrell, J. (1994). A cognitive approach to the teaching of physics. In K. McGilly (Ed.), *Classroom lessons: Integrating cognitive theory and classroom practice* (pp. 51-74). Cambridge, MA: MIT Press.

Judd, C.H. (1908). The relation of special training to general intelligence. *Educational Review, 36,* 28-42.

Keeney, T.J., Cannizzo, S.R., and Flavell, J.H. (1967). Spontaneous and induced verbal rehearsal in a recall task. *Child Development, 38,* 953-966.

Leonard, W.J., Dufresne, R.J., and Mestre, J.P. (1996). Using qualitative problem solving strategies to highlight the role of conceptual knowledge in solving problems. *American Journal of Physics, 64,* 1495-1503.

Lin, X.D., and Lehman, J. (1999). Supporting learning of variable control in a computer-based biology environment: Effects of prompting college students to reflect on their own thinking. *Journal of Research in Science Teaching, 36*(7), 837-858.

Lionni, L. (1970). *Fish is fish.* New York: Scholastic Press.

Ma, L. (1999). *Knowing and teaching elementary mathematics.* Mahwah, NJ: Lawrence Erlbaum Associates.

National Research Council. (1999). *How people learn: Brain, mind, experience, and school.* Committee on Developments in the Science of Learning. J. D. Bransford, A.L. Brown, and R.R. Cocking (Eds.). Commission on Behavioral and Social Sciences and Education. Washington, DC: National Academy Press.

National Research Council. (2000). *How people learn: Brain, mind, experience, and school, Expanded edition.* Committee on Developments in the Science of Learning and Committee on Learning Research and Educational Practice. J.D. Bransford, A. Brown, and R.R. Cocking (Eds.). Commission on Behavioral and Social Sciences and Education. Washington, DC: National Academy Press.

National Research Council. (2003). *Learning and instruction: A SERP research agenda.* Panel on Learning and Instruction, Strategic Education Research Partnership. M.S. Donovan and J.W. Pellegrino (Eds.). Division of Behavioral and Social Sciences and Education. Washington, DC: The National Academies Press.

Needham, A., and Baillargeon, R. (1993). Intuitions about support in 4 1/2 month-old-infants. *Cognition, 47*(2), 121-148.

Palincsar, A.S., and Brown, A.L. (1984). Reciprocal teaching of comprehension monitoring activities. *Cognition and Instruction, 1,* 117-175.

Thorndike, E.L. (1913). *Educational psychology* (Vols. 1 and 2). New York: Columbia University Press.

Vosniadou, S., and Brewer, W.F. (1989). *The concept of the Earth's shape: A study of conceptual change in childhood.* Unpublished manuscript. Champaign, IL: Center for the Study of Reading, University of Illinois.

Vye, N.J., Schwartz, D.L., Bransford, J.D., Barron, B.J., Zech, L., and Cognitive and Technology Group at Vanderbilt. (1998). SMART environments that support monitoring, reflection, and revision. In D. Hacker, J. Dunlosky, and A. Graessner (Eds.), *Metacognition in educational theory and practice.* Mahwah, NJ: Lawrence Erlbaum Associates.

Whimbey, A., and Whimbey, L.S. (1975). *Intelligence can be taught.* New York: Dutton.

White, B.Y., and Fredrickson, J.R. (1998). Inquiry, modeling, and metacognition: Making science accessible to all students. *Cognition and Instruction, 16*(1), 3-118.

Wood, T., and Sellers, P. (1997). Deepening the analysis: Longitudinal assessment of a problem-centered mathematics program. *Journal for Research in Mathematics Education, 28*, 163-186.

Part I

HISTORY

2

Putting Principles into Practice: Understanding History

Peter J. Lee

A major principle emerging from the work on *How People Learn* is that students do not come to their classrooms empty-handed. They bring with them ideas based on their own experience of how the world works and how people are likely to behave. Such ideas can be helpful to history teachers, but they can also create problems because ideas that work well in the everyday world are not always applicable to the study of history. The very fact that we are dealing with the past makes it easy for misconceptions to arise (soldiers and farmers are not the same now as in the seventeenth century, and "liberty" did not have the same meaning for people then as it does today). But problems with everyday ideas can go deeper. Students also have ideas about how we know about the past. If they believe, for example, that we can know nothing unless we were there to see it, they will have difficulty seeing how history is possible at all. They will think that because we cannot go back in time and see what happened, historians must just be guessing or, worse, making it up. If, as teachers, we do not know what ideas our students are working with, we cannot address such misconceptions. Even when we think we are making a difference, students may simply be assimilating what we say into their existing preconceptions.

Another principle of *How People Learn* is that students need a firm foundation of factual knowledge ordered around the key concepts of the discipline. Some of the key concepts for the study of history are concerned with the content or substance of history—with the way people and societies work. These substantive concepts include, for example, political concepts such as state, government, and power, and economic concepts such as trade, wealth, and tax. But understanding history also involves concepts of a different kind, such as evidence, cause, and change.

Historians talk and write about things that go on in the world. Their histories are full of pioneers, politicians, and preachers, or of battles, bureaucracies, and banks. They give their readers explanations, they use evidence, and they write accounts, but their books are not about the idea of explanation, or the notion of evidence, or what kind of thing a historical account is. Rather, they use their own (usually sophisticated) understandings of evidence or explanation to write books about Columbus or the Maya or the American Revolution. Nevertheless, concepts such as evidence lie at the heart of history as a discipline. They shape our understanding of what it is to "do" history and allow us to organize our content knowledge (see Box 2-1).

There is no convenient agreed-upon term for this knowledge of the discipline. It is sometimes called "metahistorical"—literally, "beyond history"—because the knowledge involved is not part of what historians study, but knowledge of the kind of study in which they are involved. Another term sometimes used is "second-order" knowledge, denoting a layer of knowledge that lies behind the production of the actual content or substance of history. Finally, because the knowledge involved is built into the discipline of history, rather than what historians find out, another term used is "disciplinary" knowledge. In this chapter, all three terms are used interchangeably to refer to ideas about "doing history." It is important to stress that the intent here is not to suggest that students in school will be doing history at the same level or even in the same way as historians. The point is rather that students bring to school tacit ideas of what history is, and that we must address these ideas if we are to help them make progress in understanding what teachers and historians say about the past.

Once we start to include ideas of this kind among the key concepts of the discipline, we can see that they also provide a basis for enabling students to think about their own learning. We thereby arrive at the third principle emphasized in *How People Learn*—the importance of metacognitive strategies (see Chapter 1). Monitoring one's own learning in history means, among other things, knowing what questions to ask of sources and why caution is required in understanding people of the past. It means knowing what to look for in evaluating a historical account of the past, which in turn requires understanding that historians' accounts are related to questions and themes. In short, it means having some sense of what counts as "doing" history.

In Box 2-1, for example, Angela is implicitly asking whether her group is making the right moves in its attempt to explain why World War II started. She is using her knowledge of what counts as a good explanation in history to question how well the group really understands why the war began. In this way, metahistorical (disciplinary) concepts allow students to begin to monitor their understanding of particular events in the past. As metacognitive strategies of this kind become explicit, they play an increasingly important role in learning.

This introductory chapter first explores students' preconceptions about history, pointing out some key concepts involved in making sense of the discipline. It considers students' ideas of time and change, of how we know about the past, of how we explain historical events and processes, and of what historical accounts are, and why they so often differ (second-order ideas). The discussion then turns to students' preconceptions of how political and economic activities work (substantive concepts). Of course, students' ideas change as their experience grows and they encounter new problems; this means we need to consider how we might expect students' ideas to develop as we teach them. Although there is a growing volume of research on students' ideas about history, one that is expanding particularly rapidly in the United States, it is important to remember that there has been much less work of this kind in history than in science or mathematics.[1] Research conducted in the United States and Europe over the past three decades appears to suggest that some of the key concepts of history (the discipline) are counterintuitive, and that some of the working assumptions about history used by students are much more powerful than others and may be developed in a systematic way over the years spent studying history in schools. The chapter ends with an exposition of how teachers can present history to their students in a way that works to develop historical understanding.

HISTORY AND EVERYDAY IDEAS

What do we mean by saying that history is "counterintuitive"? The "intuitions" at stake here are the everyday ideas students bring to history lessons. They are the ideas that students use to make sense of everyday life, and on the whole they work very well for that purpose. But people doing history are looking at things differently from the way we handle them for practical daily living.

Take the example of telling the truth. If a youngster gets home late and her mother asks where she has been, the child has a choice between "telling the truth" and "telling a lie." From the child's point of view, what has happened is a fixed, given past, which she knows very well; the only issue is whether she tells it the way it was. Often children learn what counts as "telling the truth" in just this kind of situation, where the known past functions as a touchstone; it is as if what one says can be held up against the past to see if it measures up. This idea works fine in some everyday situations, but in history the past is not given, and we cannot hold what we are saying up against the real past to see whether it matches. The inferential discipline

BOX 2-1 Understanding the Past and Understanding the Discipline of History

The three (British) seventh-grade students in the excerpt below are discussing why World War II started and whether it could have been avoided without thus far having studied this at school. All they have to work with from school history is their knowledge of World War I, along with anything they know from outside school. To understand what is going on here, we need to distinguish between two different kinds of knowledge about history: knowledge of what happened, of the *content* of history, and knowledge about the *discipline* of history itself.

Angela	I think Hitler was a madman, and I think that's what . . .
Susan	He was . . . a complete nutter, he should have been put in a . . . um . . .
Angela	He wanted a super-race of blond, blue-eyed people to rule the world.
Susan	Yeah—that followed him. . . .
Angela	I mean, but he was a short, fat, dark-haired sort of person.
Susan	. . . little person.
Katie	Could it be avoided? I don't think it could have.
Angela	No.
Katie	If Hitler hadn't started . . . I mean I can't blame it on him, but if he hadn't started that and provoked . . . you know . . . us . . . if, to say, you know, that's wrong . . .
Susan	It would have been [avoided]. . . .
Katie	Yeah, it would have been, but it wasn't.
Susan	Yeah, if you think about it, *every* war could've been avoided.
Angela	I reckon if Hitler hadn't come on the scene that would never have happened.
Katie	Oh yeah, yes, yes.
Angela	There must've been other *underlying* things, like World War I we found out there was lots of underlying causes, not only . . . Franz Ferdinand being shot. . . .
Susan	Yeah.
Angela	. . . but loads of other stuff as well.
Katie	Oh yeah, I don't think he was so far . . .

Angela	Yeah, there must've been a few other main currents. . . .
Katie	But, like that Franz Ferdinand, he didn't get, that was the main starting point for it all, that really blew it up. . . .
Angela	But I don't know whether . . . because we don't know any underlying causes. If Hitler *hadn't* been there, I don't know whether it could've been avoided or not.
Susan	Yeah but most wars can be avoided anyway, I mean if you think about it we could've avoided the First World War and *any* war . . .
Katie	. . . by discussing it.
Susan	Exactly.
Katie	Yeah, you can avoid it, but I don't think . . .
Angela	Yeah but not everybody's willing to discuss. . . .

SOURCE: Lee and Ashby (1984).

In discussing World War II, the three girls try to use what they have learned at school about World War I. Their knowledge points in two different directions. What they know about the events suggests to them that "most wars can be avoided" if people discuss their problems, so Susan and probably Katie think that World War II could have been avoided by reasonable negotiation. They have learned a "lesson" from their study of one passage of the past and, sensibly enough, try to apply it to another. Unfortunately the "lesson" does not hold. Angela has learned a different kind of knowledge from her earlier study of World War I, and it leads her to treat her friends' lesson with caution. She has learned that a historical explanation is likely to require more than a single immediate cause, and that "underlying causes" may also be at work. So even if there had been no Hitler, we need to know more about international relations between the wars before we can say that World War II could have been avoided. Angela's knowledge of how explanations are given in the discipline of history provides her with a more powerful way of thinking about why things happen. She knows what to look for.

of history has evolved precisely because, beyond the reach of living memory, the real past cannot play any direct role in our accounts of it. History depends on the interrogation of sources of evidence, which do not of themselves provide an unproblematic picture of the past.

Everyday ideas about a past that is given can make it difficult for students to understand basic features of doing history. For example, how is it possible for historians to give differing accounts of the same piece of history? (See Box 2-2.) Students' common sense tells them that the historians must be getting things wrong somewhere.

Differences in the Power of Ideas

The everyday idea of telling the truth is often closely linked to a very recent past in which people remember what they did or saw. Some students behave as if they believe the past is somehow just there, and it has never really occurred to them to wonder how we know about it. In Box 2-2, Kirsty, like many other fifth and sixth graders, does not even raise the question of how we could know about the past.

Other youngsters are only too well aware that this question may be problematic. Allison, a fifth grader, states the difficulty quite clearly: "You cannot really decide unless you were there." If one thinks like this, history becomes impossible. If knowing something depends on having seen it (or better still, having done it), one can never say anything worthwhile about most of the past. Many students stop here, wondering what the point of history is. However, while some working assumptions make history appear to students to be a futile exercise, others allow its study to go forward.

Samantha (fifth grade):

Why are there different dates?
No one knows, because no one was around then, so they both can be wrong.
How could you decide when the Empire ended?
If you found an old diary or something it might help.
Does it matter if there are two different dates?
Yes, because you can get mixed up and confused.

We can see here both the problem and initial steps toward a solution. Samantha appears to agree with Allison when she writes, "No one knows, because no one was around then." But Samantha, unlike Allison, sees the beginnings of a way out for historians. Perhaps someone told it the way it was and wrote it down, and we could find it: "If you found an old diary or something it might help." This view remains very limiting because it still sees the past as fixed, but it does make history possible. If we have true reports, historians are in business.

Of course, many students see that truthful testimony may not be easy to come by. They are well aware that people have reasons for saying what they say and the way they say it. As Brian (eighth grade) remarks, "I don't think we could find out definitely [when the Empire ended] because there are only biased stories left." Students who decide that we cannot rely on reports because they are biased or give only opinions are almost back to square one. If history is possible only when people (eyewitnesses or agents) tell us truthfully what happened, its study once more comes to a stop.

It is only when students understand that historians can ask questions about historical sources that those sources were not designed to answer, and that much of the evidence used by historians was not intended to report anything, that they are freed from dependence on truthful testimony. Much of what holds interest for historians (such as, What explains American economic supremacy in the postwar years? Did the changing role of women in the second half of the twentieth century strengthen or weaken American social cohesion?) could not have been "eyewitnessed" by anyone, not even by us if we could return by time machine. Once students begin to operate with a concept of evidence as something inferential and see eyewitnesses not as handing down history but as providing evidence, history can resume once again; it becomes an intelligible, even a powerful, way of thinking about the past.

The Progression of Ideas

Insofar as some of the ideas students hold are more powerful than others, we may talk about progression in the way students understand the discipline of history. For example, changes in students' ideas about our access to the past allow us to discern a pattern of progression of ideas about *evidence*. Working from less to more powerful ideas, we find a given past with no questions arising about how we can know; a notion of testimony, with questions about how truthful a report may be; and a concept of evidence, whereby questions can be asked that no one was intending to answer. (Medieval garbage dumps were not constructed to fool historians.)[2] Once we are able to think in terms of a progression of ideas in history, we can see how students' understandings can gradually be extended. In some cases we can accomplish this by enabling students to discover how prior conceptions break down in the face of historical problems. However workable the idea of a given past may be in everyday life, for instance, it is a misconception in history. In other cases we can build more directly on existing ideas. Thus testimony is important to historians, even if it must be used as evidence rather than simply being accepted or rejected. The goal is to

BOX 2-2 Two Different Ideas About Historical Accounts

In research by Project CHATA (Concepts of History and Teaching Approaches) into students' understanding of how there can be different historical accounts of the same events, 320 British students in grades 2, 5, 6, and 8 were given three pairs of stories and asked how it is possible for there to be two different history stories about the same thing. Each pair of stories was about a different topic, and the two stories making up any particular pair were the same length and ran side by side down a single page. Specially drawn cartoons illustrated key themes and steps in the story. Younger children tended to say that the two stories in each pair were "the same" because they were "about the same thing" but were just "told differently." Many of the students considered that the pairs of stories were different because no one has enough knowledge. Older students tended to emphasize the role of the author, some relying on relatively simple ideas of lies and bias as distorting stories, and others taking a more sophisticated view about the inevitability and legitimacy of a point of view. About 20 percent of the older students pointed out that stories answer different questions and fit different parameters (not their word). They did not see historical accounts as copies of the past and thought it natural that such accounts should differ.

One pair of stories had to do with the end of the Roman Empire, each claiming it ended at a different date. The first story, dealing mainly with the barbarian incursions, ended with the fall of the Empire in the West in 476. The second, which concentrated on the Empires' administrative problems, took the story up to the fall of Constantinople in 1453. Below are two (written) responses to the task.

Kirsty (fifth grade):
Why are there different dates?
One of the stories must be wrong.
How could you decide when the Empire ended?
See what books or encyclopedias say.
Does it matter if there are two different dates?
*Yes, because if someone reads it and it has the wrong date in it then they will be wrong and might go round telling people.**

Kirsty's view of history is that if there is more than one account, one must be wrong. The past is given (in books), and she is sure that if historians read the same books and are honest, they will come up with the same story "because they will do the same things and they are not lying." Everyday ideas are apparent here, but they do not help Kirsty solve the problem she faces. We can see how different things look for someone who has a more sophisticated understanding of what a historical account is if we read Lara's response to the same problem.

> ***Lara (eighth grade):***
> ***Why are there different dates?***
> > ***Because there is no definite way of telling when it ended. Some think it is when its city was captured or when it was first invaded or some other time.***
>
> ***How could you decide when the Empire ended?***
> > ***By setting a fixed thing what happened for example when its capitals were taken, or when it was totally annihilated or something and then finding the date.***
>
> ***Could there be other possible times when the Empire ended?***
> > ***Yes, because it depends on what you think ended it, whether it was the taking of Rome or Constantinople or when it was first invaded or some other time.***

Where Kirsty sees the past as given, Lara understands that it has to be reconstructed in that statements about the end of the Roman Empire are judgments about the past, not just descriptions of events in it. This means that a historical account is not fixed by the past, but something that historians must work at, deciding on a theme and timescale. Thus the problem of the date of the end of the Roman Empire is not a matter of finding an already given right answer but of deciding what, within the parameters of a particular account, counts as the end. Knowing when the Roman Empire ended is not like knowing when Columbus reached America.

---

*All responses in this chapter not otherwise attributed are unpublished examples of responses from Project CHATA. For published CHATA work, see, for example, Lee and Ashby (2000).

help students develop more powerful ideas that make the study of history an intelligible task, even in the face of disagreement and uncertainty, whether encountered in school or in the multiple histories at large in the wider world.

Grounds for Caution

Some caution is needed here. The notion of getting students to understand the discipline of history may appear to make life absurdly difficult for adolescents, let alone fourth graders. It is perhaps appropriate, therefore, to clarify at this juncture what we are *not* saying. We are not saying that teaching history is about training mini-historians. Second-order, disciplinary understandings of the kind we are talking about are not all-or-nothing understandings. Historians no doubt learned some science at school or college, but their understanding of science is not likely to be in the same league as that of a professional physicist. This does not mean their understanding is equivalent to that of a 7-year-old, nor does it mean such understanding is useless. Developing students' understanding of history is worthwhile without implying any grandiose claims.

It is also important to recognize that learning to understand the discipline does not replace the goal of understanding particular periods of the past. The substantive history (the "content" of the curriculum) that students are required to study is important, and so there will always be arguments about what is to be included, what should be omitted, and whether there is too much to cover. Regardless of what must be taught, however, understanding the kind of knowledge history is, its evidentially based facts, and its stories and explanations is as much a part of what it means to know some history as is knowing about the chosen periods of study, whatever these may be. Better understanding of key second-order ideas can help students make sense of any new topics they encounter. Although the quantity of research evidence available on the transfer of disciplinary ideas from one topic to another is relatively small, an evaluation of the Schools Council History Project in the United Kingdom suggests that teaching for transfer can be successful.[3] In light of the principles of *How People Learn*, this should not be entirely unexpected.

The point of learning history is that students can make sense of the past, and doing so means knowing some historical content. But understanding the discipline allows more serious engagement with the substantive history students study and enables them to do things with their historical knowledge. This is why such an understanding is sometimes described in terms of *skills*. However, the term is misleading. Skills are commonly single-track activities, such as riding a bicycle, which may be learned and improved through practice. The understandings at stake in history are complex and demand reflection. Students are unlikely to acquire second-order understandings by practice alone; they need to think about what they are doing and the extent to which they understand it. This kind of metacognitive approach is essential for learning history effectively. Building ideas that can be used effectively is a task that requires continuous monitoring and thinking on the part of both teacher and student.

The Ideas We Need to Address

Historians give temporal order to the past, explain why events and processes took place as they did, and write accounts of the past; they base everything they do on the evidence available. In this section we examine some key second-order concepts that give shape to the discipline of history: *time*, *change*, *empathy* (roughly, understanding people in the past), and *cause*, as well as *evidence* and *accounts*, mentioned earlier in passing. With any such list of second-order concepts, it is important to remember that we are using labels that refer to an adult concept to cover a whole range of understandings. When we talk about a concept such as *evidence*, as we have already seen, some of these understandings will fall far short of the kind of ideas we eventually want our students to grasp. For many students, what we present to them as *evidence* will be thought of as *information* or *testimony*. Thus if we say of a particular lesson that one of its purposes is "to teach students about evidence," we are thinking of where we want the students to arrive, not how they may actually be operating. The same considerations apply to anything we say about other ideas.

Time

The concepts of time and change are clearly central to history. Time in history is measured through a conventional system of dates, and the importance of dates is that they allow students to order past events and processes in terms of sequence and duration. The latter is particularly important if students are to understand that processes in history (for example, urbanization or shifts in the attitudes of Europeans and Native Americans toward each other) may be long-drawn-out and cannot be treated as if they were events taking place at a particular moment.

Teachers at the elementary level often say their students have no concept of time. This may mean that children foreshorten the passage of time in waiting for some anticipated event or that they cannot "work" clock time (perhaps their counting skills are defective, or they do not understand the analogue symbolism of a clock face). It seldom means that even very young children have failed to internalize their everyday basic temporal structures, such as day and night or breakfast, lunch, and dinner, let alone patterns of work and play. But they may have trouble estimating the long duration of passages of the past, and once again the attempt to transfer common-sense ideas about time from everyday life to history may pose problems.

For example, when English first-grade students were asked to sort paired pictures of people and objects into piles labeled "from long ago" and "from now," a significant majority were influenced by such factors as the physical condition of the objects portrayed and the state of the pictures. When a picture of a 7-year-old in a Victorian Little Lord Fauntleroy suit was paired with a modern photograph of an old man, most students said the Victorian picture was "from now." A picture of a beat-up and dirty modern car would be placed on the "from long ago" pile when paired with a photograph of a bright and shiny museum stagecoach. The pairing of clean and crisp pictures with bent, faded, and dog-eared pictures proved to be almost as distracting. It is clear that for these first graders, the historical distinction between long ago and now had been assimilated into the common-sense distinctions of old versus young and old versus new.[4]

With time, as with other ideas, history can be counterintuitive. Several features of history show the limits of a "clock time" understanding. Even apparently conventional terms are not always what they appear to be. Notoriously, a century in history is not necessarily a hundred years when used as an adjective (as in "eighteenth-century music"). The nineteenth century may be held to have closed with the start of the Great War of 1914–1918 or with the entry of America into the war and the beginning of the "American Century." The reason there are alternative possibilities and even disputes about such matters is obvious enough: historians clump and partition segments of time not as bits of time but as events, processes, and states of affairs that appear to belong together from certain perspectives. Thus the eighteenth century may be shorter musically than it is architecturally. Start and end dates are debatable, such that it makes no sense to argue over the beginning and end of any conventionally designated century. Much the same could be said about decades. When, for example, did "the 1960s" begin?

Of course, none of this means the conventional time markers and their normal mathematical relationships are unimportant in history or that they do not need to be understood, only that they must be supplemented by other ideas. The problem with centuries or decades is that they are linked to ideas of *period* in history (see Box 2-3). Knowing historical periods and being able to use them depends on knowing some of the history from which they are constructed. It means knowing the themes historians have chosen as a basis for thinking about the past. It may also mean knowing how people saw themselves, which presupposes that students recognize the distance of the past from our thinking as well as our time. For this reason, as well as the fact that it requires a good deal of knowledge, a sense of period is a difficult achievement for students, one that tends to come late in their study of history.[5]

BOX 2-3 Periods in History

Periods in history are not necessarily transparent, as this example from Sweden indicates. The students are responding to the teacher's question about which historical period came after the Renaissance.

Student	The Baroque Period.
Teacher	In the fine arts, yes.
Student	The Age of Greatness.
Teacher	Yes, but that was in Sweden.
Student	The Age of Freedom.
Teacher	That came a bit later.
Student	The Age of Monarchic Absolutism.
Teacher	Yes, or the Age of Autocracy. What's the period that we're reading about now?
Student	The Age of Freedom.
Teacher	In Sweden, yes.
Student	The Age of Enlightenment.
Teacher	Yes.

Halldén, who reports this exchange, comments, "It is tragic-comical that, in this particular case, the concepts that are supposed to help the students grasp the continuity of history become a problem in themselves." He adds, "It is highly probable that this is not an exceptional case."

SOURCE: Halldén (1994).

Change

Events are not in themselves changes, although this is exactly how many students see things. For children, the everyday model of change can often be simple. One minute "nothing" is happening, and then something does happen (often, someone does something). So there has been a change, and the change is that an event has taken place. It is a natural step to think of the event as a change.[6]

History tends to deal with longer scales than the moment-to-moment scale of everyday life, and historians are unlikely to subscribe to the notion of "nothing" happening. The idea that nothing happens is typically an everyday-life notion, rooted in highly conventional and agreed-upon ideas about what counts as interesting. Historians also operate with criteria of importance that include or exclude events, but these criteria are likely to be contested. Instead of the idea that no events occurred, historians are apt to work with the notion of *continuity*. This notion presupposes two other key ideas—*state of affairs* and *theme*. Change in history is generally to be understood in terms of changes in states of affairs; it is not equivalent to the occurrence of events. Consider the change from a state of affairs in which a class does not trust a teacher to one in which it does. There may be no event that could be singled out as marking the change, just a long and gradual process. Similarly in history, changes in population density, the role of the automobile industry in the economy, or attitudes toward minority cultures may change without any landmark event denoting a point in time in which the change took place. If students see changes as events, the idea of gradual, unintended changes in situations or in the context of actions and events is not available to them. Change is likely to be regarded as episodic, intentional (and hence rational or stupid), and able to be telescoped into a small compass (see Box 2-4).

As students become aware that historians must choose themes to write about (it is not possible to write about everything at once), they can begin to think in terms of patterns of change. What was changing? How? Was it changing a lot or just a little? Answering such questions involves concepts such as the *direction* and *pace* of change. One of the key understandings for students is that changes can run in different directions both between and within themes. Suppose the theme is subsistence and food production. For societies in Western Europe over a long period, food became more reliable, relatively cheaper (compared with income), more easily obtained, and available in a wider variety. Of course, in a parallel theme dealing with changes in the environment, there were costs. Here once again, students' preconceptions can cause problems. There is some evidence from research that students tend to think of the direction of change as automatically involving progress, and that this tendency may be more marked in the United States than in some other countries.[7] This misconception can lead to a condescending attitude toward the past, while also making it more difficult to grasp the complexities of change.

Two of the most common ideas likely to be encountered among students are the notion that everything gets better and that the past can be viewed in terms of deficits. Kenny (fourth grade) suggests some examples of progress:

> *Better cars, they've gone from women [now] getting the exact same thing as men; now black people have gone from being horrible people to being—they're the best athletes in*

BOX 2-4 Change as Progressive, Rational

Keith Barton spent a year in two Cincinnati clas
sons with the teachers, and interviewing students.
showed pictures from different periods of American hi
fifth graders and asked them to put the pictures in order, e
as they did so.

He found that students envisaged change as something linear
beneficial." They tended to think of change as being spatially and tem
ited in scope and "conceived of history as involving a limited number of d
events, rather than lengthy and extensive processes." They "thought of change
having come about for logical reasons" and believed that people in the past decided to make changes because they realized, usually in the face of some particular event, that change would improve matters. Hence Jenny, a fourth-grade student, explained the end of witch trials like this:

> ***When they accused like the mayor's wife or somebody's wife that they were a witch, and he said, "This has gone too far, we've killed enough innocent people, I want you to let everyone go, my wife is not a witch, and this has just gone too far," and then, just like that, everybody just forgot, and they didn't accuse people of witches anymore.***

Jenny has turned a process of change into an event. Someone important made a rational decision that everyone accepted forthwith.

SOURCES: Barton (1996), Lee and Ashby (2001).

ample
wor

> *the world, they've gone from bad to good—and the cars have gone from bad to good; everything has gotten better than before.*[8]

The idea of progress is reinforced by the idea—a very natural one acquired in part, no doubt, from parents and grandparents—of a deficit past. "Milk used to come in bottles because they didn't have cardboard." It was delivered to people's houses because "they didn't have many stores back then." Bicycles looked different because "they hadn't come up with the ideas yet."[9]

Patterns of change also provide a context for attributing *significance* in history. Significance can be attributed to changes within themes. A key idea for students is that the same change may have differing significance within different themes.[10] The significance of change in food marketing, for ex-e, may differ for a theme of changes in health and one of patterns of king life and employment.

Empathy

One kind of explanation in history involves showing that what people did in the past makes sense in terms of their ideas about the world. This kind of explanation is often called *empathy.* Here we run into some problems. The word "empathy" has more than one meaning, and it tends to be used only because finding a single word that does the job better is difficult. (Other labels are "historical understanding" and "perspective taking"; however, the former is too broad, and the latter tends to get confused with "multiple perspectives," which is more a matter of the points of view from which accounts are constructed.) The use of the word "empathy" in history education is to some extent stipulative (that is, the word is assigned a particular meaning, whatever other meanings it may have in the world outside history education). To that extent it is jargon, but there is no harm in this if it helps professionals reach a consensus on what they are talking about.

The central idea here is that people in the past did not all share our way of looking at the world. For this reason, when writing or reading history we must understand the ideas, beliefs, and values with which different groups of people in the past made sense of the opportunities and constraints that formed the context within which they lived and made decisions about what to do. Thus empathy in the study of history is the understanding of past institutions, social practices, or actions as making sense in light of the way people saw things. Why, for example, would a free peasant agree to become a serf in the Middle Ages? Southern (1953, pp. 109-110) explains an act that appears almost perverse to us now by showing how it could fit into a pattern of beliefs and values: "There was nothing abhorrent in the idea of servitude—everything depended on its object. All men by sin have lost the dignity of freedom and have made themselves, in varying degrees, slaves of their passions. . . ." He quotes St. Anselm:

> Is not every man born to labor as a bird to flight? . . . . So if all men labor and serve, and the serf is a freeman of the Lord, and the freeman is a serf of Christ, what does it matter apart from pride—either to the world or to God—who is called a serf and who is called free?

Southern continues:

It is easy to see that from this point of view secular serfdom had no terrors. The burdens and restrictions it imposed were of featherweight compared with those imposed by the radical servitude of unredeemed nature. At best, this human servitude was a preparatory discipline . . . at worst, it added only one more lord . . . to an array of lordly passions under which human nature already groaned. . . .

Southern's explanation—and of course this is only a short excerpt, not a full explanation even of the narrow issue of why people might *choose* serfdom—relies on the reconstruction of past beliefs and values using historical evidence. Empathy is not a special faculty for getting into other people's minds, but an understanding we achieve if we entertain ideas very different from our own. "Entertaining" ideas here denotes more an achievement than a special sort of process. It is where we arrive when, on the basis of evidence, we can say how someone might have seen things. It requires hard thinking and use of the evidence we have in a valid way. Empathy, however, is not just having the inert knowledge that people saw things in the way they did, but also being able to use that knowledge to make sense of what was done. This is not a matter of having an emotional bond. In history we must empathize with ideas we might oppose in the unlikely event we came across exactly the same ideas in the present. If understanding people in the past required shared feelings, history would be impossible. Understanding the hopes of the Pilgrims means entertaining their beliefs and values and knowing that they had those hopes. But we cannot now share the hopes—feel them ourselves—even if we want to, because to hope for something means to see it as a possible outcome, and our hindsight allows us to know that the outcome did not occur. Similarly, we cannot experience the fear felt by people in Britain in 1940 that Hitler might triumph and occupy their country. The same holds for a great deal of history.

None of this is to say that we do not want students to care about people in the past. If they treat people in the past as less than fully human and do not respond to those people's hopes and fears, they have hardly begun to understand what history is about.[11] But people in the past can appear to be strange and sometimes to do peculiar things (things we would not do) and so it is not always easy for students to accord them respect.

Partly because students tend to think about people in the past as not having what we have, and partly because they encounter decisions or ways of behaving that are difficult to make sense of, they tend to write off people in the past as not as smart as we are. (Evidence for the ideas described below goes back nearly 30 years and appears to have survived through a variety of changes in teaching.)[12] Students are quite capable of assuming that people in the past did not understand or do very basic things. A highly intelligent eighth grader, puzzling out why the Saxons might have used the ordeal of cold water to discover whether someone was guilty of a crime, declares, "But *we* know that nowadays if you ain't got air you're dead, but they didn't." An exchange between two eighth graders, this time about the ordeal of hot water, shows a similar disposition to write off the past:[13]

Sophie	And what about the boiling water, the boiling water—that could be hotter one time than another. I know it boils at 100 degrees centigrade, but um . . .
Mark	They wouldn't be able to get it that high, would they, in them times.

Another common way of dealing with the strange activities of human beings of the past is to assimilate those activities with our own. Often this is done in routine, even stereotypical ways. Mark, a fifth grader, explains why European monarchs paid for overseas ventures to the New World:[14] "They were greedy and wanted gold and more land, and sometimes they wanted jewels and different things." This sort of explanation is almost standard for monarchs and emperors, regardless of the period involved. Claudius invaded Britain for much the same reason:[15] "to get the pearls, the tin and the gold," or because "he wanted more land." Of course, assimilation can be more sophisticated than these examples, but may still leave problems unresolved. When, to return to our earlier example, students do not simply write off the Saxon ordeal but instead construe it as either a "punishment" or a "deterrent," they often remain dissatisfied with their own explanation.

At a higher level, students begin to think carefully about the particular situation in which people found themselves. What exactly were the circumstances in which they had to make decisions about what to do? This thinking can involve careful exploration, in which a variety of elements of the situation are related to one another. But although students who think like this make considerable efforts to understand why people in the past did what they did, they still tend to think in terms of present ideas (see Box 2-5).

Some students, however, will recognize that people in the past not only found themselves in different situations from those of today, but also thought differently, as is evident in this eighth grader's explanation of trial by ordeal:[16]

> *I think that the Saxons used the ordeal partly because of their belief in God. I think that the Saxons believed that as the ordeal was the judgment of God, and because God had power over everyone, God would heal your hand or make you sink if you were innocent, or make you float or your hand not heal if you were guilty. I think that the Saxons believed that God would save you, and God was saying if you were guilty or innocent.*

The ordeal becomes intelligible as a different way of thinking about things from our own, and our job in doing history is to understand it in past terms as well as ours. Occasionally, students even in the second or third grade think like this, but given the way parents and grandparents introduce children to the differences between the past and the present, as well as prevailing ideas about "progress," we are more likely to encounter assumptions about a deficit past. Nevertheless, with teaching that aims to develop sensitivity to past ways of thinking, one can expect to find students making moves such as the one Sarah (a fifth grader) makes in trying to work out why the Helots did not rebel against their Spartan masters:

> *We're given the training of freedom, right, we're given this ever since we grew up, and we have had freedom, in different ways. But these people never had freedom at all, so they can't imagine life without being enslaves [sic] right? They don't know what it's like, they'd be scared of it.*[17]

There is an element of condescension in this view, perhaps. But what appears to her fellow students as craven weakness on the part of the Helots in failing to rebel despite great numerical superiority, Sarah recognizes as an intelligible position.

Cause

Not all explanations in history are concerned with understanding people's reasons for acting or thinking as they did. We often want to explain why something happened that no one intended. Actions have unintended consequences, or simply fail to achieve their purposes. Historians also explain why large-scale events or processes occurred (for example, the Renaissance, the Industrial Revolution, or American westward expansion). In such cases, understanding what people were trying to do—their reasons for action—can be only part of an explanation of how events turned out, and we are likely to have to start talking in terms of *causes*. Students who have noticed this sometimes take a step too far and dismiss intentions as irrelevant since "they didn't happen." (No one intended World War I, so what people were trying to do is irrelevant.) When asked whether knowledge of people's plans is important to historians even if the plans go wrong, a typical response of students thinking this way is:[18] "No! 'Cos they didn't cause anything then if they went wrong."

Students often treat causes as special events that make new events happen in much the same way as individual people do things: causes act the way human agents act. When one fails to do something, nothing happens; similarly, if no causes act, nothing happens. It is as if the alternative to something happening is not something different occurring, but a hole being left in history.[19] Students thinking like this misconceive the explanatory task,

BOX 2-5 Exploring the Logic of the Situation

Even young children may sometimes give quite sophisticated explanations of apparently puzzling actions in the past, but they tend to rely on our modern ways of thinking to explain why people did as they did.

Twenty-three second graders in three schools in England were interviewed to explore how far and in what ways their ideas about history changed as they went through school. The CHATA researchers interviewed them twice in grade 2 and again at the end of grades 3 and 4. The students were asked to explain actions that appeared puzzling according to modern ways of thinking. They were given information about the people concerned and the circumstances they faced, including the broader context of the situation. The materials also included information about ideas and values held by people at the time.

In grade 2, 6 children were baffled in the face of a puzzling action, and 12 gave explanations of action in personal terms (e.g., the emperor Claudius ordered the invasion of Britain because he "wanted gold"). By grade 4 there was a shift: 2 children remained baffled, but more than half had moved to or beyond explanations appealing to roles (e.g., explaining the invasion by appeal to the kinds of things that *emperors* do). Four children explained by examining the situation in which people were acting.

One fourth grader (Carol) tried to reconstruct the situation and values of Elizabeth I to explain why she delayed so long in ordering the execution of Mary, Queen of Scots, in a way not characteristic of many eighth graders.*

Carol	Well, there're a number of reasons. Well, one, Mary was Elizabeth's cousin, and she couldn't desert her just like that, even though, well, their differences; and also I think she wanted to hold the favor of the Catholics in England and Scotland for as long as she could, and also, she didn't want to have a civil war, as I said, she didn't really have the money to, er, well, get together an army to fight.
Interviewer	So, erm, hang on . . . so she wanted to avoid civil war?
Carol	Yes.

Interviewer	Who would she have had the civil war with?
Carol	Well, as she was a Protestant, she might have had a civil war with the Catholics.
Interviewer	Ah, right, right, anything else?
Carol	Er, well, it partly . . . it might have been to do with the other countries, the Catholic countries, France, Spain, Holland. And she might have, even though they weren't sort of joined together, united as friends, I think she wanted to avoid a war, at least very bad relations with those countries.
Interviewer	Right . . . and why would she want to avoid a war with those?
Carol	Well, as I said before, there's the money, the . . . she wanted to keep, and also, well, I suspect she wanted to keep on good relations with the whole of Europe.
Interviewer	Right, any other points?
Carol	Er, not really. I don't think so, at least.
Interviewer	No, Ok. Does anything puzzle you about Elizabeth delaying for so long?
Carol	No, no.
Interviewer	Nothing at all?
Carol	No.

Carol's achievement here is considerable. She takes into account Elizabeth's relationship with Mary, the possibility of clashes between Protestants and Catholics at home, the danger of war with other European countries, and the financial burdens of war. But none of these considerations goes beyond present-day ways of thinking about Elizabeth's decisions. Despite having relevant information at hand, Carol does not, for example, take account of Elizabeth's reluctance to execute another monarch, and shows no sign of understanding what a serious step this would be.

---

*Interview from unpublished CHATA longitudinal study, Lee, Dickinson, and Ashby (1996b).

seeing it as explaining, for example, why the Civil War happened as opposed to "nothing" happening. But the task for historians is to explain why the Civil War occurred rather than other possibilities (such as a compromise solution or the gradual demise of slavery).

Another idea connected with seeing causes as special kinds of events is that causes are discrete entities, acting independently from each other. Construed this way, they can be thought of as piling up so that eventually there are enough causes to make something happen. Hence students make lists, and the more causes are on the list, the more likely the event is to happen. (The bigger the event, the longer the list needs to be.[20]) Some students, while still seeing causes as discrete events, go beyond the idea of a list and link the causes together as a linear chain. The first event impacts on the second, which in turn causes the third, and so on down a line. Should a textbook tackle the question of why Europeans went exploring with brief sections on the Renaissance, the rise of nation states, demand for luxury goods, and technological developments, some students will see these as interchangeable items. Others will try to order them in a linear chain, seeing the Renaissance as leading to nation states, which in turn led to demand for luxury goods, which in turn led to technological changes in navigation and ship design. This is a more powerful idea than simply piling causes up, but still makes it difficult for students to cope with the complex interactions that lie at the heart of historical explanations.[21]

The notion of causes as discrete events makes it difficult for students to understand explanations as dealing with relationships among a network of events, processes, and states of affairs, rather than a series of cumulative blows delivered to propel an outcome forward. In the textbook example of the question of why Europeans went exploring, the Renaissance helps explain developments in technology and astronomy, the rise of the nation state helps explain both demand for luxury goods from the east and the technological developments, and those technological developments in turn made it possible to meet and indirectly further stimulated the demand. There is a network of relationships involved, not a simple chain. In historical explanations, the relationships among the elements matter as much as the elements themselves—it is how they came together that determined whether the event we want to explain happened, rather than something else. Within this network of interacting elements, a key idea is that there are some elements without which the event we are explaining would not have occurred. This idea provides a basis for understanding that historians tend to select necessary conditions of events from the wider (sufficient) set. If these necessary conditions had not been present, the event we are explaining would not have happened; it is often these that are picked out as the "causes." This in turn gives students a means of thinking about how to test explanations. If causes in history are usually necessary conditions and necessary conditions

BOX 2-6 Causes as Necessary Conditions

Researchers in Project CHATA gave British students in grades 2, 5, 6, and 8 cartoon and text material on Roman and British life prior to the Roman conquest of Britain and a short story describing Claudius's invasion. They were then given two explanations of why the Romans were able to take over most of Britain. One said, "The Romans were really able to take over most of Britain because the Roman Empire was rich and properly looked after." The other said, "The Romans were really able to take over most of Britain because they beat the Britons at the battle by the River Medway." They were then asked how we could decide whether one explanation is better than another.

James, an eighth grader, shows that he is thinking of causes as necessary conditions. (He replies using his own labels—A and B for the two rival causes he is considering and X for the event he was asked to explain.)

> ***If without A, X doesn't happen, but it does [happen] even without B, then A is more important than B.***
>
> ***If point A [the Roman Empire was rich and properly looked after] wasn't true, could the Roman takeover of Britain still happen?***
>
> ***If point B [the Romans beat the Britons in a battle by the River Medway] wasn't true could the Roman takeover of Britain still happen?***
>
> ***A good explanation would mean the Roman takeover of Britain couldn't really happen while a bad explanation wouldn't stop it happening even if the explanation wasn't there/wasn't true.***

In a further example, in which James is testing the explanation that the Romans took over Britain because they had good weapons, he asks:

> ***If the Romans didn't have good weapons, would they have been able to take over Britain anyway? If they could, then [the suggested explanation] is wrong.***

SOURCES: Lee (2001, p. 80), originally in Lee and Ashby (1998).

are the ones that must be present for the event to happen, we can test an explanation by asking whether the event could have happened without the causes selected to explain it (see Box 2-6).

Historical explanations place some relationships in the foreground as causes and treat others as background conditions. A "cause" in history is frequently chosen because it is something that might have been different or is not to be found in other ("normal") situations. This perspective, too, connects with everyday life, but this time more helpfully. The cause of a rail disaster is not the fact that the train was traveling at 80 mph but that the rail was broken, or the driver went past the signal telling him to stop. Our ideas about what is normal help us decide what is a background condition and what is a cause. Trains often run at 80 mph without coming off the rails. But a broken rail is not present in those cases in which the incident did not happen, and drivers might be expected to stop when signals tell them to. Thus it is these states of affairs, events, or actions that tend to be identified as "causes."

It is easy for students to assimilate this distinction between background conditions and causes into the everyday distinction between long- and short-term causes. When they do so, they are likely to try to differentiate causes by attempting to assign them dates, fastening on arbitrary cut-off points between long and short instead of understanding the more context-related ways in which we pick "causes" out from the mass of interconnected antecedents to particular events.

If students think of causes as discrete events that act to produce results, they have difficulty recognizing that it is the questions we choose to ask about the past that push some factors into the background and pull others to the foreground to be treated as causes. We select as a cause something absent in other, comparison cases. The question of why the Roman Empire in the west fell is a classic case. The question may be answered in at least two different ways: first, "when it had successfully resisted attack for hundreds of years," and second, "when it didn't end in the east." In the first case we look for events or processes that were present in the fifth century but not (to the same degree) earlier. In the second we look for factors present in the west in the fifth century but not at that time in the east. What counts as a cause here, rather than a background condition, is determined in part by what question we ask.[22]

Evidence

We have already noted the way some ideas about how the past can be understood bring the study of history to a halt while others allow it to move forward. The concept of *evidence* is central to history because it is only through the use of evidence that history becomes possible. Even when students ask themselves how we know about what happened, however, it does not follow that they will recognize source material as evidence to be used differently from the notes or textbook accounts they may encounter on other occasions.

Research suggests that for some students, the question of how we can know about the past does not arise.[23] Younger students in particular are likely to assume that history is just known; it is simply information in authoritative books, such as encyclopedias. Forced to consider the question of *how* we know, they may slip into an infinite regress (bigger and better books) or assume that a witness or participant wrote down what happened on "bits of paper," in diaries, or in letters, or even carved it into the walls of caves (see Box 2-7). The assumption that the past is given on authority makes any encounter with multiple sources problematic. If sources are simply correct or incorrect information, all we can do is accept or reject what is proffered. Sources either get things right, or they do not. Common sense suggests that if two sources say one thing and a third says something different, the third must be wrong. And once one knows which sources are right, why bother with reading two that say the same thing?

The idea that what we can say about the past depends on eyewitnesses can provoke apparently similar reasoning, although it has a different significance. Students still count sources to decide what to believe (the majority wins), but there is an implicit understanding that the question of how we know about the past is at stake. We may still just have to accept or reject what we are told (after all, we were not there, so how else can we know), but we have a more sophisticated basis for making a choice. We can begin to ask questions about whether the witnesses agree, whether they are truthful or not, and even whether they were in a position to know. Once students ask such questions, further questions arise about why people lie or distort the truth in partisan and selective ways. Here a further everyday idea comes into play—the notion of bias.

The trouble is that students are likely to hold well-established everyday ideas about personal bias, which often surface in the statement "He would say that, wouldn't he." Students know only too well that people have their own agendas and may twist what they say to fit them or that people tend to take sides, whether personally or as part of a social group. One study found that even many students aged 16–18 who were taught about the importance of detecting bias in historical sources behaved as though bias were a fixed property of a source that rendered it useless. Once they managed to find any sign of a point of view, the students jettisoned the source; there was no point in considering it further.[24] This kind of idea again rests on the assumption that historians can repeat only what past sources have truthfully reported. And since students know that most people's reports must be taken with a grain of salt, they regard history as a dubious activity.

The preconception that history is dependent on true reports also encourages students to think of the reliability of a source as a fixed property, rather than something that changes for different questions. This notion in turn can lead students to take the historian's distinction between primary

BOX 2-7 Finding Out About the Past: Received Information or Evidence?

Denis Shemilt explored U.K. students' ideas about evidence. He found that for some students the question of how we know about the past does not arise, whereas others understand that historians used evidence to produce knowledge about the past. Research conducted under Project CHATA more than a decade later found very similar patterns of ideas.

When students stick with common-sense ideas they can run into difficulties. This is clear in the following excerpt, in which Annie, a ninth-grade student, responds after being asked how she knew that Hitler started World War II:

Annie	**I've read it.**
Interviewer	**How did the author [of the book] know?**
Annie	**He might have been in the war or have been alive and knew what happened.**
Interviewer	**How do people who write books know about cave men?**
Annie	**The same . . . only they've to copy the books out again and translate some of 'em.**
Interviewer	**Are you saying that cave men wrote history books?**
Annie	**No, they'd carve it on the rocks.**

Contrast this with Jim, an eighth grader, who can see that sources must be interrogated if we are to say anything about the past.

Interviewer	**Is there anything you have to be careful about when you're using sources to find out what's happened?**

and secondary sources to mean that the latter are less reliable than the former. The recognition that someone writing a long time after an event has occurred is not in as good a position to know about it as someone writing at the time is useful as a broad principle. The danger is that students will mistakenly generalize the principle to historians, as if their histories were also reports from the past rather than attempts to construct pictures of the past on the basis of evidence. This misconception is all the easier to fall into

Jim	You have to think about how reliable they're going to be . . . either if they're a long time after the event they, they're not likely to be, erm, primary sources of evidence, there's going to be more passed on either by reading something or having a story told to you, which if its told you it's less likely to be accurate because details. . . .
Interviewer	. . . Details go in the telling?
Jim	Yeah, and also if it's a particularly biased piece of evidence [we] might have to look at it and compare it to another piece of evidence, and it might not be much good on its own to get information, just opinion—it would only be good if you wanted an opinion of how people saw the event.
Interviewer	Right.
Jim	So you have to look at what context you're looking at the evidence in and what you want to find out from it.

Jim makes the point that reports can be damaged in transmission over time, and shows he is aware that we must weigh how far we can trust reports about the past. However, he also distinguishes the value of a source as a report of what happened from its value as a means of shedding light on a different kind of question—how people saw what happened. He is beginning to show signs of recognizing that we can ask questions about the past that the sources we have were not meant to answer.

SOURCES: Shemilt (1987); Lee, Dickinson, and Ashby (1996a).

when both contemporary reports and historians' inferential arguments are called "sources."

In any case, the distinction is a difficult one, and presupposes that students already understand it is the questions we decide to ask that determine whether something is a primary or a secondary source. Thus Gibbon's book *The History of the Decline and Fall of the Roman Empire* may be either a primary or a secondary source, depending on whether we are asking questions about Rome or about eighteenth-century ideas. Much the same sort of issue arises for Frederick Jackson Turner's argument before the American Historical Association in 1893 that the frontier was closed. Even the idea that a primary source is contemporary with whatever it addresses encounters difficulties with something like Bede's *History*. In the face of these difficulties, some students develop their own categories; as one sixth grader said:[25] "I can tell this is a primary source because it doesn't make any sense."

A crucial step for students in shedding everyday preconceptions and making real headway in understanding historical evidence is therefore to replace the idea that we are dependent on reports with the idea that we can construct a picture of the past by inference. Historians are not simply forced to choose between two reports, but can work out their own picture, which may differ from both.[26] With this understanding goes the recognition that we can know things about the past that no witness has reported. What matters is the question we are asking. Gibbon and Turner were not *reporting* anything about the beliefs and values of their time, but historians may use what they said (and other evidence) to produce an account of those beliefs and values. Jim, in Box 2-7, shows signs of thinking like this when he says you have to remember what you want to find out from any piece of evidence you are using.

Once students understand two parallel distinctions—between relic and record and between intentional and unintentional evidence—they can escape from the trap set by some of their everyday preconceptions. A record is a source that intends to tell us, or someone else, something about some event, process, or state of affairs. Relics are sources that were not intended to tell us what happened, or sources that are used by an investigator to answer a particular question in ways that do not depend on what they intend to report but on what they were part of. Coins, tools, and acts of Congress do not report the past to us, and so cannot be more or less "reliable." They are the traces of human activities, and we can use them to draw inferences about the past. Even deliberate reports of the past can be used to answer questions in this way when we do not ask about what they meant to report, but what they show about the activity of which they were a part.

One final point is worth making in connection with students' ideas about evidence. Common sense dictates that claims must be *backed up*, so students understandably look for evidence that does this: the more, the better. This is perfectly acceptable, but students also need to understand that however much evidence they gather in support of a claim, one piece can be enough to refute it. Learning to try to disconfirm claims may be difficult initially, but disconfirmation can be a highly efficient strategy in the face of a multiplicity of claims. We say "can be" because in history matters are seldom clear-cut, so the single piece of knockout evidence may be difficult to find, and there is always a danger that students will try to short-circuit difficult problems demanding judgment simply by trying to discredit whatever is put before them.

Accounts

The concept of a historical *account* is related to that of evidence. Whereas with evidence the focus tends to be on the establishment of particular facts, with accounts we are more concerned with how students view historical narratives or representations of whole passages of the past.

Many younger students appear to work with the idea that what makes a "true story" true is that all the component singular factual statements within it are true. As a first move in distinguishing between true stories and fiction, this idea is reasonable enough, but as a characterization of a true story, it will not stand up even in everyday life. All the component singular factual statements in an account may be true, but the meaning of the account may still be highly contestable. The meaning of a story is more than the sum of its parts. In history this point is of great importance, as the following account demonstrates.

Adolf Hitler

In 1933 Adolf Hitler came to power in Germany. In elections held soon after he became chancellor, he won a massive majority of the votes. Pictures taken during his chancellorship suggest his popularity with the German people. He presided over an increasingly prosperous nation. A treaty signed with France in 1940 enabled Hitler to organize defenses for Germany along the Channel coast, and for a time Germany was the most militarily secure power in Europe. Hitler expressed on many occasions his desire to live peacefully with the rest of Europe, but in 1944 Germany was invaded from all sides by Britain, the United States, and the Soviet Union. Unable to defeat this invasion of his homeland by superior numbers, Hitler took his own life as the invading Russian armies devastated Berlin. He is still regarded as one of the most important and significant figures of the twentieth century.

Every component statement in this account is true, but the story would not be accepted by most people as a "true story," and no historian would regard it as a valid account. Given that its title indicates a general survey of what is important about Hitler and his political career, the most obvious defect is the omission of clearly germane material that would give a different implicit meaning to the story. Moreover, what is said carries implications that would normally be specifically ruled out if they did not hold. If we are told that a politician won a massive majority, this normally means that voters had choices and were not under duress. The point of saying, without qualification, that someone has expressed a desire to live at peace is that it shows what he or she wants, and Hitler did not—in any straightforward sense—want peace. The account puts matters in ways that would normally suggest certain relationships, but in this case the relationships are highly questionable.

Students tend to deal with the problem that true statements do not guarantee acceptable historical accounts by using concepts employed in everyday life. If accounts are not clearly and unambiguously true or untrue, they must be matters of opinion. This view carries with it the idea that it is impossible to choose between conflicting accounts and, for some students, the idea that therefore anything goes. History is reduced to an arena in which opinions are freely exercised, like dogs in the park.[27]

Another preconception that can cause difficulties for students is the idea that a true account is a copy of the past rather than something more like a picture, or better still, a theory. If students think true stories are copies of the past, there will obviously be a problem when different stories exist. One way students explain this is by saying that different stories must arise when historians make mistakes. Another explanation is that part of the story has not been found. It is as if stories lie hidden like mosaics buried beneath the sands, waiting to be uncovered, but when historians sweep aside the sand, they find that some pieces are missing. Either way, the view is that historians do not know the real story (see Box 2-8).

Some students think alternative historical accounts are created when people deliberately distort the truth, usually because they are "biased." The everyday idea of bias as something like taking sides allows students to attempt to solve the problem by looking for accounts written by someone neutral. This approach makes sense for everyday clashes between two people with clear interests in some practical outcome (Who started the fight?), but it does not work for history, where alternative accounts may have nothing to do with taking sides over a practical issue. The ideal of neutrality is sometimes broadened into writing from a "perspective-free" stance.[28]

Such ideas will cause difficulties for students until they can see that stories are not so much copies of the past as ways of looking at it. The key notion here is that stories order and make sense of the past; they do not reproduce it. There can be no "complete" story of the past, only accounts within the parameters authors unavoidably set when they decide which questions to ask (see Deirdre in Box 2-8). All this means that accounts demand selection, and therefore a position from which selection is made. A point of view is not merely legitimate but necessary; perspective-free accounts are not possible. Research suggests that some students already understand this point by the end of eighth grade.[29] They know we can assess the relative merits of alternative accounts by asking the right questions. What are the accounts claiming to tell us? What questions are they asking? Are they dealing with the same themes? Are they covering the same time span?

How do they relate to other accounts we accept and to other things we know?

SUBSTANTIVE CONCEPTS

Second-order, disciplinary concepts such as *change* and *evidence*, discussed above, are involved in any history, whatever the content. Other concepts, such as *trade*, *nation*, *sachem*, *protestant*, *slave*, *treaty*, or *president*, are encountered in dealing with particular kinds of historical content. They are part of what we might call the *substance* of history, and so it is natural to call them "substantive concepts."

Such concepts belong to many different kinds of human activity—economic, political, social, and cultural. They are numerous and fit together in many different ways, which makes it difficult to form a coherent picture of student presuppositions about these concepts. As teachers, however, we tend to be much more aware of the substantive preconceptions students bring to lessons than of their disciplinary ideas. As part of the content of history, substantive concepts are usually central to what we think of ourselves as teaching, and if we forget to pay attention to students' ideas, they often remind us by revealing the misconceptions that can be so frustrating (and sometimes entertaining).

Concepts are not the same as names and dates. It is important to remember that understanding concepts—such as *colony*, *market*, or *migration*—involves knowing a rule (what makes something a migration, for example) and being able to identify instances of that rule. The substantive concepts we encounter in history can come from any walk of life or any discipline, but each denotes a cluster of *kinds* of things in the world. Names and dates are not like this; they are particulars that students must know about as individual items. Moreover, names are not limited to people. Some denote particular things, such as the Constitution, or France, or Wounded Knee. Some, like the American Revolution, denote a cluster of events and processes not because they are one kind of thing, but because they make up a greater whole to which we wish to assign a name. Of course, *constitution* is a concept that we want students to understand and apply across a range of cases, but the Constitution is the name of one particular case. Similarly while *revolution* is a general concept, the American Revolution is the name of a particular instance, although in this case exactly what it denotes can be disputed. This kind of dispute is a frequent occurrence in history (consider the Renaissance, the Age of Discovery, and the Industrial Revolution), and one that we need to help students understand if they are to be able to make sense of differences in historical accounts.

Substantive concepts in history involve a complication not often encountered in the practical concepts of everyday life: their meaning shifts

BOX 2-8 Historical Accounts Are Not Copies of the Past

While some students think of history stories as copies of the past (provided we know enough to get things right), others think of them as alternative ways of answering questions and making sense of the past.

In CHATA research exploring students' ideas about historical accounts, researchers gave 320 students in grades 2, 5, 6, and 8 two different stories of the Saxon invasion of Britain, one concentrating on the arrival of the Saxons and one taking the story right through the period of settlement. The students were then asked to say whether they agreed or disagreed with the following statement:

History really happened, and it only happened one ***way, so there can only be one*** proper ***story about the Saxons in Britain.***

Amy, a second grader, was interviewed:

Interviewer	You said "because it happened or we wouldn't know it." So, do you think history only happened one way?
Amy	Yes.
Interviewer	Yeah? And do you think there's only one proper history story about the Saxons in Britain?
Amy	Yes.
Interviewer	How come we've got all these other different stories then, Amy, do you think?
Amy	Because they don't know which one's the real one.
Interviewer	Right.
Amy	And they just make them up.

over time as well as space. An eighteenth-century king is not the same as a fifteenth- or a twenty-first-century king, and students who think they are likely to behave in the same way and have the same powers and roles are likely to become confused. Conceptions of presidents, church leaders, and even the wealthy or beautiful differ in different times. Thus while students can learn, for example, what a president is, they may run into difficulty if they gain this knowledge in the context of Thomas Jefferson and go on to assume when they deal with Lyndon Johnson and the Great Society that

Interviewer	Who makes them up?
Amy	The historians.

Amy is convinced that if there is more than one story, there must be something wrong. Not all students go as far as Amy in their dismissal of historians, but many share her view that if only one thing happened, there can only be one story. Annabelle, a sixth grader, writes:

> ***Something in history can only happen one way. I got up this morning. I wouldn't be right if I wrote I slept in. Things only happen one way and nobody can change that.***

These students think of history stories as copying the past: one past gives one true story.

Deirdre, an eighth grader, takes a very different view. She recognizes that different stories fit different questions and is therefore able to see that there can be more than one historical account of the "same" events:

> ***Yes, history really did happen. Yes, there was an outcome. But lots of different factors and things may have affected it. A history story may emphasize one particular point, but it doesn't mean that that is the only correct history story. They can say different things to answer certain questions. They can go into more detail on a certain point. They may leave out certain points but it doesn't mean it is right or wrong. There can be many different history stories about one thing.***

SOURCE: Lee (2001).

presidents are just presidents. The full significance of Jefferson can be understood only through the historical accounts of his presidency. Indeed, learning about historical particulars always involves studying historical accounts; in other words, it means knowing some historical content.

The concepts that enable us to operate in the world are not neatly defined, closed capsules. We cannot expect students to learn definitions and examples, however thoroughly, on a particular occasion and then simply apply them to other cases. Students' social concepts emerge out of current ways of life and fit into patterns of behavior that may not be fully understood, but are so "normal" that for students they are just the way things are. Students carry these concepts with them into the past. Apparently harmless concepts, such as *town* or *painter*, can be burdened with present associations, never deliberately taught, that may cause serious difficulties. When students learn of the Pilgrims coming upon an abandoned Native American "town," some assume that the Pilgrims were on to a good thing: at least they would quickly find shelter in some of the empty buildings. But even when a concept is not one that is salient in their everyday lives, students may assimilate it into known patterns of behavior that are. One of the first things beginner history teachers learn is that for most youngsters, a monk is likely to be a pretty safe source of evidence. How could it be otherwise? Monks spent their time worshipping God and living a Christian life. Clearly they would not tell lies.

Research suggests that while there may be differences in the development of relevant political and economic concepts in different societies, there may be commonalities in the United States and Western Europe.[30] There is some evidence from Europe that between second and fifth grade, the idea of someone in charge, a "boss," develops, although politicians are often not distinguished from other forms of boss. Students are likely at this age to think of people in power giving commands through direct personal contact.[31] Research provides some support for a pattern in which political and military affairs are understood by students first as the actions of individuals or collectives without structure (such as a crowd) and later in terms of systems and structures (such as armies and nation states).[32] A recent study found that before fourth grade, many Italian students believe wars are begun by individual fighters and end when people are too tired to go on or are enslaved or killed.[33] From the fourth grade on, students are more likely to see war as a clash between nation states and to believe that political authorities begin and end hostilities. Even within a particular society and school system, however, students' political concepts may develop in very different ways, depending on what experiences they have had, as well as on what they have been taught.[34]

In economic matters (money, profit making, banking, ownership, poverty, and wealth), students tend to transition from ideas based on moral norms to more overtly economic ideas in which people and actions are considered in terms of their potential as opportunities to increase personal wealth. Youngsters tend to think that shopkeepers exist to make people happy and will be pleased if prices drop, since that means people can save their money. By fourth grade, most students should be beginning to integrate ideas about, for example, buying and selling, so as to understand the workings of economic life. But an understanding of these things at the level of everyday life does not necessarily carry over into other areas. Ninth or tenth graders may have difficulty understanding how banks make profits, and the fact that sixth graders can cite profit as a motive for starting a factory does not necessarily mean they understand how shops, let alone factories, make profits[35] (see Box 2-9).

We need to remember that even when students have a quite sophisticated understanding of political and economic concepts, they may find it difficult to transfer those concepts from one case to another in history. A consequence of changes in the meaning of concepts in history is that learning history means paying attention to details and to contexts because they often determine what can and cannot be transferred. This is a point made at the beginning of the chapter in describing students who tried to apply ideas about the origins of World War I to the origins of World War II. (Both World Wars I and II are historical particulars, of course, even though both fall under the concept of *war*.) In short, students need to know some substantive history well: they need to have a deep foundation of factual and conceptual knowledge and to understand these facts and ideas in a broader framework. The qualification "some" history is important because what students do know must be manageable. And for what students know to be manageable, it must be organized so they can access and use it, knowing how to make cautious and realistic assessments about how far and in what circumstances it is applicable. We therefore need to consider the kind of history that will allow this to be achieved.

HISTORY THAT WORKS

In the previous section, the focus shifted from second-order understandings of the kind of discipline history is to substantive understandings of the content of history. Students certainly need to know some history well if they are to see, first, that there are nuances and complications within any particular topic or period that may or may not apply outside it, and, second, that however much they know, it may still be necessary to know more. But as they begin to make connections between how people in the past saw things on the one hand and actions, policies, and institutions on the other, it becomes possible for even young students to begin to appreciate something of the complexity of historical understanding. For such understandings to develop, a topic (and preferably more than one) must be studied in depth. But not everything has to be thus studied. As long as the scope and scale of a particular in-depth study are workable, students can be introduced to the kinds of thinking required. Here such concepts as *empathy* and *evidence* are central, and time must be allowed for students to begin to develop their ideas of how we can make claims about and understand the past.

While understanding something in depth is a necessary part of learning history, however, it is not enough. Moving from one in-depth topic to an-

BOX 2-9 Substantive Concepts in History: Payment for Work

As part of a broad investigation of students' ideas about a range of economic concepts, Berti and Bombi interviewed 60 Italian students aged 6 to 14 to explore their understanding of payment for work. They found that some second graders envisaged payment for work as an exchange between just two figures: one person providing goods or services and another consuming them. They saw "pay" as an exchange of money, but had no clear idea of the direction of the exchange, seeing the relationship as comparable to that of friends who give each other money. ("Change" was seen as money given to the purchaser of goods, and the youngsters thought it may often be more than is tendered in the first place.) Chiara (age 6) explained how people get money at the drugstore.

> ***When you go to get medicine, then the money they give you for the medicine you keep for getting something to eat.***

The interviewer asked whether her father, who owned a drugstore, gave people more or less or the same amount as they gave him. Chiara replied:

> ***My daddy gives them different amounts. . . . [He] gives more than they gave.***

Most third graders understood payment for work in terms of a "boss" figure paying people for work, seen either as a private owner of a business or the council or state (understood as a much richer version of the private owner). They knew that the money goes from boss to worker, but did not necessarily understand how the boss acquires the money used to pay the workers or whether the boss is also paid.

Massimo (age $6^1/_2$), having said that people who organize work pay the workers, explained how these people in turn get their money:

Massimo	**Sometimes they get it from home, maybe they ask their wife for it and . . . sometimes they find it in their wallet, if they don't have much then they go and get it from those who have.**

Interviewer	And the man who pays the bus-driver, how does he come to have the money?
Massimo	He could go to the bank and get it.
Interviewer	What is the bank?
Massimo	Where they go and put money, and when they need it they go and take it. . . .
Interviewer	To get the money does this man have to put some in the bank already or does the bank give him some all the same?
Massimo	The bank gives it to him.

More than half the fifth graders and all the seventh graders could fit the idea of payment for work into a framework of relationships whereby bosses, too, receive money from other business people or customers who buy goods and services from their business. Giovanni (aged 10 $^1/_2$) was asked who pays factory workers:

Giovanni	The owner of the factory.
Interviewer	And how does he get the money?
Giovanni	Because while others work to produce various objects, the owner sells them at a higher price, then he gives a small percentage to the workers, and he himself keeps the greater part of the money he's made.

Of course, American children may not have exactly the same ideas as Italian children. The point is not that all students, in whatever culture, will have the same range of ideas, although this is a possibility in Western industrialized countries; research in Britain, for example, appears broadly to fit the pattern suggested by Berti and Bombi. The importance of research of this kind is that it makes us aware that we cannot assume students share adults' assumptions (even at a very basic level) about how the economic, social, and political worlds work. Teaching history without recognizing this may have serious consequences for students' ability to make sense of the history they encounter.

SOURCE: Berti and Bombi (1988, pp. 32, 34, 38).

other and illuminating each in the historical spotlight only begins to develop historical understanding if such topics are set in a wider historical framework. Students will be unable to make much sense of historical change if they examine only brief passages of the past in depth. The snapshots of different periods they acquire will differ, but it will be impossible to say why the changes occurred. Moreover, if students need study only short periods of history, they will have no opportunity to come to grips with a central characteristic of historical accounts—that the significance of changes or events varies with timescale and theme. A long-run study is therefore essential for students both to understand the kind of discipline history is and to acquire a usable framework of the past.

Working through a narrative sequence of events of the history of the United States may not be the most effective way of helping students acquire a framework that can be adjusted to accommodate to or assimilate new knowledge. To provide something students can use and think about, we may need to teach a big picture quite quickly, in a matter of two or three weeks, and keep coming back to it. Such a framework focuses on large-scale patterns of change, encompassing students' in-depth studies so they are not simply isolated topics. For a temporally extended topic such as migration, exploration, and encounter, students can derive a broad picture of migration to and within America, at first picking out just the main phases of population movement to America (the land bridge crossings, the Arctic hunters, the Europeans). As in-depth studies of Native American settlement and later European arrivals (including Columbus, later Spanish exploration, Virginia, and the Pilgrims) are taught, they can be fit into this broad picture. But if it is to be a usable framework, the original broad picture will have to be adapted and made richer as it expands to include new in-depth studies. The original three phases will become more complex. Patterns of movement within America can be taught (again quickly), and changes in population movement from outside can be studied, so that, for example, differences in the kind of European migration over time are recognized.

Such a framework is not just a long narrative of events and cannot be organized in the same way as an in-depth study, bringing together all aspects of life in their complex interrelations. Instead the framework must allow students to think in terms of long-run themes, at first rather isolated from one another, but increasingly linked as students' understanding increases. Population change, migration, and cultural encounter provide themes for a framework, but these themes will be taught at the level of a big picture of change. It is the in-depth studies nesting within the framework that allow students to explore how the themes play out at the level of events.

If such a framework is to avoid overloading students with information, it must give them a range of large-scale organizing concepts for patterning change. It is the ability of such concepts as *internal* and *external migration*, *population density*, and *life expectancy* to "clump" information in meaningful ways that allow students to handle "the long run" in history rather than becoming overwhelmed by a mass of detail. The in-depth studies chosen to nest in the long-run study remind students that the details of those studies' complex interrelations matter too, and can serve as tests for the adequacy of the framework developed in the long-run study. But the latter must concentrate on the big picture, not degenerate into a series of impoverished would-be in-depth studies. Part of learning history is learning the effect of scale, and the difference between big generalizations (which can admit of exceptions) and singular factual statements.

Taking stock of the ideas presented thus far, we can say that students' substantive knowledge of history should be organized in a usable form so they can relate it to other parts of the past and to the present. This means students need to acquire a usable framework of the past, a big picture organized by substantive concepts they increasingly understand and can reflect upon. It also means they need an in-depth knowledge of contained (not overlong) passages of the past, with time to explore the way of life and world view of the people they are studying. This in turn allows them to begin to be aware of the complex interrelations involved and to be thoughtful and reflective about analogies they draw with other times and places. But learning history also requires an understanding of history as a discipline, evidenced in students' increasing understanding of key second-order concepts. Without this understanding, students lack the tools to reflect on their own knowledge, its strengths, and its limits.

Any picture of the past to which students are introduced inside school is likely to encounter rival and often opposed accounts in the wider world outside.[36] As soon as singular factual statements are organized into historical accounts, they acquire meanings within the stories in which they figure. Such stories may already be part of students' apparatus for thinking about the world before they encounter competing accounts in school. Teaching multiple perspectives, or critiquing particular accounts, is a valuable step toward facing up to students' predicament, but it is not enough.

To understand this point, consider these students' responses when faced with two alternative historical accounts. Laurence, an eighth grader, insists that the differences between the stories do not matter "because it is good to see how other people thought on the subject and then make your own mind up. Everyone is allowed to hold on to his own opinions, and no matter what the evidence, people believe different things." Briony, another eighth grader, claims that the differences are just a matter of opinion, and it does not matter "because it's up to you to express your opinion unless there are sufficient facts that prove a story. . . . I think it really is a matter of opinion." Rosie, a sixth grader, says accounts will differ "because some people are biased and therefore have different opinions of how it happened. . . . People are always going to have different opinions of how something happened." If students think like this, multiple perspectives are simply different opinions, and people can believe what they want. Xiao Ming, also in the sixth grade, sums up: "There can be many different opinions from historians so there can be different stories. Of course one *has* to be true but we don't know which one." Critiquing accounts will not make much sense to Xiao Ming when, despite our critiques, we can never know which is true.

Without explicit teaching and reflection on the nature of historical evidence and historical accounts, as well as the different ways in which various types of claims can be tested for validity, multiple perspectives become just another reason for not taking history seriously. If students are to go beyond helpless shoulder shrugging in the face of contested histories, they must have an intellectual toolkit that is up to the task. There is a danger that "toolkit" implies something overly mechanistic, so that it is simply a matter of applying the tool to get the job done. Such a simple analogy is not intended here. What is meant is that some tasks are possible only if certain tools are available, and in this case the tools are conceptual. Students need the best tools we can give them, understandings that enable them to think clearly about, for example, what kind of evidence is needed to support a particular kind of claim or what questions are being addressed in competing accounts. Once they understand that accounts are not copies of the past but constructions that answer a limited range of questions within a chosen set of boundaries, students can begin to understand how several valid accounts can coexist without threatening the possibility of historical knowledge or leading to a descent into vicious relativism.

Students have ideas about the past, and about history, regardless of what and how we teach them. The past is inescapable; it is built into our ways of thinking about ourselves. What would we say of someone who, when asked what the United States is, could define it only as a geographical entity? Our notion of what the United States is incorporates a past; it is a time-worm. Nor should we think that, because we are often told students do not know this or that piece of information about the United States, they have no version of its past. They certainly have one, but the question is whether it is the best we can give them. And while "the best" here does not mean "the one best story," because there is no such thing, the fact that there is not just one best story most certainly does not mean that any story will do. What we should give our students is the best means available for making sense of and weighing the multiplicity of pasts they are offered in various accounts. To this end, students must learn to understand the discipline of history—the one offering school can make that the busy world outside cannot. Schools could hardly have a more important task.

The study of history is often portrayed as learning an exciting—and sometimes not so exciting—story. This chapter has attempted to show that there is more to learning history than this. But we are not thereby absolved from asking how the history we teach can engage our students and what they might feel about what they are getting from it. History offers students (albeit at second hand) strange worlds, exciting events, and people facing seemingly overwhelming challenges. It shows students the dark and the light sides of humanity. It is one of the central ways of coming to understand what it is to be human because in showing what human beings have done and suffered, it shows what kind of creatures we are. The past is, as has often been said, a foreign country.[37] Its strangeness provides endless puzzles and endless opportunities for students to widen their understanding of people and their activities. An important part of understanding what appears strange is the disposition to recognize that we must try to understand the situations in which people found themselves and the beliefs and values they brought to bear on their problems. If students fail to see that there is anything to understand or do not care whether they understand or not, history will appear to be a senseless parade of past incompetence and a catalogue of alien and unintelligible practices. Empathy, in the very specific senses discussed earlier in this chapter, is central here. Historical imagination needs tools.

History can also offer another very human motivation—a sense of mystery and adventure. One source of adventure is to follow the experiences of people who were moving into unknown territory. Such study can be quite literal, when focused on people who explored lands they had not known existed, or metaphorical, when focused on those who attempted what no one had done before in some aspect of life. In the case of one of the topics discussed in the next chapter—the Pilgrims—the sense of the precariousness of their situation and the sheer scale of the challenges they faced has long been understood by teachers to offer obvious opportunities for the engagement of students' imagination. For older students, a dawning understanding of the enormity of the choices Native Americans had to make, in circumstances in which the future could only be guessed at, can offer a more complex and morally difficult stimulus to the imagination. But beyond adventure, strangeness, and a sense of awesome challenges, there is mystery. Young children—and many adults—love the mystery of the unknown. The voyage of St. Brendan (a topic in the next chapter) appeals to just this sense of mystery. What happened so long ago? What can we make of such a weird but sometimes plausible tale? Even better, the mystery arises in circumstances in which St. Brendan was having real adventures, too.

Of course, if history is the tale of things known, a fixed story that simply must be learned, then mystery can be reduced to waiting for the next installment. If we teach history as simply a set of facts to be imparted to our pupils, the mystery is a phony one. The teacher knows the answers, so where is the mystery? It can only be in deciphering the workings of the teacher's mind, in finding out what he or she wants to hear—in short, in getting the right answer. In history there are unending opportunities for students to be given tasks that leave room for them to maneuver, and to be more or less successful in finding a valid answer to an open question. Knowing the facts then becomes an urgent and meaningful business because they are essential for beginning to answer the question, and the question is worthwhile because it is a real question.

For a long time, and not just in history, schools have tended to keep a kind of secret knowledge from all but their oldest and most able students. Knowledge is contested, is provisional, and is subject to continuous change. Mystery never stops, and there is always a job for the next generation to do. The authors of this and the following chapter still remember, as one of the high points of their teaching lives, the excitement of the moment when a group of students whose main subject was science realized that science was not "all sewn up." In learning the history of medicine, they came to see—quite suddenly—that the whole way in which scientists approached and understood disease had undergone major shifts. *They* had a future in science beyond tweaking the textbooks. If they could devise new questions, they could begin new projects. Knowledge was not closed but open and open to them, too, if they mastered what was known well enough to understand what was not.

As we learn more, we should begin to see that mystery does not fade away as we come to know things. The more we know, the more questions there are, and the more there is that we need to understand. History must look like this to students as well. There is excitement in finding oneself in a richer, more open world than one thought one inhabited, but there is even more excitement in suddenly finding oneself empowered by a flash of understanding. It is not only that one has some stake in the answers and the right to a view. One can actually see that it is precisely what one is learning that gives one the right to the view, as well as the means to improve upon it. Understandings of this kind must be taught precisely because they are not things one picks up in everyday life. Generations of people have had to fashion the conceptual tools that really make a difference in the way we see the world. The only institutions whose central task are to hand those tools on and encourage the next generation to develop them are schools and universities, and the only people whose professional job it is to do this are teachers.

NOTES

1. This reservation is important, but it should also be pointed out that there has been considerable agreement among independent research teams in the United Kingdom; moreover, some recent U.S. work, as well as research in places as diverse as Portugal, Spain, and Taiwan, appears to point in a similar direction.

   There is a strong U.S. tradition of research into the ways in which the meaning of particular history stories and topics is viewed by school students, but there has been rather less focus on students' understanding of the discipline. Where such research has been undertaken, many of the researchers, such as Jim Voss, have worked mainly with college students. However, Keith Barton, Linda Levstik, and Bruce VanSledright have all done extensive research on the ideas of younger school students. Peter Seixas in Canada has carried out wide-ranging research with older school students. Sam Wineburg has worked with school and college students and with historians, and has recently begun to pay particular attention to ideas acquired outside school. Other U.S. researchers, such as Gaea Leinhardt, have investigated the differing approaches of history teachers to classroom history teaching, and investigation of students' understanding of textbooks has been widespread.

   Students' understanding of second-order concepts has been explored by Isabel Barca and Marilia Gago in Portugal; Lis Cercadillo, Mario Carretero, and Margarita Limón in Spain; and Irene Nakou in Greece. Research in this area outside the United States and Europe is also beginning to expand. Early findings from a Taiwanese study by Liu Ching Cheng and Lin Tsu Shu suggest that students in Taiwan share many ideas about historical accounts with British and Portuguese students. Mario Carretero has carried out some of his research in Argentina, and Angela Bermudez and Rosario Jaramillo have investigated ideas about causation in Colombia.

   Lists of this kind can only hint at the range of work, and any brief selection of names is necessarily invidious. This list, for example, omits a whole new generation of U.S. researchers whose work is beginning to be published. (See, for example, the authors in O.L. Davis Jr., Elizabeth Anne Yeager, and Stuart Foster (Eds.). *Historical Empathy and Perspective Taking in the Social Studies*, Lanham, MD: Roman and Littlefield, 2001.)
2. Lee et al., 1996a.
3. Shemilt, 1980.
4. Shemilt, 1994.
5. Shemilt, 1983, pp. 11-13.
6. Ibid, 1983, p. 7.
7. Barton, 1999, 2001.
8. Barton, 1996, p. 61.
9. Ibid, 1996, p. 56.
10. Cercadillo, 2000, 2001.
11. Levstik, 2002; Walsh, 1992.
12. Dickinson and Lee, 1978, 1984; Shemilt, 1984; Ashby and Lee, 1987; Lee et al., 1997; Lee and Ashby, 2001.
13. Ashby and Lee, 1987, p. 71.

14. Brophy and VanSledright, 1997, p. 130.
15. Lee et al., 1997, p. 236.
16. Lee et al., 1996a, 1997.
17. Dickinson and Lee, 1984, p. 134.
18. Shemilt, 1980, p. 33.
19. Shemilt, 2000, pp. 89-92.
20. Shemilt, 1980, pp. 30-32.
21. Lee et al., 1998.
22. Martin, 1989, pp. 58-61.
23. Shemilt, 1987; Lee et al., 1996a.
24. Thomas, 1993.
25. Ashby, 1993.
26. Wineburg, 1998; Wineburg and Fournier, 1994.
27. Lee and Ashby, 2000.
28. Barca, 1997; Cercadillo, 2000.
29. Lee and Ashby, 2000.
30. Furnham, 1992; Berti, 1994; Delval, 1992; Torney-Purta, 1992.
31. Berti and Andriolo, 2001.
32. Berti and Vanni, 2002.
33. Ibid., 2002.
34. Berti and Andriolo, 2001.
35. Furnham, 1992, pp. 19, 25, 26.
36. Seixas, 1993; Penuel and Wertsch, 1998; Wertsch and Rozin, 1998; Wineburg, 2000.
37. Lowenthal, 1985.

REFERENCES

Ashby, R. (1993). *Pilot study on students' use of evidence.* Unpublished study, Essex, England.

Ashby, R., and Lee, P.J. (1987). Children's concepts of empathy and understanding in history. In C. Portal (Ed.), *The history curriculum for teachers.* London, England: Falmer Press.

Barca, I. (1997). *Adolescent ideas about provisional historical explanation.* (Portuguese translation for publishing at CEEP.) Braga, Portugal: Universidade do Minho.

Barton, K.C. (1996). Narrative simplifications in elementary students' historical thinking. In J. Brophy (Ed.), *Advances in research on teaching: Teaching and learning history, vol. 6.* Greenwich, CT: JAI Press.

Barton, K.C. (1999). *Best not to forget them: Positionality and students' ideas about significance in Northern Ireland.* Paper presented at the Annual Meeting of the American Educational Research Association, Montreal.

Barton, K.C. (2001). A sociocultural perspective on children's understanding of historical change: Comparative findings from Northern Ireland and the United States. *American Educational Research Journal, 38,* 881-891.

Berti, A.E. (1994). Children's understanding of the concept of the state. In M. Carretero and J.F. Voss (Eds.), *Cognitive and instructional processes in history and the social sciences.* Mahwah, NJ: Lawrence Erlbaum Associates.

Berti, A.E., and Andriolo, A. (2001). Third graders' understanding of core political concepts (law, nation-state, government) before and after teaching. *Genetic, Social and General Psychology Monograph, 127*(4), 346-377.

Berti, A.E., and Bombi, A.S. (1988). *The child's construction of economics.* Cambridge, MA: Cambridge University Press.

Berti, A.E., and Vanni, E. (2002). Italian children's understanding of war: A domain specific approach. *Social Development, 9*(4), 479-496.

Brophy, J., and VanSledright, B. (1997). *Teaching and learning history in elementary schools.* New York: Teachers College Press.

Cercadillo, L. (2000). *Significance in history: Students' ideas in England and Spain.* Unpublished doctoral thesis, University of London.

Cercadillo, L. (2001). Significance in history: Students' ideas in England and Spain. In A.K. Dickinson, P. Gordon, and P.J. Lee (Eds.), *Raising standards in history education: International review of history education volume 3.* Portland, OR: Woburn Press.

Delval, J. (1992). Stages in the child's construction of social knowledge. In M. Carretero and J.F. Voss (Eds.), *Cognitive and instructional processes in history and the social sciences.* Mahwah, NJ: Lawrence Erlbaum Associates.

Dickinson, A.K., and Lee, P.J. (1978). Understanding and research. In A.K. Dickinson and P.J. Lee (Eds.), *History teaching and historical understanding* (pp. 94-120). London, England: Heinemann.

Dickinson, A.K., and Lee, P.J. (1984). Making sense of history. In A. K. Dickinson, P.J. Lee, and P.J. Rogers (Eds.), *Learning history* (pp. 117-153). London, England: Heinemann.

Furnham, A. (1992). Young people's understanding of politics and economics. In M. Carretero and J.F. Voss (Eds.), *Cognitive and instructional processes in history and the social sciences* (pp. 19, 25, 26). Mahwah, NJ: Lawrence Erlbaum Associates.

Halldén, O., (1994). Constructing the learning task in history instruction. In M. Carretero and J.F. Voss (Eds.), *Cognitive and instructional processes in history and the social sciences* (p. 187). Mahwah, NJ: Lawrence Erlbaum Associates.

Lee, P. (2001). History in an information culture. *International Journal of Historical Teaching Learning and Research, 1*(2). Also available: http://www.ex.ac.uk/historyresource/journal2/journalstart.htm [Accessed January 14, 2003].

Lee, P.J., and Ashby, R. (1984). *Making sense of the Second World War.* Unpublished study of seventh grade students' historical explanations carried out in 1984 in Essex, England. Data were collected using video recordings of groups of three students discussing possible explanations, with no adults present, University of London Institute of Education.

Lee, P.J., and Ashby, R. (1998). *History in an information culture.* Paper presented at the Annual Meeting of the American Educational Research Association, San Diego, CA.

Lee, P.J., and Ashby, R. (2000). Progression in historical understanding among students ages 7-14. In P.N. Stearns, P. Seixas, and S. Wineburg (Eds.), *Knowing, teaching and learning history*. New York: University Press.

Lee, P.J., and Ashby, R. (2001). Empathy, perspective taking and rational understanding. In O.L. Davis Jr., S. Foster, and E. Yaeger (Eds.), *Historical empathy and perspective taking in the social studies*. Boulder, CO: Rowman and Littlefield.

Lee, P.J., Dickinson, A.K., and Ashby, R. (1996a). Progression in children's ideas about history. In M. Hughes (Ed.), *Progression in learning*. Bristol, PA: Multilingual Matters.

Lee, P.J., Dickinson, A.K., and Ashby, R. (1996b). Research carried out by Project CHATA (Concepts of history and teaching approaches), funded by the Economic and Social Research Council, Essex, England, 1991-1996.

Lee, P.J., Dickinson, A.K., and Ashby, R. (1997). "Just another emperor": Understanding action in the past. *International Journal of Educational Research, 27*(3), 233-244.

Lee, P.J., Dickinson, A.K., and Ashby, R. (1998). Researching children's ideas about history. In J.F. Voss and M. Carretero (Eds), *International review of history education: Learning and reasoning in history, vol. 2*. Portland, OR: Woburn Press.

Levstik, L., (2002). *Two kinds of empathy: Reasoned analysis and emotional response in historical thinking*. Paper presented at the Annual Meeting of the American Educational Research Association, New Orleans, LA.

Lowenthal, D. (1985). *The past is a foreign country*. Cambridge, MA: Cambridge University Press.

Martin, R. (1989). *The past within us*. Princeton, NJ: Princeton University Press.

Penuel, W.R., and Wertsch, J. (1998). Historical representation as mediated action: Official history as a tool. In J.F. Voss and M. Carretero (Eds.), *International review of history education: Learning and reasoning in history, vol. 2*. Portland, OR: Woburn Press.

Seixas, P. (1993). Popular film and young people's understanding of the history of Native-white relations, *The History Teacher, 3*(May), 351-370.

Shemilt, D. (1980). *History 13-16 evaluation study*. Edinburgh, Scotland: Holmes McDougall.

Shemilt, D. (1983). The devil's locomotive. *History and Theory, XXII*(4), 1-18.

Shemilt, D. (1984). Beauty and the philosopher: Empathy in history and the classroom. In A.K. Dickinson, P.J. Lee, and P.J. Rogers (Eds.), *Learning history*. London, England: Heinemann.

Shemilt, D. (1987). Adolescent ideas about evidence and methodology in history. In C. Portal (Ed.), *The history curriculum for teachers*. London, England: Falmer Press.

Shemilt, D. (1994). Unpublished research, University of Leeds, United Kingdom.

Shemilt, D. (2000). The Caliph's coin: The currency of narrative frameworks in history teaching. In P.N. Stearns, P. Seixas, and S. Wineberg (Eds.), *Knowing, teaching and learning history*. New York: University Press.

Southern, R.W. (1953). *The making of the Middle Ages*. New Haven, CT: Yale University Press.

Thomas, J. (1993). *How students aged 16-19 learn to handle different interpretations of the past.* Unpublished study, University of London Institute of Education, 1990–1993.

Torney-Purta, J. (1992). Dimensions of adolescents' reasoning about political and historical issues: Ontological switches, developmental processes, and situated learning. In M. Carretero and J.F. Voss (Eds.), *Cognitive and instructional processes in history and the social sciences.* Mahwah, NJ: Lawrence Erlbaum Associates.

Walsh, P. (1992). History and love of the past. In P. Lee, J. Slater, P. Walsh, and J. White (Eds.), *The aims of school history: The national curriculum and beyond.* London, England: Tufnell Press.

Wertsch, J.V., and Rozin, M. (1998). The Russian revolution: Official and unofficial accounts. In J.F. Voss and M. Carretero (Eds.), *International review of history education: Learning and reasoning in history, vol. 2.* London, England: Woburn Press.

Wineburg, S. (1998). Reading Abraham Lincoln: An expert/expert study in the interpretation of historical texts. *Cognitive Science, 22*(3), 319-346.

Wineburg, S. (2000). Making historical sense. In P.N. Stearns, P. Seixas, and S. Wineburg (Eds.), *Knowing, teaching and learning history.* New York: New York University Press.

Wineburg, S., and Fournier, J. (1994). Contextualized thinking in history. In M. Carretero and J.F. Voss (Eds.), *Cognitive and instructional processes in history and the social sciences.* Mahwah, NJ: Lawrence Erlbaum Associates.

3

Putting Principles into Practice: Teaching and Planning

Rosalyn Ashby, Peter J. Lee, and Denis Shemilt

It has been argued thus far that the learning of history can be accelerated and deepened through consistent application of the key findings from *How People Learn*, and that these findings should be applied in ways that acknowledge what is distinctive about the historical enterprise and the particular challenges it poses to students (see Chapter 2).

The first key finding of *How People Learn* emphasizes the importance of students' preconceptions. Teachers must take account not only of what students manifestly do not know, but also of what they think they know. This finding is confirmed in the study of history by both research and experience.[1] Much of the gap between what we teach and what students learn is attributable to the fact that students link new knowledge about the past to preexisting but inappropriate knowledge derived from everyday life. Thus, for example, an account of the growth of medieval towns may be linked to existing knowledge about the growth of trees; that is, students assume medieval buildings got bigger, and so the towns grew. More significant still, students have critical misconceptions—about how we know about the past, about the relationship between historical accounts and the past they represent, about what counts as an answer to a "why" or a "how" question, and so on—that are more difficult to access but that impact profoundly the ways in which students construe what they are taught. To the extent that we are able to identify the preconceptions held by students, we may preempt misunderstandings about the substantive past and, more important, seek to modify and develop the conceptual tools students need to make sense of history.

The second key finding of *How People Learn* emphasizes the importance of providing students with conceptual structures and tools with which to organize and manipulate factual knowledge. Students must have a deep foundation of factual knowledge, but this is not tantamount to saying that they must learn all there is to know about any topic or set of topics. Because history is an information-rich subject, it is easy for students to flounder in a sea of facts that cannot be contained or controlled. And because history is about people and events that are halfway recognizable, it can sometimes be viewed as a series of weird soap operas. Thus, the foundations of factual knowledge must be deep in the sense that its layers of historicity are understood; in other words, the rules by which communities work and people interact are likely to shift according to time and place. In addition, as is argued in Chapter 2, the substantive facts and ideas of history must be understood in the context of a conceptual framework that includes second-order concepts such as those associated with time, change, empathy, and cause, as well as evidence and accounts. Indeed, it has been argued that the systematic development of such concepts is essential for students to be able to organize knowledge in ways that facilitate retrieval and application.

The third key finding of *How People Learn* emphasizes the importance of metacognitive approaches that enable students to reflect on and control their own learning. This finding relates to the development of second-order concepts noted above. Students can acquire and refine the conceptual tools necessary to organize and manipulate information only to a limited extent until they are explicitly aware of what they are doing. In order, for example, to determine that a given source is reliable for some purposes but not for others, or to decide that a source can yield evidence of things that it purports to neither say nor show, students must be able not merely to draw inferences, but also to know that they are doing so and to make those inferences objects of consciousness that are evaluated against rules. This level of metacognitive awareness is unlikely to be achieved in the lower grades, but its achievement may be accelerated if teachers of third and fourth graders focus their attention on such questions as "How do we know?" "Is this possible?" and "If this could have happened, can we say that it did happen?"

This chapter examines what these three key findings entail for the ways in which we work with students in the classroom and for the strategies used to plan history teaching. The first section sets the stage for what follows by addressing the issue of the extent to which these findings can realistically be applied in the classroom. The next two sections demonstrate the applicability of the findings by presenting two detailed example classroom case studies.

THE REALITY TEST

The three key findings of *How People Learn* and the arguments advanced in the preceding chapter may be thought to reflect too favorable a view of the realities of teaching in some classrooms. Indeed, we may not always have carte blanche in what is taught, but feel obliged to work within the narrow space between national standards on the one hand and locally adopted textbooks on the other. In consequence, the second key finding may appear to presume that we have more freedom in what we teach than is always allowed us. Worse still, the emphasis placed in the previous chapter and in the first key finding on the identification and systematic development of preconceptions and second-order concepts assumes that we have more in-depth knowledge of how and what students think than may be the case. At the start of the school year, we may know names and test scores but little else. Students must still be taught even if we lack in-depth analysis of their existing knowledge of pre-Columbian civilization or their ability to empathize with predecessors. Last but not least, the exhortation to take "a metacognitive approach to instruction" may appear overly optimistic for some students, who by the end of the year still have not acquired any kind of coherent story. What chance do they have of becoming metacognitively aware?

These are fair points, and can serve as acid tests of the value of what is presented below. At the same time, the reader must keep in mind that a chapter such as this cannot provide a simple recipe for instant success, as any experienced history teacher will know only too well. A lesson plan for unknown children in unknown classrooms invites disaster. This is not just because all students are different personalities; both research and experience tell us there are more specific reasons. Individual students have different prior conceptions of history, the past, and how things happen in the world. In addition, students at any given age are likely to be working with a wide range of ideas (see Box 3-1). We can make some informed predictions about what ideas are likely to be prevalent among students in a particular grade, but research makes it clear that in any given class, some students are likely to be thinking in much more sophisticated ways, perhaps even using the sorts of ideas more common among students many years older. Likewise, some will be operating with much simpler ideas.

Moreover, if we talk here about "fourth graders" and "youngsters" or "seventh graders" and "older students," we are not implying that changes in ideas are an automatic consequence of age. Many seventh graders will happily go on thinking in much the same ways as fourth graders if they are not made aware of the problems their everyday ideas create. Teachers are not the only impetus for changing students' ideas, but it is part of our job as teachers to act as if we were. Because we cannot predict the starting points of any particular class of students, the discussion of example lesson tasks in the following case studies must be qualified by "ifs," alternatives, and conditional moves. At the same time, however, practical moves with real teaching materials used by the authors and by serving teachers in both the United Kingdom and the United States are suggested.[2] They nevertheless remain

BOX 3-1 The 7-Year Gap

The CHATA research discussed in Chapter 2 reveals the conceptual understandings of *some* 8-year-old students to be more advanced than those of *many* 14-year-olds. For example, when asked to explain why one account of the Roman invasion of Britain conflicts with another, *some* 7- and 8-year-olds suggest that the authors may have chosen to record "different facts" because they were asking different questions about the invasion, while *many* 14-year-olds claim that one or other author "made mistakes" in their account. It follows that when working with typical mixed-ability classes, teachers must accommodate a "7-year gap" between the ideas of the lowest- and highest-attaining students.

Two other CHATA findings are significant in this connection. First, ideas about different second-order concepts do not develop in lockstep. A student's understanding of evidence and accounts may be the most advanced in the class, but her grasp of causal and empathetic explanation may not be as good, and her understanding of time and change may even be below the class average. Second, students' ideas about history do not develop as a necessary consequence of maturation. Many seventh and eighth graders are happy with their mental furniture and see no need to rearrange or replace it. To some extent, this is because they lack metacognitive awareness and conclude that they "are no good at history." It is one of the more difficult jobs of teachers to show such students how they can "get good" at the subject, albeit at the cost and effort of ongoing mental makeover.[3]

examples only, and do not offer "the best way" to teach these or any other topics.

Two case studies are presented in this chapter. Each involves a specific task—comprising teaching materials and questions—in the context of how the task might be used in developing students' ideas about historical evidence. The focus of the first case study is a familiar topic, "The Pilgrim Fathers and Native Americans"; the second deals with a more unusual topic, "St. Brendan's Voyage." It might appear illogical to start with the Pilgrim Fathers, since the topic chronologically precedes the Brendan voyage. The fact that the task in the Brendan case study is written for fourth graders, while that in the Pilgrims case study is for sixth graders, may make the order appear even more wayward.

Given appropriate teaching, we would expect sixth graders on the whole to outperform fourth graders in their understanding of historical evidence. If their teaching has been designed to develop their understanding of evidence, older students will, on the whole, apply more powerful ideas than younger ones. However, we have already seen that the "7-year gap" means there is considerable variation in students' ideas, and in any case, students' ideas will depend in part on what they have already learned. Moreover, historical questions can be answered at very different levels of sophistication, so that students from a range of different grades can profitably tackle the same materials and questions. Students need not wait until they reach a certain grade to benefit from trying to weigh the evidence for the claim that St. Brendan reached America a thousand years before Columbus, but more conceptually sophisticated students will give different answers than less sophisticated ones.

Of course, the language we use in designing our questions and materials is likely to set limits on the range of students who will be able to work with them, and we cannot expect young students to have the same understanding of the adult world—even in the present—as older students. Thus, it still makes sense to talk of designing tasks for a particular grade, at least as far as setting limits below which use of the task would be unwise. But if we encounter students from sixth or seventh grade who have not developed ideas about evidence that we would normally begin to teach in fourth grade, we might profitably use the "fourth-grade" task with them.

We therefore begin with the Pilgrim Fathers and Native Americans case study, on the grounds that it will be a much more familiar topic for most teachers than the Brendan voyage. The discussion of evidence work in this first case study assumes that reference is made to a standard textbook and that we have no privileged knowledge about student preconceptions and misconceptions. The case study aims to illustrate, first, how it is possible to identify and work with student preconceptions during the process of teaching; second, how student ideas about a second-order concept, that of *evidence*, can be developed in ways that support, not supplant, the teaching of substantive history; and third, how it is possible to promote metacognitive awareness among students who have no special ideas and abilities.

While the materials and questions in the Pilgrim Fathers and Native Americans case study are designed for students who already have some acquaintance with ideas about evidence, the aim of the second case study—on St. Brendan's Voyage—is to introduce less sophisticated students to some key ideas about evidence in the context of an adventure without losing them in masses of content. There is also a difference in focus between the two case studies. Discussion of the first emphasizes the identification and refinement of previously acquired ideas about evidence, whereas the second case study concentrates on the teaching of students who have yet to reach first base and, in particular, who cannot yet make clear and stable distinctions between well-founded and speculative accounts of the past.

Although the tasks in the two case studies were designed with students in grade 4 (St. Brendan) and grade 6 (Pilgrim Fathers) in mind, materials and questions from both can be and have been used from grades 4 through 8 and beyond. This notwithstanding, decisions about how—and even whether—materials and questions are used with given classes must be informed by the ideas the students are already working with and the kind of responses we expect. In any case, nothing in what follows is about learning that can be accomplished in a single or even several short sessions. Even when students appear to have understood what has been taught in one context, we will need to return to it in other topics. Changes in students' ideas take time, patience, and planning.

WORKING WITH EVIDENCE: PILGRIM FATHERS AND NATIVE AMERICANS

Exploring the Basis for Textbook Claims and the Nature of Sources

The choice of the arrival of the Pilgrims as a topic for discussion here implies no claims about what should or should not be taught. However, it is clearly a popular topic in textbooks, and one with which readers are likely to be familiar. It is also relevant to the broader topics, such as "Exploration and Encounter" and "The Settlement of New England" that are regularly taught. Moreover, it is a topic that offers opportunities to explore the Pilgrims' significance for later generations in America, and supports an examination of the complex relationships between the newcomers and the native inhabitants that can help break down stereotyping. There is also a very rich record available from the testimony of the Pilgrims that can provide worthwhile and exciting learning opportunities, particularly in connection with understanding the nature of historical evidence.

The questions in the Pilgrims' task work at two levels. First, they can expose the assumptions students appear to be working with, and second, as a consequence, they provide the teacher with a basis for a learning dialogue with the students.[4] As will be seen, such a dialogue can challenge the misconceptions that become apparent and encourage the development of more powerful ideas, while at the same time providing the teacher with information about future learning needs. Testimony of the kind provided in the materials associated with this task needs to be understood evidentially, and part of the teacher's task is to encourage students to think in more complex ways about the experiences, ideas, and beliefs of these "eyewitnesses."

The source materials can interact with the textbook so as to transport students from the security of a few historical particulars and descriptions of the arrival of the Mayflower in Cape Cod Bay in 1620 to the more precarious circumstances of William Bradford and John Pory and the early seventeenth-century world they inhabited. The time and place can be richly explored through the materials left behind, and the legacy of the events considered through their impact on later societies. The search for access to this world through these materials is likely to be halting and problematic for young students; good storytellers may well be tempted to believe they can open it up to their students without involving the testimony of those involved more directly. Working with students, who are happy to grapple with the difficulties inherent in materials of this kind, provides us with a different perspective. Learning experiences of any kind, however, need structures, with clear objectives.

An approach of this kind can be used for a wide range of age and ability groups. The format can remain the same but the task made to differ in its language level; the nature, length, and quantity of the sources used; and the extent of visual material needed to support ideas. The task was initially designed for sixth graders but was taught to U.K. sixth and eighth graders as a whole-class lesson. The examples quoted are of two kinds: written answers to the teachers' whole-class questions, and excerpts from a recorded follow-up discussion with a small group of three sixth graders. (The small-group recording offers a more detailed picture than written answers can provide of how students responded to the questions.) U.K. students' perspective on the Pilgrims is likely to differ from that of equivalent students in the United States, but the focus here is on students' evidential understanding.

Five sources have been chosen. The extracts taken from William Bradford's journal have been set out separately in Sources 1 and 3, separating the arrival of the Mayflower from the expedition ashore, so as to allow students easier access. The extracts have also been edited to limit the difficulty for these 12- and 15-year-olds.

The three written sources provide testimony from William Bradford about the arrival and settlement of the Pilgrims at Plymouth in 1620 and testimony from John Pory, a visitor to the settlement in 1622. Through these sources, the teacher is able to explore students' existing understandings of "eyewitness" accounts, and to encourage students to look behind this testimony to consider the circumstances, ideas, and beliefs of the people directly involved.

The two paintings depicting the arrival of the Pilgrims allow the teacher to explore and challenge students' misconceptions about these sources as a record of the actual events of the time. They also give the teacher an opportunity to encourage students to recognize that while the paintings may not provide evidence of the events of 1620, they do provide evidence of the significance attached to the arrival of the Pilgrims in 1620 by later generations.

The Pilgrims' task begins by presenting students with extracts from their textbooks and a map showing them the location where the action takes place. The second textbook extract provides an opportunity to introduce the testimony of William Bradford and the evidence it may not have been intended to provide.

How do we know about the arrival of the Pilgrims in America? The Mayflower finds land, and the Pilgrims look for a place to settle.

One textbook tells us:

> On November 11, 1620, after 10 weeks at sea, a small, storm-battered English vessel rounded the tip of Cape Cod and dropped its anchor in the quiet harbor of what is now Provincetown, Massachusetts. The people in the ship were too tired and sick to travel farther. While the Mayflower swung at anchor in Provincetown harbor, a landing party looked for a place to settle. These men explored a small bay on the western edge of Cape Cod. They found a swift-running stream with clear, fresh drinking water. The area seemed ideal for a settlement. In December, the Pilgrims anchored the Mayflower in the bay and began building Plymouth Plantation.[5]

Another textbook tells us:

> They found a spot on the inner shore of Cape Cod Bay and promptly named it for the town from which they had sailed—Plymouth. At Plymouth the Pilgrims found abandoned cornfields. Their leader, William Bradford, sadly described their situation. "What could they see," he wrote, "but a hideous and desolate wilderness...what could now sustain them but the spirit of God and his grace?"[6]

Here is a map to help you locate the places the textbook is talking about.

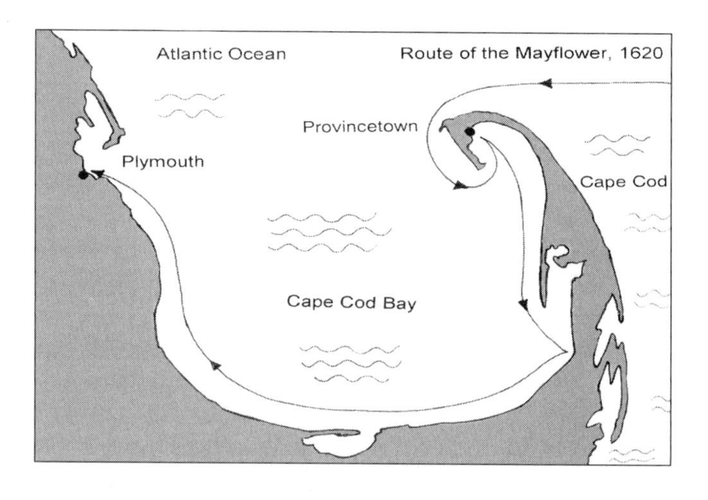

Once the students are familiar with this basic material from the textbooks, the teacher can give them a briefing sheet. This briefing sheet has three main purposes: to introduce the students to their inquiry, to encourage an enthusiasm for the work, and to provide them with an ultimate goal—the production of their own *substantiated* account of the arrival of the Mayflower and the decision to settle in Plymouth. The briefing sheet enables the students to focus on the instructions, to which they can return if necessary; the teacher works through the instructions with the class, clarifying, checking understanding, and reinforcing them as necessary.

Source 1: An extract taken from William Bradford's personal journal, finished in 1650. Bradford was one of the leaders of the English Separatists whom we now call the Pilgrims.

> *Having arrived in a good harbor, and brought safe to land, they fell upon their knees and blessed God who had delivered them. They had no friends to welcome them and no inns to refresh their weather beaten bodies; no houses to go to for food. When St. Paul (in the bible) was shipwrecked the barbarians were kind to him and his friends but the barbarians here when they met with the Separatists and their friends were readier to fill their sides full of arrows. And it was winter, and they knew the winters here to be subject to fierce storms, and dangerous to travel to known places, much more to search an unknown coast. They could only see a desolate wilderness, full of wild beasts and wild men—and what multitudes there might be of them they knew not. What could now sustain them but the Spirit of God and his Grace?*

Source 2: "The Mayflower on Her Arrival in Plymouth Harbor" by William Formsby Halsall. Painted in Massachusetts in 1882.

Briefing Sheet

Things for you to think about and things for you to do

How do the people who wrote the textbooks know about these events when they happened nearly 400 years ago?

The second of these textbook writers gives us a clue about how they found out.

✦ Can you spot it?

The first textbook tells us more than the second textbook, but the second textbook helps us understand how the writer knew about the Pilgrims' arrival.

✦ You are going to carry out your own inquiry about "The Arrival of the Pilgrims" so that you can write your own version in a way that shows how you know these things.

Your inquiry will involve looking carefully at some *sources* and doing some hard thinking.

Source 3: Another extract taken from William Bradford's personal journal, finished in 1650.

> *Arrived at Cape Cod on the 11th of November and a few people volunteered to look for a place to live. It was thought there might be some danger but sixteen people were given permission to explore. They were well armed and led by Captain Standish. They set off on the 15th of November; and when they had marched about a mile by the seaside, they spotted five or six persons with a dog coming towards them, who were savages; but they fled from them and ran up into the woods, and the English followed them, partly to*

Source: A source is something that has survived from the past that we can use to find out about the past. Sources help us work things out that we wouldn't otherwise know.

✦ Read the sources carefully, and as you do this, write down questions that come to your mind.

(These questions will be useful to your teacher because they will help her understand how you are thinking.)

✦ Then answer the questions your teacher thought about, set out on a separate sheet.

(While you are answering your teacher's questions, she will collect your questions and think about how to find answers to them.)

Words you might need to know about:

Pilgrims: These people were looking for a place to live so that they could worship God in their own way without interference. They were called Separatists at the time because they separated themselves from the official ideas the priests in England taught about God. Later people called them the Pilgrims, and sometimes the Pilgrim Fathers.
Shallop: A small boat. This was used to get close to land because the Mayflower could not safely go into shallow water.

see if they could speak with them, and partly to discover if there might be more of them lying in ambush. But the Indians left the woods and ran away on the sands as hard as they could so they followed them by the track of their feet for several miles. When it was night they set up a guard and rested in quiet that night; and the next morning followed their track till they had headed a great creek and so left the sands and turned another way into the woods. They followed them by guess, hoping to find their dwellings; but they soon lost both them and themselves. At length they found water and refreshed themselves, being the first New England water they had drunk.

Then they changed their direction to get to the other shore, and on the way found a pond of clear, fresh water, and shortly after a large area of clear ground where the Indians had formerly set corn, and some of their graves. And further on they saw new stubble where corn had been set the same year; also they found where lately a house had been, where some planks and a great kettle was remaining, and heaps of sand newly paddled with their hands. Which, they digging up, found in them Indian baskets filled with corn of different colors, which seemed to them a very goodly sight (having never seen any such before). This was near the place of the river they thought they might find and they found it where it opened itself into two arms with a high cliff of sand in the entrance but more like creeks of salt water than fresh, and they saw a good harbor for their shallop. Then they returned to the ship lest the others might be in fear of their safety; and took with them part of the corn and buried up the rest.

Source 4: "The Landing of the Pilgrims" by Michael Felice Corne. Painted in Salem, Massachusetts, between 1803 and 1806.

Source 5: Written by John Pory, an official from the settlement at Jamestown, farther south in Virginia, after he had visited Plymouth in 1622.

Whether it was because of the wind or the backwardness of their ship's captain they did not arrive where they had planned. Instead they reached the harbor of Cape Cod, called Pawmet by the Indians. After some dangerous errors and mistakes, they stumbled by accident upon the harbor of Plymouth where it pleased Almighty God (who had better provided for them than they could imagine) to land them where there was an old town, which several years before had been abandoned by the Indians. So they quietly and justly settled down there without having to push any of the natives out, so not so much as one drop of blood was shed. Even the savages themselves did not claim any title to it so that the right of those planters to it is altogether unquestionable. The harbor is good for shipping both small and great being land-locked on all sides. The town is seated on the ascent of a hill. There is plenty both of fish and fowl every day in the year and I know no place in the world that can match it.

The briefing sheet is designed to encourage students to record their own questions during their initial examination of the sources. This is done to make transparent any difficulties the students might encounter with the sources, and to encourage them to generate their own questions as part of the longer-term goal of developing their independent learning strategies. After their initial perusal of the sources and the recording of their own questions, the students are asked to respond to their teacher's questions. It is useful to explain to the students that these questions may well look similar to those they have raised themselves, demonstrating that questions are not necessarily the special province of the teacher. Normally the teacher will promise to collate the questions raised by the students and pursue answers to them in the following session. Students may raise the point that none of the sources directly record the thoughts of the native population at the time; this creates the opportunity to ask the students to think about why that is and what those thoughts might have been.

Students' written responses to the teacher's questions are used to provide the teacher first with an understanding of the students' preconceptions about evidence, and second with an opportunity to begin a learning dialogue about the nature of these sources and their potential as evidence (see questions 1, 2, 3, and 4). In addition, the questions provide a means to support the first steps in developing students' understanding of the beliefs that influenced the Pilgrims' actions (see questions 5 and 6). These questions are simply examples, and there are many other ways in which the selected sources could be used to both diagnose and develop students' thinking.

Teacher Question 1.

The first textbook writer describes the Mayflower's arrival. He tells us that "a small storm-battered English vessel rounded the tip of Cape Cod." Source 2 is a painting showing the Mayflower arriving at Cape Cod. We know that when the ship's master sailed it back to England, it quickly fell into disrepair and rotted. So how would the person painting the picture in Source 2 have been able to work out what the Mayflower looked like?

What is this question trying to find out about students' existing understanding?

The question is designed to check whether students understand that

(a) The painter is not an eyewitness to the arrival of the Mayflower.
(b) There was a time difference between the source and the event.
(c) The Mayflower was not available to the painter as a relic from the time.

The question also probes whether students understand the ways in which the painter might have knowledge of the Mayflower, and whether they see the painting as providing direct information about the arrival of the Mayflower or as evidence of its significance to later generations.

What is this question trying to encourage students to reflect on as a means of developing their understanding?

The question is trying to develop students' understanding of evidence by encouraging them to see:
(a) That the painting is better evidence of the *significance* than the *fact* of the Mayflower's arrival.
(b) That the absence of relic evidence or of trustworthy descriptions by eyewitnesses is not an insoluble problem. We can find good grounds for saying what the Mayflower could not have looked like and for working out its probable appearance.
(c) That it is possible to work out the extent to which the representation of the Mayflower should be trusted by checking whether it is typical of ships of the period.

The responses of two particular groups of students—aged 12 and 15—to some of the questions exemplify the kinds of moves students make. (If no age is given for a quotation, the example comes from the younger group.)

You need to be able to see for yourself.

Simon assumed that the painter might have seen the Mayflower before it left England, ignoring the time gap between the painting and the event it depicted. He claimed that "the person who drew the picture knew what the boat looked like because he might have seen it in the port before she set sail for America." Jennifer, recognizing a time difference, believed there would still be something left of the Mayflower, and was convinced that "the person painting the picture in Source 2 was able to work out what the Mayflower looked like by visiting the remains." Some 12-year-olds saw that the painter could not have been an eyewitness, but argued that it was therefore not possible to know what the ship looked like. As Adam explained, "The person painting Source 2 wouldn't have known what the Mayflower had looked like as he wasn't even there."

If you weren't there to see for yourself, then you need access to someone who was.

Typically, many students felt the need to connect the painter with the subject matter of the painting by creating a direct link with an eyewitness. Peter said, "The painter could have got the information from a person who actually saw the Mayflower." In saying this, however, Peter stretched the age of the possible witness to an improbable extent to accommodate his thinking, while simultaneously shrinking the amount of time that passed between 1620 and the production of the painting in 1882. "Since it was a hundred years after, there may have been people alive from the vessel to describe it." The importance to *some* students of an eyewitness as a way of knowing about the past is clearly considerable.

Contact could be maintained with the eyewitness by means of knowledge handed down through the generations.

Students can, of course, be more realistic about the time difference. Elliot pointed out that the painting "was painted 262 years after the voyage." He looked for a different kind of link to the original witness, the handing down of knowledge within a linear sequence. He suggested, "It must have been told by the voyagers to their children, and then to their children, and then to their children, what it looked like." He recognized that this might have created difficulties for the artist and claimed, "The painter is probably drawing partly from what he's been told and partly from his imagination." In a similar vein, Edward recognized the difficulty of both a drawing of the Mayflower surviving over a long period of time and this kind of information being available as oral evidence over such a long period. He wrote:

> *I don't think he could have [worked out what the Mayflower looked like]. The only way he could was if there was a drawing that had remained for over 250 years which is unlikely. It also says that the artist painted it in 1882 so it couldn't have been spread about by word of mouth.*

In recognizing the problems, however, Edward provided no solution for how we might check the appearance of the Mayflower and thus the accuracy of the information in the painting. The absence of a direct link and uncertainties of transmission make a determination of accuracy difficult.

You can use a scissors-and-paste approach.

When faced with the difficulties of direct access or transmission error, many students operate with a scissors-and-paste approach to piece together what is available and what they can trust. Robert explained that "the person who painted it knew what the Mayflower looked like because another artist had probably provided it in Britain and he altered the angle and scenery." He was working with the idea that the picture of the Mayflower needs to be an exact copy of its arrival in the bay, almost a photograph of the event, and saw the possibility of piecing information together to produce this result. Robert believed that the details of the ship might have been available to the artist through a previous picture of the Mayflower in England, but that the American painter would have been able to create the setting needed to portray this event, perhaps from his own personal geographical knowledge.

You have to work it out from other sources or knowledge available to you.

The awareness of a broader range of records available to the historian can help students recognize that we are not left totally helpless without eyewitnesses (or indeed, as some believe, without the recovery of the Mayflower itself). Julie, aged 15, suggested, "The artist may have studied pictures of other early seventeenth-century ships and drawn one. The painter might have incorporated knowledge from these into his painting." Melanie, also 15, claimed in her written answer to this question, "There would have been blueprints, paintings and maybe even a sister ship to the Mayflower."

Students' need for a direct link with the events, however, can remain very strong. Peter was particularly keen on having access to something tangible from the period.

Peter	They have this age testing machine and they can test how old things are.
Teacher	What would they be testing with that?
Peter	Maybe things on the ship.
Matthew	Yes, but then that would only tell us when it was manufactured and not when it circled round Cape Cod, and it still wouldn't tell us what it looked like.
Peter	Well that would be in William Bradford's diary.
Matthew	I think it was based on what was probably a regular design and all that would have changed was mast shapes so it could have been like a regular ship.
Peter	The archaeologists might have got it up from the sea, with all sorts of cranes and things.
Matthew	But it had rotted.
Peter	Well the basic shape might be there just not all the fine details.

Even when he came under pressure from his teacher and Matthew, Peter remained convinced that the recovery of the ship or a direct description of it is essential. He was clearly familiar with the way in which science, archaeology, and technology might assist the historian.

Teacher Question 2.

In Source 3, William Bradford is talking about the first people who went ashore. He tells us that it wasn't until they had "marched about a mile by the seaside" that "they spotted five or six persons with a dog coming towards them." He tells us they "fled and ran away into the woods, and the English followed them." But Source 4 shows the Native Americans waiting on the shore to meet them. How do I solve this confusion?

What is this question trying to find out about students' existing understanding?

The question explores whether students are making decisions simply on the basis of whether someone was there or not (Bradford was, the artist wasn't), or they understand that people's intentions in producing the sources also need to be taken into account.

What is this question trying to encourage students to reflect on as a means of developing their understanding?

The question is designed to encourage students to reflect on:

(a) Whether, and under what circumstances, the accuracy of the picture matters.

(b) What the artist was trying to portray about the encounter between the Pilgrims and the Native Americans.

(c) Whether the encounter portrayed by Bradford would have been described in the same way by the native people at the time.

Trust the source who was in a position to know.

We must expect many students, convinced of the need for an eyewitness, to respond in a direct and uncomplicated way to this question. George, for example, wrote, "William Bradford was there and the painter wasn't." Given the claim being made, this is a perfectly justifiable answer. Jack also made the point about Bradford being in a position to know, and explained the conflicting information in the painting by pointing out that stories change over time:

> *I think that Source 3 was right, as he was one of the leaders of the Pilgrims. In his own personal diary he was probably writing the events that happened when they happened, whereas Source 4 was drawn almost 200 years after the events. Over 200 years stories change.*

These students did not question whether Bradford was among the actual party that first went ashore. They made the assumption that he was there. The idea of "being there" is often generalized by students and taken as sufficient to validate a great deal. Sometimes they use "from the time" regardless of the distance between the person providing testimony and the event itself. In this case, however, the students made a legitimate distinction.

You need to understand the purpose of the artist.

In pursuing this question with students, an important goal is to help them understand that the painting is not meant to be a photographic image of an exact moment in time, and that although it is "just a painting," it can often yield information about how past events were seen by later generations.

Some 12-year-olds considered the artist's purpose in relation to the information contained in the painting. Daniel, for example, said, "I think that the Indians are in the picture to show that they were there first, and that they were watching for them even if they weren't seen." Daniel's response is interesting in two ways. First, it suggests a specific purpose on the part of the artist, showing that Daniel was aware that this intent must be considered if the painting is to be understood. Second, the response introduced a perspective not yet suggested by the text extracts and the sources, nor at this stage by the questions. Daniel was sensitive to the position of the Native Americans. In the questions he had recorded when first looking at the sources, he had written about the painting (Source 4), "Were the Indians watching them from the land?" About John Pory's testimony (Source 5), he raised the question, "Why didn't the native Indians attack them?"

When Adam began to muse on the production of both paintings (Sources 2 and 4) in a follow-up classroom discussion, the teacher used Daniel's written response to explore the issue further.

Adam	It's funny that it's done in Massachusetts the same as the other one.
Teacher	Yes. Let me just run this past you all and see what you think about this. This answer by someone in your class says, "In this picture I think the Indians are in the picture to show that they were there first, and that they were watching for them, even if they weren't seen."

Matthew recognized the point being made when the teacher confronted the students with Daniel's response, and he elaborated on it. Although both Matthew and Daniel were making assumptions about the artist's actual intentions, they clearly recognized that the artist was not necessarily attempting a historical reconstruction.

Matthew	I think that's very good 'cos art isn't always total fact it's usually symbolism because you couldn't put tiny men on there showing that they are far away, it could very well symbolize, yeah, that these Native Americans are here first and its not really the Pilgrims' land at all.
Adam	I think the Indians would be very territorial, like protect their land and their territories and say, like, "This is my territory, go away!"

The teacher probed the students' ideas further by getting them to consider the possibility that the painting might provide evidence of the importance of the event to future generations, and might not necessarily be an attempt to recognize the Native Americans' first claim to the land.

Teacher	You remember the part where we said that those who arrived on the Mayflower become known as the Pilgrim Fathers later on. And that kind of means that the painting might really be trying to say these people are really important because they established, it was the beginning, they are the "Fathers" who made this part of America what it was at the time the painting was done. So what might the artist want to portray about these people—the Pilgrim Fathers? Would the painter be concerned to portray the Native Americans' position? Would the historical accuracy matter that much in this case?
Matthew	Like they would want to show them as great because they founded the white part of America.
Adam	Maybe it was to make the Pilgrims look good.
Peter	Yeah, make the Pilgrims look like they are fending off the Indians, make the Pilgrims look good.

Matthew took the point further, and an awareness of past attitudes and perspectives came into play.

Matthew	I think this painting could be somewhat racial and that they are kind of trying to say that these Pilgrims are the white fathers and that the Native Americans shouldn't be there, its just for these people which isn't fair, its very racial, but that's what could be portrayed—it could be a racial statement.
Teacher	That's interesting, but what would we need to know to interpret the painting? It may not have been intended to be racial, but merely to focus on the arrival of the Pilgrims, and the Native Americans are just there as part of the scenery. The racial aspect may be more unconscious than we are supposing, or the artist may have wanted to reflect this as a peaceful encounter.

Adam	You would need to know about the painter who actually painted it. You need some background information.
Peter	Then we could find out the truth about what it's saying.
Teacher	Would the information you need be just information about the painter? What else would you need to know?
Matthew	What period of time it was painted and whereabouts it was painted. They could be changed with society, like giving in to society [meaning agreeing with predominant ideas?] because, like, most people in Salem, Massachusetts, which is where this was painted, were white, so he wanted to portray the white people as the great greats . . . or however you want to interpret it.
Teacher	There was some very good thinking there actually, and I think you got us on to that point, didn't you, Matthew, about symbolism, and therefore what you're saying to me seems to be that the painting is not supposed to be *exactly* what happened at the time but may be more about what it means to people later on, and at a particular time and place.

In this excerpt, the teacher sought to discover whether Matthew was close to adopting a more subtle approach than his initial position had suggested, and his response showed a growing awareness of the complexities of interpreting the intentions of the painter and the kind of knowledge one needs about the society in which the painter was working (see Box 3-2). This is a strong hint that Matthew will be able to use any new information and source materials judiciously and to understand the significance of the Mayflower's arrival for future generations. The materials to be used in future lessons with these particular students will need to explore the different relationships among groups of people at the time and the complexities of the Mayflower legacy.

Teacher Question 3.

The writer of Source 5 tells us, "The harbor is good for shipping both small and great, being landlocked on all sides" and "The town is seated on the ascent of a hill." How did the writer know this?

BOX 3-2 Interpreting Sources in Context

The disposition to interpret historical data with reference to the social contexts within which they were produced and intended to be used is slow to develop and, even when developed, may be difficult to activate. Working with a group of "college-bound" seniors who "represented the successes of our educational system," Sam Wineburg found that they were disposed to take at face value a "patently polemical" account of the skirmish between British soldiers and colonial farmers at Lexington Green in 1775. Wineburg concludes that these able seniors "failed to see the text as a social instrument skillfully crafted to achieve a social end."[7]

It is necessary to account for the disparity in ideas and assumptions between the "college-bound" seniors and the more sophisticated sixth graders who engaged with the Pilgrim Fathers materials and tasks. Three factors are significant in this connection. First, it may be easier for students to construe pictorial rather than textual sources within a supplied or inferred context of social meanings and intentions. Second, the text used by Wineburg carried the received authority of a textbook account and, as Wineburg notes, "the textbook, not the eyewitness accounts, emerged as the primary source." Teaching of the sixth graders, on the other hand, had systematically diminished the credibility of the Mayflower painting by pointing out that the artists could not possibly have witnessed the events depicted. Third, and perhaps most significant, the teachers who worked with the Pilgrim Fathers materials and tasks had the development of students' understanding of evidence concepts as their principal objective. The seniors, as Wineburg observes, should not be "overly" criticized since "these aspects of text, while central to the skilled reading of history, are rarely addressed in school curricula."

Teacher Question 4.

John Pory, the writer of Source 5, tells us that when the Pilgrims reached the harbor of Cape Cod, they found "an old town, which several years before had been abandoned by the Indians." The writer was not one of the people who arrived on the Mayflower, so how did he know this?

What are these questions trying to find out about students' existing understanding?

These two questions work together. They are designed to check whether students understand that "being in a position to know" is not just a matter of whether someone was there at the time, but also depends on the kind of knowledge we are asking about.

What are these questions trying to encourage students to reflect on as a means of developing their understanding?

The questions encourage students to:

(a) Recognize that different kinds of information may be given in people's testimony.

(b) Think about how these differences affect the way we can verify testimony (using other sources in some cases, and judging likelihood and plausibility in others).

(c) Think about why the circumstances at Plymouth might be important to John Pory and perhaps speculate about the nature of his visit.

These kinds of reflections can encourage students to move beyond the face value of testimony and begin to draw inferences, getting sources to yield what they did not set out to reveal.

You need to make distinctions among kinds of claims.

Pory's claim in Source 5 that "the harbor is good for shipping both small and great, being landlocked on all sides" and that "the town is seated on the ascent of a hill" are based on his own observation of the geographic advantages of Plymouth during his visit in 1622. Students who have become familiar with source work are likely to look at the source caption and recognize this. Pory's claim that the town was one that "several years before had been abandoned by the Indians" is, however, of a different kind, and may well have rested on word of mouth from either the native population or more likely the Pilgrims' own story of their arrival, told to him during his visit. The circumstances at Plymouth may indeed have reached him by word of mouth at Jamestown, but his written account of Plymouth is in the context of his visit. The advantages of Plymouth's geographic location and the Pilgrims' relationships with the Native Americans would no doubt have been a subject of discussion between someone from Jamestown and the leaders of the Plymouth settlement, and Pory's account helps the teacher introduce students to the importance of these advantages for the Plymouth settlers.

We should expect many 12-year-olds, and perhaps most 15-year-olds, to be able to distinguish between the different claims addressed in these two questions. Jonathan's written answers demonstrated his ability to make this distinction:

> *Question 3: The writer of Source 5 would know this because he visited Plymouth two years after the Pilgrims' settlement and not many changes of this kind would have happened.*
>
> *Question 4: John Pory probably asked William Bradford about this because they were both in Plymouth in the same decade.*

Jonathan understood that Plymouth's geography was unlikely to change quickly and that Pory would have been able to see these features for himself. He was also aware, like many in his age group, that Pory's knowledge base for the second claim might have depended on what others at Plymouth had told him.

Generalizing.

Some students will suggest William Bradford's journal as the basis for John Pory's knowledge of Plymouth and pay little attention to the information attached to Source 5 about the visit to Plymouth in 1622, or decide that this information is not relevant to the question. David's responses are illustrative:

> *Question 3: The writer would have known this by the personal diary of William Bradford which they found.*
>
> *Question 4: He could have known this because of the diary of William Bradford.*

Students like David may not take into account that Bradford's journal was not published until 1650, and may therefore not ask themselves whether Bradford would have shown Pory any records he had made or whether, during a visit in the circumstances of early settlement, these things would have been an important matter for discussion between the two men (and indeed others). David did not get behind this source to the circumstances surrounding its production. If he had looked at the source caption, he did not use it to inform his response.

Another kind of response is to recognize that a site visit could provide this kind of evidence, but not to think about the difference between the geographic features of the site, which are unlikely to have deteriorated, and the signs of an abandoned town, which may well have been obliterated by the activities of the 2 years between the arrival of the Pilgrims and Pory's visit. The concept of "town" here is also likely to be important: if students imagine a Native American settlement as consisting of brick or stone buildings, an answer such as Vincent's makes more sense.

Question 3: The writer might have known this by going to the site and finding ruins.

Question 4: This question has the same answer as question 3.

Vincent was presumably assuming that Patuxet (the name used by the native population for the abandoned town on which the Plymouth Plantation was built) would still have been visible in the way the ruins of a modern town might be. Although there may have been signs of a settlement, it is more plausible that the abandoned town would have been an important topic of the conversations that took place between Pory and the settlers, particularly given the comparative advantage an "abandoned town" had for the Pilgrims in their relationship with the native population.

If we return to one of the groups of students reflecting on these questions with their teacher and look at a substantial portion of their discussion, the importance of understanding exactly what students mean becomes very clear. Unless we know the distinctions that matter here—the ones that indicate crucial steps in students' understanding—we can blur students' ideas and fail to help them move forward.

In discussion with his teacher, Peter—forever enthusiastic—suggested a range of possible sources that Pory might have used as a basis for his claims, while Matthew tried to pin down the circumstances of the visit, and made a distinction between what Pory would have been able to see for himself and what he might have been told by the people of Plymouth. Adam challenged Pory's second claim by suggesting it rested on hearsay. Their teacher triggered this discussion by focusing on questions 3 and 4.

Teacher	We need to look at Source 5. It says the harbor is good for shipping both small and great, being landlocked on all sides. Some people asked about what landlocked meant. Do you understand what that means now?
All	Yes.
Teacher	Pory also tells us that the town is seated on the ascent of a hill. And one question there is how does he know that? And a further question is that he also tells us that when the Pilgrims reached the harbor of Cape Cod they found an old town, which several years before had been abandoned by the Indians. So I want to know how the writer knew that, because he wasn't on the Mayflower. Can you explain *each* of those to me?

Peter	Well maybe for the second one it could have been that the leader, William Bradford, maybe it was in his journal, and maybe also that he's been to see that place and he has found signs of markings, like Indian words and statues of their gods.
Matthew	Yeah because it says here "Written by John Pory an official from the settlement at Jamestown, further south in Virginia, after he has visited Plymouth in 1622," so he had actually visited, so that explains the geographical point, and then it could have been from word of mouth from the people who were actually on the Mayflower so they are talking to each other. That's how he finds out about the old town that several years had been abandoned by the Indians.
Adam	Yeah, that's probably true but that doesn't make his source as reliable as it could be then, because his source is not based on pure facts, it's probably not based on pure fact, it's probably based on word of mouth and what he's been told.

Perhaps Adam used the phrase "not based on pure facts" in an attempt to distinguish between the physical environment available for all to see, and as a consequence easily testable, and the kind of knowledge that comes secondhand to someone, resting on another's word about what he or she had seen or heard. The teacher checked the students' understanding of this distinction, but it was Matthew who responded.

Teacher	Which one of these things can you say that for? Both of those questions?
Matthew	No. I believe like I said before, that where it says the harbor is good for shipping both small and great, being landlocked on both sides, you can see through your eyes, so you don't need to be told about that, but in order to be told about the old town it has to have been by word of mouth which can sometimes be twisted like we managed to find that paintings can be twisted by social . . . surroundings.
Peter	Even if he did get it by word of mouth people do twist the truth as you go along.
Adam	Like *Pass it on.*

This discussion goes beyond the parameters of questions 3 and 4 in a search for some general principles. Matthew's notion of "twisting the truth" appears to appeal to a familiar, everyday understanding of intentional distortion, but his reference to "social surroundings" may indicate an understanding that "twisting" may be less deliberate. Adam's analogy with the game *Pass it on* reflects the same ambiguity between transmission errors as a consequence of the very nature of word-of-mouth information and deliberate distortion (although Peter's comment was clearly about the latter).

The teacher explored how far the students could think more precisely about intentions, because the second of John Pory's claims is not of the sort likely to have come about through a deliberate attempt to twist the truth. The students nevertheless continued to pursue the issue of deliberate distortion.

Teacher	If you are going to use the word "twist," can you make distinctions between the kind of things people are likely to twist and those they aren't?
Peter	If it was something important and they didn't want anybody to find out about it they twist it so they think it was something else.
Matthew	It depends who they are supporting, um, say the Pilgrims did something really bad. Say they murdered Indians while they were sleeping just out of want for their land, they would make it sound a bit better, like that the Indians did so many horrible things to them that they didn't actually do, so that it was even a good deed to go and murder them while they were sleeping.
Adam	They wouldn't even say they were sleeping. They would say the Indians came to them so they killed them in battle and so they were great warriors.

These speculations brought Peter back to the sources they were examining. Despite the previous discussion about the status of the painting in Source 4, he used this source as a stimulus to articulate his concerns about the Native American perspective.

Peter	Yeah, and you know where it says abandoned by the Indians, well in Source 4 it shows that the Indians were actually still there, so whether

	maybe the Indians were slaughtered or maybe they were hiding, because they did not want those people to come over and take the land and change their cultures, and then these people just found their land, and they are threatened by it, and they think they are going to take over their culture.
Adam	Yeah, leading on from what Matt says about the way they exaggerate things, it says they was abandoned but the people could have done, like, invaded their culture and slaughtered them, and therefore they would say there were no Indians there so it was abandoned to make them sound, like, not so bad.
Matthew	So it would be to look like they were great.
Peter	Supposedly.
Matthew	In American people's eyes they *were*, because they founded their land and would see it as their land.

The students had begun to think of the general context of what an encounter of this kind might mean to the Native Americans, and as a consequence found it difficult to believe in the convenience of the "abandoned" town (all the more convenient if the "town" is still conceived of as a collection of permanent structures in which the new arrivals could find shelter). They also believed that the Pilgrims would have felt some need to justify their claim to Plymouth. At this point, the students, as well as their teacher, had begun to recognize the need for material that would enable some of these questions and assumptions to be pursued.

Teacher	Well, before you can answer all those kinds of questions you need to know some more things perhaps, some more background information.
All	Yeah.
Teacher	But just let me get clear what you are saying that you have got in this source written by John Pory. You made the important point didn't you, that some things he could have seen for himself, but that he would not have been able to see for himself the bit about the abandoned town, and you are saying he might have heard about that from the people who were there. The point then that Matthew is making is that it would be difficult to see *that*

first hand, and that he would be relying on the Pilgrims for that information, and so Matthew is just saying that there might be an issue here, that he might be a bit worried about doing that and that it may not be quite right. It may be that if we know something more about John Pory and the Pilgrims we can think about this point further.

You need to get behind the record to the concerns of the people who produced them.

The teacher then pursued the further objective involved in these questions—that concerned with thinking about the kinds of things particular people might record. An attempt was made to encourage the students to consider why the advantages at Plymouth had a particular resonance with John Pory.

Teacher	Why is Pory concerned with these things anyway, this kind of information? Why would he record *this kind* of information? If I told you that he came from the settlement farther south, and that the settlement farther south, when *they* got to America there wasn't any abandoned land and they were having a lot of problems. So why might that make him want to mention this?
Adam	Probably to let his settlement know, and they have probably got friends and allies, that they *have* got abandoned land, and maybe they could share with those who haven't actually got any.

It is clear that the knowledge base with which students are working is unlikely to be sufficient to pursue this matter further at this stage. The need for additional information exists on a more or less continuous basis in history lessons. It is vital in this task not to crowd out the evidence objectives by providing too many factual details too soon, but at this point it is difficult to advance understanding without further contextual understanding. Some details can be provided without risk, as the students will be in a position to assimilate them and use them effectively to shed light on the problems they have already identified. These details have a context that will give them meaning.

The teacher, aware of these difficulties and of the overall scheme of work, was able to tell the students that a comparative study of the settlements at Plymouth and Jamestown would be part of their future work and would shed light on John Pory's concerns. In addition, she explained that the following lesson would use further source material to explore other matters: the circumstances of the abandoned town; the relationship between the Pilgrims and the Wampanoags, who lived in the immediate area; and the changing nature of the relationships between the settlers and the native populations with the arrival of a Mr. Weston and his attempt to create a settlement at Wessagusett. The teacher also knew (but did not tell the students at this time) that they would be learning about the changes in these relationships in the context of patterns of white penetration into the lands populated by the native peoples of the eastern lands of North America over a longer time span.

Understanding what is likely to get recorded and under what circumstances: diaries.

Students in the sixth, seventh, and eighth grades tend to be quite aware that we depend on traces from the past in order to say anything about it; as we have seen, however, they are likely to assume that if this testimony is less than accurate, we will face difficulty. When testimony is still the main idea in the students' toolkit, one of the first things they suggest as a good source for historians is a diary. The following exchange indicates why.

Teacher	Perhaps we could come back to the things in William Bradford's diary because several people in the class asked how Bradford knew the Native Americans—Bradford calls them barbarians—were ready to fill them full of arrows. The question people wrote down when they were looking at this source was, "How did he know they were ready to do this?" So what I want you to do is to try to shed some light on this for us.
Adam	It's very strange really because you know when you write a diary, no one would lie to a diary because that would be just like lying to yourself. It would be a ridiculous thing to do.
Peter	I think he might lie in his diary, maybe because he knows that one day or another, people some how or another are going to find his diary, and he wants to, maybe, twist this so that people hear what he wants them to think.

The teacher had returned to William Bradford's testimony to encourage the students to consider how the language of such a text can help us recreate the circumstances in which records are made and hence the subject matter that is likely to be recorded, and to examine the further question of how a diary becomes a publication. The aim was to see how far the students were thinking beyond the simplistic dichotomy of "telling the truth" or "lying" that came out in the exchange between Adam and Peter. The students were aware that we can make moves that go beyond testimony, but it is precisely testimony that they confronted in this material. The teaching objective was therefore to help them see that even when we have testimony, we have to use it in quite subtle ways. In other words, we have to use it as *evidence*, not just as testimony. This means thinking about how the testimony arose. The teacher explored the students' ideas to provide herself with an informed starting point for the next exercise.

Teacher	What about us thinking about the way diaries get written, we need to think about the circumstances in which diaries get written.
Matthew	Yes, because you're not exactly, it's like talking to a really good friend, because mostly people start it off like "Dear Diary" so they're not really leaving it for someone else to find. It's just like having someone to talk to, because I know they are not there, but you just feel better after you have written it down.
Teacher	Do you think people might write their diary up every day?
Adam	Well some people do, like Anne Frank, she did.
Teacher	But she was in a room with nothing else—she was restricted in what else she could be doing. In what sort of circumstances might people not write their diary up every day?
Matthew	Oh, if there is something exciting happening they probably wouldn't do it so when they were on the ship then he probably would have filled it in, but by the time they had landed he would probably be so excited he wouldn't, that would be the last thing on his mind, he probably wouldn't be able to do those things.
Adam	And if he did it would be like dear diary too excited to write we just did this and that, right see you tomorrow, so he might have written it a lot later.

Teacher	It would be nice to go into this further, but we are not going to have time to do that today. But what I was trying to do was to get you to think about how when the Pilgrims arrived they had an awful lot of things to cope with because they had had this dreadful journey, they were exhausted, and clearly some of them are very ill or dying, and maybe William Bradford was very busy when they arrived. He might not have had time to write up his diary on a regular basis, and if you write a diary later on, what are you likely to write about compared with if you write a diary every day?
Adam	Pick out all the good points, because if you have had some really down times you don't want to make it worse by writing about the bad things.
Peter	And I think if you write in your diary every day you just write what happened today, and if you, say, write up a date a week later you think, "Wait a minute! I'll only write this," because you don't want people going through your stuff and finding this. "I want them to find good things."
Teacher	Do you think he is just writing this out personally for his own benefit? I mean this is a man who eventually becomes the Governor of Plymouth.
Matthew	I suppose it could be for both, because personally, like, maybe other people know what Indians are really like, and maybe they all put their ideas and extracts into this diary so that it can be passed down so that everyone can remember the story of the Pilgrims and we do now. Maybe they had plans so that everyone would remember who they were and what they did.
Adam	And how great they were.
Teacher	So in the extract you were looking at, by William Bradford, Source 1, what does it say at the top?
Adam	I think he sort of writes it in the past tense, he says "having arrived."

Teacher	And what does it actually say about the source?
Adam	Personal journal finished in 1650, and they arrived in 1620, so that's, like, a 30-year diary.
Peter	I don't think anyone would have a 30-year diary.
Matthew	Well if he is a great man . . .
Peter	Maybe it's not for personal use, because for personal use it would be more like a child, and when you are 20 you are more mature, so you wouldn't really bother. Not many adults keep diaries for personal use, so maybe he just thought, "Oh, I will leave it for future generations."
Teacher	If you know you are a small group of people who have gone all the way across the Atlantic Ocean creating a new settlement . . .
Matthew	Yeah, you are going to want people to take notice of it. If there is a small number they might not even survive, or like reproduce and they are going to want other people who come to the land to think, "Oh my God, these people were great," and, like, other people from the past, like, think that if you won a battle God was on your side so they might think, "Oh my God, God was on their side so he must be the true God!," so he is increasing their religion which would still make their name.
Peter	And it may even have worked because like in America they have carved out of rock the foreheads of the forefathers so it probably even worked.

The teacher was aware that in future lessons, her students would need to develop more subtle understandings about the nature of diary accounts, their relationship to record keeping, and the level of awareness of authors of these accounts with respect to the possible legacies they were creating. In particular, the students would need to understand the responsibility that William Bradford, as governor of a settlement of this nature, would have had for keeping particular kinds of records. Within this context, they would need to be able to differentiate, even within the same document, among different kinds of information and whether the document is being used as a record or relic source.

Ideas, Beliefs, and Attitudes

Although the focus of the Pilgrims' task as discussed here is on the concept of *evidence*, an important connection exists between that concept and some aspects of *empathy*. If students are to know what a source may be used to argue, they need to understand two closely related things. First, they must understand what sort of thing a source is as an object that has social meaning at a particular time—in this case a diary (or, more precisely, a journal). Second, they must be able to begin to understand the ways of seeing the world, and the associated values, manifested by the source.

In the above discussion, Matthew introduced an opportunity to consider how religious beliefs, particularly that of "providence," actually work. In explaining that winning a battle would actually be evidence of God being on your side, Matthew also suggested that successes of this kind would reinforce such a belief. This is a complex understanding, and it will be valuable to him when in further studies he is asked to give explanations of some of the later actions of the European settlers on the eastern coast of America. The Pilgrims' task contains two questions that would provide an introduction to such later work. The first is a simple question asking students to use Sources 1 and 5 to identify who the Pilgrims believed was helping them when they arrived at Cape Cod.

Teacher Question 5.

The writer of Source 1 and the writer of Source 5 seem to share the same beliefs about who was helping the Pilgrims when they arrived at Cape Cod. Who did they think was helping them?

What is this question trying to find out about students' existing understanding?

This question explores students' understanding of:

(a) The distinction between how people at the time would explain the advantages they had and how we might explain these things now.

(b) How Bradford's and Pory's beliefs provided them with an explanation of their circumstances.

What is this question trying to encourage students to reflect on as a means of developing their understanding?

The question encourages students to:

(a) Reflect on how the interrogation of sources can give us access to understandings beyond the immediate information that the source intended to provide.

(b) Think about the distinction between the way in which the Pilgrim Fathers would have explained what was happening and the way in which we might explain it.

This question is also an opportunity to introduce the specific idea of "providence."

A majority of sixth graders were able to identify God as the agency the Pilgrims believed was helping them, but another response we are likely to encounter is that it was the Native Americans who really helped the settlers. In many ways, students are quite right to say this (and indeed in the evidence work that followed, the students were introduced to Squanto), but the issue here was how the Pilgrims would have seen things, and in particular how they would have interpreted the help they received from the Native Americans as the manifestation of divine providence. Later the students often emphasized the practical support the Pilgrims received as a consequence of either the good will of the native population or the food stores of the native population that the Pilgrims found. Sean, for example, wrote, "I think the Indians helped them because why would they suddenly have a grudge with someone they just met." This response was illuminating because it turned the question into one about who *he* thought provided the help, rather than one about who the writers of the sources thought was helping. In claiming that "in Source 1 and 5 they have the Native Americans helping them," Colin was being less than precise, but appeared to have picked up the discovery of the supplies from Source 3, together with Pory's remarks to the effect that the native population made no objection to the settlement in Plymouth, and to have seen this as important practical help.

Other students made the distinction between our way of seeing things and the beliefs of people such as Bradford and Pory. These students were ready to recognize that it is *past* ideas that count here. Alex drew inferences from the religious practices of the Pilgrims to their beliefs. She wrote, "They thought God was helping them as they blessed God when they arrived." Janine, aged 15, saw as a routine consequence of their religion that they would believe the help was from God: "They thought that God was helping them because the Pilgrims were supposed to be very religious so God would help them." In discussion with Peter, Matthew, and Adam, the teacher explored this question further.

Matthew	I think that is pretty obvious. I'm sure they believed it was God helping them; it's quite easy to figure that out. [He then quoted Bradford.] "They fell upon their knees and blessed God who had delivered them."
Adam	And then it says, backing up Matt's idea, in Source 5, "After some accidents and mistakes he stumbled on the harbor of Plymouth where it pleased Almighty God who had better provided for them than they could imagine."
Teacher	What do you think he meant by "than they could imagine"?
Adam	I think he means, like, they got better land than him because they got an abandoned town, so John Pory's group in South Virginia didn't have that, so God had provided them better.
Peter	And in those times most things were based round religion, religion was very important in those days.
Teacher	What kind of religion is this that you are talking about?
All	Catholic? Christians?
Teacher	Did you read the bottom of that page about the Pilgrims? [pointing to the definition of Pilgrims on the briefing sheet]
Adam	Oh no. They're Protestants, and they're getting away from the English church because they don't want to abide by their laws.
Teacher	Do you know the word "providence"? If I said people believed in "divine providence" would you know what I meant? If I said you believe that God lets you know whether what you are doing is OK, would you know what I meant?
Adam	Like in a vision?
Teacher	What kind of things could you use to decide how God is going to let you know?
Adam	He could come to you in a dream.
Teacher	What is God likely to do to people that please him?
Matthew	Give them good weather and be nice to them.
Adam	Give them what they want.
Teacher	So how do you know?

Adam	If you have got a good life.
Teacher	Yes, if something good happens to you.
Adam	Then you know.
Teacher	How are you going to see that?
Adam	As an act of God.

The teacher drew their attention to the particulars of the Pilgrims' situation.

Teacher	Right, so what about this abandoned village?
Matthew	To them it's like an act of God because its more than they could have imagined possible.
Peter	They might have said, like English kings, they say, like God chose me to be king. So the Pilgrims could be saying, well, God has told me that I have to live here.

Teacher Question 6.

Why did religious people like the Pilgrims think they had the right to take over land that wasn't theirs?

What is this question trying to find out about students' existing understanding?

This question explores the extent to which students:
(a) Make stereotypical assumptions about religious beliefs.
(b) Are able to use their understanding about the Pilgrims' religious beliefs to explain the Pilgrims' actions in this particular case.

What is this question trying to encourage students to reflect on as a means of developing their understanding?

The question is designed to:
(a) Open up a discussion of the different ways in which past events can be explained.
(b) Develop an understanding that the Pilgrims' values and practices were not the same as ours and help explain what they did.

This question of how people see things is important for understanding what to make of evidence and is central to any kind of empathy (whether understanding patterns of belief and values or explaining particular actions; see Box 3-3). The Pilgrims' task allows this understanding to be taken further, and question 6 pursues one major thread, presenting students with a paradox.

Students' answers to question 6 revealed attempts to make what today appears to be rather indefensible behavior less unpalatable. Sean explained:

> *The Pilgrims wanted to discover more land and find out what the world looked like. They were not aiming to take over land when they set off, they were just aiming to discover more land and find out if the land around them was inhabited or if they were the only people existing along with other people they knew existed such as the French and Scandinavians.*

Sean actually avoided explaining the relevant action of the Pilgrims, or at least justified it as not intentional, suggesting that the Pilgrims were in fact part of a larger movement of people who were benign explorers.

In the small-group discussion we have been following, the teacher drew the attention of Peter, Adam, and Matthew to this question.

Teacher	Let's think about this right they think they have to take the land.
Adam	They believe they had the right like Peter said, because they needed to get away and after some errors and accidents like they stumbled across a harbor, whether it was because of the wind or the backwardness of their ship's captain they did not arrive where they had planned, so they therefore believed that God did not want them to live where they had planned, so whether it was the ship's captain or the wind, God changed it around, so that instead they reached the harbor of Cape Cod, so therefore they believed that God wanted them to live there.

Peter took this argument further, suggesting they would need to justify the action in terms of the Native Americans' religious "failings," and Matthew was concerned that their religious beliefs should not go unrecognized. Peter, however, reinforced the point more precisely by talking about how the Pilgrims might justify their action in their own terms, rather than according to the way we would look at this situation now.

BOX 3-3 Did People Think Like Us in the Past?

A major step for young students of history is to recognize that they cannot rely on our modern ways of thinking to explain why people in the past acted as they did.

In action research in U.K. schools carried out by Dickinson and Lee and by Ashby and Lee, groups of three students in grades 5 to 8 were asked to explain why the Anglo-Saxons used the ordeal to find out whether someone was guilty or innocent of a crime.[8] Their discussions were recorded on videotape.

Some students dismissed the ordeal as absurd, but others tried to make sense of it by turning it from a form of trial into a method of punishment aimed at deterrence. Their reaction was that, given any reasonable—i.e., modern—ideas and values, it could not have been a trial, so it must have been something else. If it was so deliberately unfair (by our standards), then it must have been doing what *we* would do if *we* behaved like that. As one group of eighth graders said, "If this is as unfair as we seem to make out it is, no one's going to steal anything," because they will be "scared they'll get caught." Students thinking like this cease to think of the ordeal as part of a trial, and reduce it to a form of deterrent. Some students slip into calling the ordeal a "punishment."

Another move made by students is to recognize that the Anglo-Saxons held different religious beliefs from ours, but then to treat this as part of the problem: the ordeal is the sort of absurd thing you would expect from their religion.

A few eighth graders, however, not only were able to use the different ideas held by the Anglo-Saxons to explain why the ordeal took the form it did, but were even prepared to switch perspective to judge present institutions in what they thought of as Anglo-Saxon terms.

Tim	They'd probably say that their system then, with God, is better than ours, because, well people can muck around with the truth, but God . . .
Lawrence	But God doesn't.
Tim	They'd probably say theirs was better than ours.

Peter	They might have even thought that God was punishing the Indians because the Indians weren't very religious.
Matthew	Weren't they, they had Gods, other Gods, didn't they?
Adam	Yes, they had statues and things, totem poles and things?

Peter	The Pilgrims could have said in, like, their defense, that you have not been worshiping the right God, so you have been bad, so you can go away.

The Language of Sources, Interpretation, and Other Perspectives

At the end of the discussion with Peter, Adam, and Matthew, their teacher wanted them to consider more carefully the different ways in which actions may be interpreted.

Teacher	Do you think when Bradford talks of the group of native people as "running away" that the native people would have described it as "running away"?
Adam	I wouldn't think so. I think they would say [sic] it as "going back to your tribe to tell them what was happening."
Matthew	To tell them.
Adam	They might say, "We've got white people with different ideas and a strange language. We need back-up, we've got to get ready for these people or otherwise they could change our entire habitat our entire . . ."
Teacher	So you are saying that if you don't attack someone as soon as they land and you go away, you don't have to see that as "running away." I know I'm probably putting words in your mouth here, but would you see this kind of "running away" as being scared or being sensible?
Matthew	Being sensible because like it says they were greeted by five or six people with a dog, and how are five or six people and a dog going to take on the people with the firearms?
Peter	Maybe they can sense, like, these people are dangerous so it might be a mixture of both really.
Teacher	So sensible people have to work out what's going on before they make decisions?
Peter	Well maybe it's a mixture of being sensible and being scared.

Teacher	Have you heard that expression, "Fools rush in where angels fear to tread"?
Adam	Yes. Angels are smart so they back off but fools they rush in and get killed.
Teacher	So this may have been not "running away" in the way we might understand it, as it is described, but making sure that they could assess the situation in their own way in their own time.

In the absence of testimony from the Native Americans, this conversation about how to understand a relatively concrete and simple action opens up the possibility of helping students think about the way our picture of the actions of the Native Americans is mediated by the cultural assumptions of the settlers.

The exploratory approach exemplified by this task and the ensuing dialogue enables us to gauge our students' understanding of historical evidence, particularly their understanding of how to use testimony as evidence. We can then engage more confidently in direct teaching, knowing that we have a clearer understanding of the ideas with which particular students are working. The evidence work was not, of course, detached from gaining knowledge of the topic. In fact, the richness of the sources generated a great deal of excitement and a wealth of questions. Students were keen to know more about what happened: to understand the opportunities that were available to the Pilgrims, the nature of the difficulties they faced, and how they dealt with those difficulties. They raised questions about the native population: Who were they? What kinds of beliefs and ideas did they hold? How did they live? Were they friendly? How did they feel about the arrival of the Pilgrims? Did they mind them taking the corn? Did they help them? Did they attack them? Did they feel threatened? While some waited with anticipation for the next lesson, others went off to search the Web for answers to their questions. Work focused on developing ideas about how evidence had simultaneously opened up opportunities to explore the historical content. It was as if, in grappling with the sources, they had acquired a vested interest in knowing.

WORKING WITH EVIDENCE: THE ST. BRENDAN'S VOYAGE TASK

The Pilgrim Fathers' case study exemplifies how several important things can be happening at once in the classroom. Developing an understanding of key second-order concepts and learning about the past can go hand in hand. At the same time as they are learning about evidence, students can acquire knowledge ranging from relatively straightforward matters, such as the physical conditions the Pilgrims faced on their arrival in America, to more sophisticated ideas, such as seventeenth-century conceptions of Providence.

We can try to understand students' ideas and at the same time build on or reshape those ideas. As we probe students' use of source materials to discover their preconceptions about how one can know about the past, we have an opportunity to develop their understanding of testimony by encouraging them to think about how it may have arisen. Encouraging such thinking in turn opens up new opportunities to consider what kinds of beliefs are involved, so that the students begin to consider the nature of the source. Students capable of discussing these matters are not far from an understanding of how sources may be used as evidence.

Of course, the ideas about evidence that surface in the Pilgrims' case study give us only a snapshot of students' ideas at one point in time. Such ideas may be more or less well consolidated and stable; they may be accessible to students in one context but not in another. We cannot assume that any changes that take place in one lesson have been fully grasped, so it will be important to return to them in other encounters with history. Still more important, the ideas we uncover in our probing will depend partly on what has been taught in previous grades. The students' ideas might have been different if their earlier teaching had been different.[9] The point is not that someone might have taught the students about the Pilgrims already in an earlier grade, but that they could have begun to learn about evidence much earlier, through different content—something exciting that we think is appropriate for youngsters and still fits into our overall content framework (in this case that of migrations, explorations, and encounters). Equally, we may sometimes want to help a group of older students who happen not to have had the opportunity to confront ideas about historical evidence, or whose understanding remains weak.

The St. Brendan task is an example of one possible way in which we might begin much earlier than sixth grade to develop students' ideas about how one can know the past. The story of St. Brendan's voyage in the sixth century allows us to raise the question, "Did an Irish monk land in America about 1,000 years before Columbus?" This is a question of the kind many students enjoy, and the different layers of evidence available make it highly suitable for addressing the problems of making valid statements about the past. As historical "content," its importance lies in helping students see that—even if it were true that Brendan reached America—"firsts" of this kind often lead nowhere. However, the discussion here focuses not on historical significance, but on learning about historical evidence, and serves only as an example of how such a task might work, not a prescription to be followed as "the right way to teach."

The story of St. Brendan may appear to be a matter of peripheral interest to a grand theme such as migration, exploration, and encounter, but it is possible to use very small amounts of content to tackle big ideas. We must avoid swamping *any* students with content, but this is especially important with younger or less sophisticated students. They need space to think, and teachers need time to help them. The purpose of the St. Brendan task is to develop students' ideas of historical evidence, not to give them large quantities of information. We must not repeatedly ambush students with things they *do not* know when the point of the task is to equip them with ideas to help them think more effectively about what they *do* know. This is an important reason why the—relatively—self-contained St. Brendan story is used. The voyage of St. Brendan is also useful because it is likely to be unfamiliar to students (see Box 3-4).

The St. Brendan task is designed primarily for young students from fourth grade up. (How far up will depend on what targets we set; students can respond to open-ended questions at very different levels.) It differs significantly from the Pilgrims' task, in part because it is designed to put teaching first rather than to aid in the "diagnosis" of students' ideas. Nonetheless, teaching and diagnosis must go hand in hand.

Preparing for the Task

Before proceeding with the St. Brendan task, we must consider both the preconceptions the students will be bringing to the task and just what we might achieve with them.

The student quotations used in the Brendan case study are from written work done after whole-class teaching in the United States and the United Kingdom, and also from recorded oral work with small groups. The group work (with U.K. children) was important because it allowed students' discussions to be recorded so as to give an accurate and detailed picture of some of what was said, and as a result, the majority of the examples are taken from the recordings. But it is important to emphasize that the Brendan task is not designed particularly for group work, and has been used in the United States and the United Kingdom with full classes from grades 2 to 6.

Preconceptions About How We Know About the Past

Research and experience suggest that the preconceptions we are likely to encounter will be something along the following lines.[10] Many students between fourth and sixth grades will not have thought about how we know of the past and will have no settled ideas about how we can gain such knowledge. They may treat the matter as being about *where we find the information*—which books or encyclopedias we consult or whom we ask—

BOX 3-4 The Dangers of What Appears to Be Familiar

Students are frequently resistant to teachers' attempts to change their ideas. One reason for this is their lack of metacognitive awareness, which can make it difficult for them to distinguish between what they think they already know about a topic and new information presented by a teacher or inferred from evidence.

VanSledright set out as researcher and teacher to teach fifth graders American history, while at the same time developing their understanding of historical enquiry.[11] He presented the students with Hakim's conjecture that local Powhatan Indians withheld food and supplies from Jamestown, perhaps laying siege to the stockade for much of the winter of 1609–1610. He provided the students with primary source materials and a framework for questioning those materials. The task was to test Hakim's claim. VanSledright reports the difficulties some students experienced in having to put aside their everyday ideas and prior assumptions to focus on the available evidence.

Having picked up on the testimony of Governor George Percy—who spoke of "great plenty" in 1605 in contrast to Captain John Smith, who reported starvation at Jamestown in 1624—the students resolved this conflict by depicting Percy as someone covering up the truth. Many of the students used the testimony as evidence that Percy had survived the famine. Ignoring the temporal context (perhaps influenced by Disney's character in "Pocahontas," the rather fat and greedy Governor Ratcliffe, whose dog was called Percy, the students decided that George Percy had hoarded and eaten all the food and was therefore responsible for the famine. This position was difficult to shake. As VanSledright tells us, "Given the documents at our disposal, it was likely that either poor leadership in hunting and gathering food over the winter or a siege by the Powhatans was a more palatable, evidence-based interpretation of the Starving Time. However, the die appeared to be cast. The popularity of 'liar Percy,' who hoarded food for himself, became the interpretive mantra of all but . . . four students."

It follows that much may be gained by working with topics that are completely new to students and do not figure in folk histories, and about which films—by Disney or anyone else—have not been made.

not about what evidence we examine. Others will have given the matter some thought and will assume *we cannot really know because we were not there*. For some students, this is where their thinking will stop.

A majority of the students who have thought about how we gain knowledge of the past are likely to think that true reports (typically diaries or accounts handed down in families) may allow us to know what happened.

But many will recognize that there may be problems in obtaining such reports. Typically they will point out that people do not always tell the truth. They are also likely to suggest the possibility of transmission errors (a conception modeled on the party whispering game, where a message changes as it is passed on). They may also assume that we cannot know whether reports are true or not. Older students—and some fourth graders—may mention exaggeration and bias as additional problems. Even among those students who have some idea about links with the past, many will think the only way to check the truth of reports properly would be to go back into the past to witness what happened; thus in the end, these students, too, are likely to come back to the position that we cannot really know about the past because we were not there.

Box 3-5 summarizes the range of student assumptions about how we know of the past that we are likely to encounter in our teaching. Our goal is to help students see that knowing about the past is a problem of working things out using evidence, but we may have to be content with less: if some students move from seeing the problem in terms of information to thinking of it in terms of testimony, we will have achieved something important.

BOX 3-5 Common Student Assumptions About How We Know of the Past

It's an information problem.	Where do we find the stuff?
It's a problem about access to the past.	We can't know because we weren't there. We didn't see it.
It's a problem about finding true reports.	We can know about what happened, but only if we can find something where someone "told it like it was." They would probably have had to see it happen.
It's a problem about trusting "true" reports.	We can't really know if someone did tell the truth, and anyway things get changed as they are passed down. People tell lies and exaggerate. Some are biased.
It's a problem about working things out using evidence.	We don't depend on people telling us what happened. We can work it out from clues we have, even if no one told us what happened. We can ask questions of a source that it wasn't intended to answer.

What Are We Trying to Achieve?

As teachers we could choose to do all sorts of things with the Brendan story, but in this discussion we focus on some key shifts in ideas. First is the shift from the idea that we just have *information* about the past that is usually true (but sometimes false) to the idea that any claim about the past needs testing and some sort of backup. Second is the shift from the idea that we cannot say anything about the past unless someone from the time left us a true report (testimony) to the idea that we have to work out what happened using evidence.

By the end of the Brendan task, fourth graders who started with little experience of working with historical evidence should understand (at least in this context) that the past is not given information, fixed by books or authorities; that we have no direct access to the past; and that we do not rely on someone from the time telling us truthfully what happened. Nonetheless, we can work out what happened; indeed, a discipline called "history" exists precisely because we *have* to work it out. Students should also understand that often we cannot be certain about what happened, but this does not mean guessing is sufficient: when we cannot be certain, we can still produce stronger or weaker arguments about what answers make most sense. This understanding is likely to remain highly unsophisticated after just one task, and students will find it difficult to articulate what counts as a "stronger" or "weaker" argument. This is why it is important to return frequently and explicitly to what makes an argument work or fail in a range of contexts.

This level of understanding is likely to be enough for many fourth-grade students. However, some youngsters may already be working with much more sophisticated ideas than most of their classmates, and eventually we want *all* our students to go beyond the above shifts in ideas. Thus it is worth thinking about how to take students' ideas about evidence a little further should such opportunities arise.

Only when we are clear about the question we are asking can we say what evidence is available, and it is our question that allows us to begin to consider whether a source of evidence is reliable. People often talk of written sources as more or less "reliable" as though these accounts are reports to be judged on what they are deliberately telling us—mere testimony that we must accept or reject (whether in part or as a whole). Students often think of reliability as inherent in the source instead of asking themselves, "Reliable for what?" We might expect some students to go further, and understand that we can ask a question that is not about what the source is reporting at all. All this indicates the importance of helping students understand that it is *questions* that lie at the heart of using evidence. Students also tend to think of reliability as an all-or-nothing property of a source rather than as a judgement about how far the source can be used as evidence to answer a particular question. They should understand that some questions place heavier burdens on a source than others. In other words, the burden of proof resting on a source varies according to both the nature of the source and the demands and precision of the question. For example, answers to the question, "Did Bjarni Herjólfsson accidentally reach Labrador in the tenth century?" may impose a greater burden of proof on a source than does the question, "Could the Vikings have reached America?"

Students can begin to tackle these problems by considering something close to their lives. How reliable is a school report? Can we answer that question without knowing what it is supposed to be evidence for? Is it as reliable for providing evidence of a student's school behavior as for providing evidence of the teacher's attitude toward the student? Many fourth graders are well able to appreciate the importance of the question we ask if we begin with everyday examples:

Teacher	If I say "Here's your teacher's report, on you, what are the things I *can* learn about you, and what sort of things *can't* I find about you from this report?" what would you say?
Jeff	You could learn how we act around our teacher.
Carly	If we chat, and not listen.
Teacher	What wouldn't we be able to learn?
Jeff	How we act at home, what sort of games we play on our Playstation.

An extension of these ideas is that our questions need not ask about what the source is trying to tell us. Moreover, some sources are not trying to give us any kind of true story about something that happened; they are relics of an activity, not reports on it.

Teacher	OK, supposing I get one of your exercise books. Is there anything in it about you? There's nothing in it telling a story about you? Does that mean I couldn't say anything about you on the basis of what's in the book?
Carly	Our handwriting and spelling . . .
Jeff	You could say I'm not very good at writing.
Teacher	So if a historian picked up your exercise book, she could tell something about you even if you weren't trying to tell her anything.

The Brendan task actually sidesteps talk about "reliability," precisely because it can too easily lead youngsters to think in terms of accepting or rejecting something as a true or false report rather than thinking about how to use it as evidence. There is a sense in which it is doubly misleading to think of the Brendan story as a true report of something. How could this story possibly be testimony that Brendan reached America? There was no "America" when the story was written, so no one could write a report of his reaching it. This is another reason why the whole tenor of the task is one of working out the best answer we can get to what is our (twenty-first-century) question.

If the Brendan task were used with students in the seventh grade and beyond, we would be thinking in terms of more sophisticated understanding (even fourth or third graders who started with more powerful ideas than those we assumed in the previous section would be capable of making real gains here). In particular, it would be worth developing the idea that to make sense of a piece of evidence, we must know what kind of thing it is. The account of the voyage of St. Brendan is not a failed attempt to give a factual report of an exploration, but a story about a saint. There is not a necessary conflict between its inclusion of supernatural events and its having a basis in fact, because if the author were writing for an audience that expected wonders, their absence would simply weaken the story. So even in the unlikely event that the writer had access to an oral tradition that gave a detailed account of a more modern kind, we would scarcely expect the story to have been written in that way. The teaching target, then, is to help students see that we cannot decide whether the Brendan story will help answer the question "Did Brendan get to America?" by dismissing it as a "made-up" story, any more than they can simply accept it as a "true story." We are trying to get them beyond this simple dichotomy and encourage them to ask, "What kind of story is this?"

How can we know what inferences we are entitled to draw from a source? At this point, we are touching on ideas generally labeled "empathy" or "perspective taking." The link between evidence and empathy is the general principle that, if we are to be able to use any particular source of evidence to answer a question, we must know what kind of thing the source is. And we cannot know what kind of thing a source is if we do not know what it meant to the people who produced it. Only if we understand that a source is, say, a piece of religious exhortation rather than a news report can we avoid making serious mistakes in the way we argue from it. And knowing what a source is means knowing what people at the time saw it as, which in turn requires knowing about people's world view at the time. Students may find it easy to deal with this issue in the context of everyday items with which they are familiar, especially if those items have a place in the students' culture that is not always obvious to adults. For example, students would likely have little trouble in seeing how a future historian who assumed that a high-status brand of sneaker was just a shoe might find it difficult to understand how someone would commit a crime to obtain it.

However, a task designed to tackle students' ideas about understanding people in the past would have to offer them more material about Brendan's world than is required in the evidence task on which we are focusing here. We must not confuse our goals by attempting too much at once, and in any case, there are other specific ideas that students need to learn in connection with empathy. It is enough in the Brendan task to help students see that they need to ask what kind of story they are dealing with before they can safely use it as evidence.

Preconceptions About People, Society, and How the World Works

It is much more difficult to predict what assumptions students will have about the substantive past than what they will assume about the discipline of history. This is so because in the former case, so many assumptions are possible in so many different areas, even with relatively circumscribed content such as the Brendan story.

The problem of identifying students' assumptions is complicated enough when we confine ourselves to their ideas about what is physically possible. Some will expect wooden objects to last for thousands of years and think it possible for submarines to search the entire seabed of the Atlantic in a week or two to find the remains of a small wood-and-leather boat. Many will have no idea what an ocean current is or why it might have made a difference in what destination a sailing boat with a steering oar could reach. Some will imagine icebergs to be rather small objects, a few yards across. (And of course few will know the location of the Faroe Islands, Iceland, or Newfoundland. Here, however, it is easier for the teacher to list essential knowledge and make sure it is available.)

Predicting students' prior conceptions is even more difficult when it comes to ideas about what people do. The one thing we can be fairly sure of is that students will assume people in the past thought as we do. Thus in teaching about Brendan, we are likely to find students arguing that the story may have been exaggerated so that it was more exciting, and that one reason for this was that the writer could make a better profit. Behind this argument, of course, is a picture of a world that has always had widely available books, mass literacy, and a capitalist economic system.

What all this means is that as teachers we need to be sensitive to students' substantive assumptions as we proceed—hence the importance of lessons in which students have room to express their ideas so that there is some chance of discovering what those ideas are. But it is important to remember with something like the Brendan task, which is designed to develop understandings about the discipline of history, that not all students' substantive misconceptions actually matter for the task at hand. For this task, the focus is their thinking about how we know about the past, not on correcting every minor misconception about geography or even about how society works.

Working Through the Task

The Question

We begin with the question:

Did an Irish monk land in America about 1,000 years before Columbus?

As teachers we need to be very clear in our own minds about the question right from the start, even if it is not necessarily sensible to pursue this with the students as an abstract issue at the outset. This particular question is asking about what happened, not just what was possible. Since in history it is always the question that decides what can be evidence and how that evidence can be used, this is an important point.

We tell the students that they are going to look at some important historical sources and that they will use these sources as evidence to try to obtain the best answer they can to the question. The idea of "the best answer you can get" is something that can be woven into the discussion as it proceeds.[12] By the end of the task, we will want all the students at least to understand that "the best answer" means the one for which we have the best evidence. Some students will be able to think in more sophisticated terms—perhaps something more like "the answer that makes the best sense of the most evidence and is not knocked out by anything."

The Story

We next give students an introduction to the story of St. Brendan's voyage and the story itself to read. (This material can be read by the teacher, but preferably should not be read around the class by students since doing so tends to break up the picture, especially if the students read in a halting manner.) Issues about the meaning of words or sentences can be addressed at the end, but not in a way that preempts interpretation. For example, there should be no hint that the supernatural elements in the story might also be interpreted naturalistically or that they are somehow signs of the story's being discredited or "untrue." At this stage, we normally try to avoid offering any views of our own on the nature of the story or its veracity. We need to find out how our students see it.

Introduction: The Story of St. Brendan

(All the underlined words are explained at the end.)

Sometime between the year 900 and the year 1000, someone wrote down an amazing story. It was written in the Latin language.

The story described how an Irish monk called St. Brendan went on a long voyage lasting 7 years to a land called the Land of Promise. We know that Brendan lived in Ireland between (roughly) 486 and 578. There are things in the story that make some people think Brendan might have crossed the Atlantic Ocean and reached America.

It is quite likely that the story comes from even earlier times than 900, but we don't know that. There are more than 120 versions of the story in Latin and more in other languages. They all say almost the same things.

Time Line

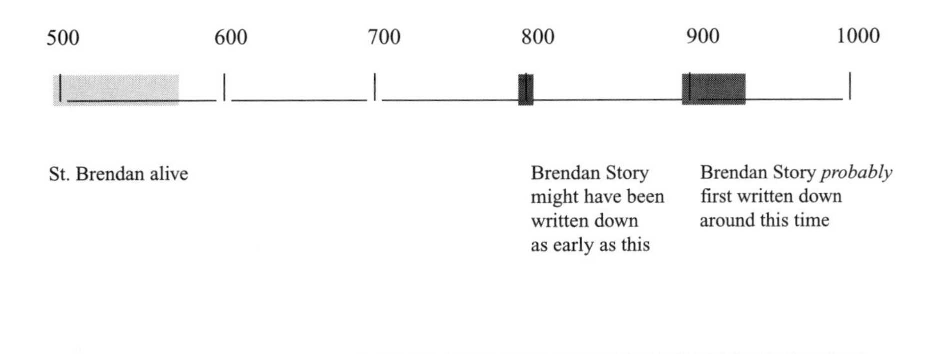

The Voyage of St. Brendan

(This is a shortened version of the story. It misses out some of the adventures of St. Brendan and his crew of monks. All the underlined words are explained at the end.)

St. Brendan lived at Clonfert in Ireland. He was head of a community of 3000 monks. One day a monk called Barrind visited Brendan and told him about a Land of Promise across the sea in the west. It was a wonderful place, special to God.

Brendan decided to go and find this Land of Promise. He and his monks built a boat with a wooden frame, covered in tanned leather. He put food and drink in the boat to last for 40 days, and also spare leather and fat for greasing it.

1. An Irish boat, copied from a carving done on a stone pillar some time between 700 and 800.

Brendan set out with 17 other monks and sailed west. After 15 days they landed on a tall rocky island. A dog led them to a settlement, where they found a meal waiting for them. They stayed for 3 days without seeing anyone, but food was always set out on the table for them.

Next they landed on an island with lots of streams, all full of fish. It was called the Island of Sheep, because flocks of sheep roamed over it all year round. A man gave them food.

Then they visited another island that was rocky and bare. They made a fire to cook food, when suddenly the "island" began to move. The monks quickly jumped into their boat, just in time to see the "island" swim off with the fire still burning. St. Brendan told the monks that it was the biggest fish in the ocean, and its name was "Jasconius."

2. The monks land on Jasconius. A picture painted between 600 and 700 years after Brendan's time.

After this the monks sailed to an island called The Paradise of Birds. They hauled their boat almost a mile up a narrow stream, and found a huge tree covered in white birds. A bird flew down and told Brendan that the birds were men's spirits, and that he would have to search 7 years to find the Land of Promise. The birds sang hymns and chanted prayers at the right times of day. A man called the Steward brought food across to the monks. (He was the man who had given them food on the Island of Sheep.)

The monks were at sea for 3 months before they came to another island. They were so exhausted that they could hardly row the boat against the wind. On the island they found monks who had agreed to keep silent (so that they could concentrate on thinking about God). The monks had been there 80 years, and none of them had been ill. They showed Brendan how their lamps were lit by a miraculous flaming arrow each evening.

The monks had many adventures before they found the Land of Promise. Many times they found themselves back at the Island of Sheep. But they still continued their search. Once they found a column of crystal sticking up out of the sea. It was surrounded by a mesh that was the color of silver and as hard as marble. They found an opening in the mesh and took the boat close to the column. St Brendan and his monks measured the column. Its four sides were each 700 yards long. The monks then took hold of the mesh and pulled the boat out to the open sea.

3. A modern picture of what we think Brendan's boat might look like.

Another day the monks were blown towards an island, and Brendan was worried. He heard the sound of a <u>*forge*</u>*, with the thud of a hammer on an* <u>*anvil*</u>*. As the monks came near the island, an islander came out and threw molten metal and hot stones at them. A lump flew 200 yards over their heads and fell into the sea. The sea round it boiled, and smoke rose up. Then more islanders rushed down to the shore and threw hot stones at the monks. Soon it looked as if the whole island was on fire. The sea boiled, the air was filled with a howling sound, and there was a terrible smell. Brendan told his monks they had reached the edge of Hell. They sailed away as fast as they could.*

In the end the Steward from the Isle of Sheep had to help them find the Land of Promise. They left the Isle of Sheep again, and after 40 days at sea they sailed into a great fog. The Steward said the fog always encircled the Land of Promise.

At last they saw a great light, and the boat came to the shore. The land was full of fruit trees. They explored for 40 days, but still did not come to the end of the land they were exploring. Finally they reached a big river, which Brendan said they would not be able to cross. A man came to them, spoke to them by name, and said the land would eventually be made known to all people at a time when Christians were being persecuted.

Brendan gathered samples of fruits, and sailed home with his monks.

Explanation of Words in the Story

<u>*Latin*</u>

Latin was the language people used for writing in Brendan's time. Almost the only people in Europe who could write were Christian monks and priests. Christian priests continued to use Latin for most of their writing for more than 1,000 years after Brendan's time.

Monk

Monks are men who spend their lives studying God, worshipping him, and trying to do what God wants. They live together in communities called monasteries, helping each other and worshipping God together.

Communities

Communities are groups of people who live or work together.

Land of Promise

This means a land where everything is right for people to live a great life. It's the sort of land where it is easy to find food, where all the plants and flowers are beautiful and grow well, and the climate is comfortable.

Tanned leather

This was specially toughened leather. It was soaked in juice from the bark of oak trees to make it stronger.

Column

A column is shaped like a pillar or a fat post, usually taller than it is wide.

Crystal

The monks meant the column was hard, bright, and semitransparent.

Mesh

A mesh is like the sort of pattern you get with a net: squares with lines or gaps between them.

Marble

This is a very hard kind of stone, often used for expensive buildings or for gravestones.

Forge

A forge is where blacksmiths make tools or weapons out of hot iron.

Anvil

This is a big block (usually made of iron) that blacksmiths use. When they are beating some hot iron into shape with a hammer (to make a tool or a weapon), they rest the hot iron on the anvil.

Working Things Out for Ourselves

Once the students have read the story and preferably had a chance to talk to each other about it, we can ask, "What do you think? Did St. Brendan get to America? What's your hunch?" After time for a free discussion, part of the point of which is to discover the way students are thinking about how we know the past or about how the Brendan story might be tested, we can press for justifications. "How can we take this further? What kind of backup can you give for your hunches? It needs to be something that might persuade someone else."

The first target is to build the idea that claims about the past cannot be taken simply as (given) information, true or false. We have to be able to justify them, and this may raise problems for us. The kinds of moves students are making will need to be made explicit and weighed. What exactly are they doing to test the claim here? What is helpful? What does not work? Are they treating the sources simply as information? (See Box 3-6.)

We need to encourage students to think about their own strategies and arguments as much as about Brendan. Some group work may be valuable here, although whole-class discussion can be highly effective if students are used to really listening to each other.

We also want to begin to counter the idea that we are totally dependent on someone in the past telling us a true story. We can try to make students

BOX 3-6 Going Beyond Face Value

When they start using historical evidence, students seldom pay much attention to the provenance of the sources, especially when they are looking at pictures. But faced with a paradox and a little encouragement to look more closely, they can often take major steps beyond treating sources as information.

Teacher	The boat was made of leather wasn't it? So how come *that* boat [points to Jasconius picture] is made of wood? Before you answer, just read what it says under the picture.
Don	So if it was painted after all *them* years, perhaps the painter never knew what his boat looked like, he just thinks, "Cor blimey, I don't know what to paint, so I might as well just pretend his boat's wood."
Rachel	The painter wouldn't know that his boat was made of leather 'cos the painter weren't a scientist, and he would've had to read something like this, what we've read, to find out.
Jilly	Because it was 700 years later, they didn't think, like, you'd have leather boats in that time, because they would've had wooden boats.

Box 3-7 Being Aware of How You Are Thinking

Youngsters are not generally accustomed to thinking about the kind of knowledge they have and how they are using it, so although they are well aware of the concrete suggestions they have made, getting them to consider these ideas reflexively may be difficult.

Teacher	You've given some good reasons. Where were they coming from?
Sonny	My brain?
Joe	What we've learned.
Teacher	Well, let's look at the things Sonny was saying, because what he actually said was they'd have run out of food, because if you count the number of days they were on the voyage. . . . Now, what sort of test is that? Where's that idea come from? What is it that you know, to have asked that question?
Sonny	I just wondered how could they survive without food.
Teacher	OK, but what is it that you know, to make that a good question?
Charlene	Because in this story it said nothing about food.
Teacher	Right, but why is Sonny right to say, "Hang on a minute, they haven't got enough food"? Where does that knowledge come from that he has?
Joe	It says in the first part they only had enough food and drink for 40 days.
Teacher	So he's looked very closely at the story, but then he's testing it by asking a question that's not from knowledge about the story. What's it knowledge about? When you say, "Could they have survived without food?", what knowledge are you using?
Joe	Oh! Using the knowledge that everyone knows that you can't survive without food!

This exchange among third graders is the start of a process, not a secure achievement at this point.

aware of the kinds of criteria they are already using that are not dependent on authority (given information) or on testimony (see Box 3-7). They raise such questions as "Could this incident have happened?", "Do birds sing hymns?", and "Isn't the Atlantic a bit rough for a little leather boat?" The fifth graders in the following (written) examples provide plenty for their teacher to go on, but the key point to emphasize is that we are not completely helpless if someone is not "telling the truth."

Greg	I think St. Brendan did get to America. But the story would sound more real if they took out all of the talk birds. You could find out by going to a library, and if the library doesn't have it, ask somebody else.
Barbara	I'm not sure [if Brendan got to America]. To me he could have just sailed to another part of Ireland he didn't know about. I don't even think this story is true, because the stewardess [sic] was also before them, so he could have reached "America" before them. When they first met him, how did they know they weren't already in America? The way the story is told just sounds fake. If no one had been to America, how did they know about it, and why did it take so long to write about it? If we wanted to find out, we would have to take everybody who thought about this back in time, because one person could lie.

Many students, like these third graders, distinguish between "true stories" and "fake" or "made-up stories."

Charlene	If they wrote it like 300 years after he'd done something, it couldn't, it might not be true 'cos they don't actually know.
Joe	How would they know this would've happened all those years after?
Sonny	The story could be carried on by other people.
Charlene	But it might be made up.
Sonny	It might be not true, it might be, like . . .
Charlene	Made up. It might be, what do they call, is it fiction or nonfiction?
Teacher	It's fiction if it's made up.
Charlene	Yeah, fiction.

We need to be sure students are clear that factual stories try to say true things, whereas fiction is invented, and does not have to be true. But this is just making sure that everyone is starting from the same point because, as noted earlier, we need to get students beyond this simple dichotomy. Youngsters often have problems in conceptualizing something that is not straightforwardly true or untrue. Take the following discussion among third graders.

Teacher	What sort of story do you think this is?
Ricky	I think it's like sort of true, and not true, sort of story, between that.
Teacher	Half way between true and not true? And why do you think that?
Ricky	It might be, in that bit, they, he might [much hesitation and repetition of start of sentence] . . . I don't know what I'm going to say now [laughs].
Teacher	[Laughs] No, keep going. . . .Sounded interesting.
Ricky	I'll start again. I think it's between that because he might not get there, and it's like sort of made up, some of this, I think.
Teacher	What makes you think some of it is made up?
Ricky	Because there couldn't be a giant fish—there's no giant fishes around now.
Lenny	You know that fish, it could be a whale-shark.

The idea that Brendan may possibly have reached America or that his doing so may be more or less likely tends to be expressed in terms of Brendan going part of the way. Halfway between true and made up is turned into part of the way to America.

Bill	He could've gone somewhere near America.
Steve	He might have done it to Canada.
Naomi	Yeah, but America just doesn't fit.
Steve	I think it was Canada.
Teacher	They're including all that as America. It's the continent of North America, not the country—there wasn't one called America then.
Naomi	I think it was round about America but not America.
Teacher	So where was it then? That's not a good move, because now you've got a worse problem, because you've got to say where it could have been, and there isn't anywhere it could have been.
Steve	What's under America?

Teacher	More of America.
Bill	Mexico! Might be Mexico.
Steve	Could've gone to Cuba.
Teacher	But if he got that far, he could have got to America.
Bill	America's so *big*. He could've gone *that* side of the world [pointing to Indian Ocean].

Note that the problem here is not that the students' geography is shaky (although that may be true), but that they have a desperate need to find something Brendan might have reached that is not America. If the story cannot be accepted but cannot be dismissed, the answer must be that Brendan got part of the way, or even went a different way. This notion is a proxy for talk of possibility or likelihood. Mitch, a fifth grader, may be thinking in this way when he suggests, "I think it's not possible because he might have went in circles, there might have been another way to get to America to go the opposite way, or it might not work because of the wind and currents."

Much of the discussion will be based on plausibility, partly because the task is deliberately designed so that initially it gives little else to go on; thus students are able to make judgments without having to master a mass of material. They generally will not use the word "plausible," but it is valuable to introduce the term here to make them more aware of their own thinking. As students are introduced to new evidence, we can then keep returning to the question, "How plausible do you think the story is now?"

Most students at this stage talk in terms of "everyday" plausibility—what would be plausible if the story were written today. Ideas that appeal to what was likely then do not usually emerge until later, when we turn to the kind of story the Brendan voyage is. The distinction is highly sophisticated, but occasionally a few students will hint at it. Such responses need reinforcing—not necessarily at this point if doing so discourages other responses, but as something to return to should the chance arise.

Thinking About the Story from the Outside

To build on the general ideas students use to make their first judgment about Brendan's voyage, we can ask a simpler question: "Is it even *possible* that a boat like Brendan's could make a journey across an ocean?" Because we want to know how the students are thinking, we can also ask, "How could we find out?"

If the students are to make good progress in answering these questions, they will need to consider more specific knowledge, namely other relevant things we know about Brendan and his times. But students often suggest making a copy of the Brendan boat to see what it can do, and because Tim Severin did exactly that, this is a good time to introduce his reconstruction and his crossing of the North Atlantic.[13] Shirley, a fifth grader, immediately saw the possibilities: "I don't think Brendan got to America. We could find out by remaking the events, finding how possible each is and when they might have been."

How far could a leather boat have managed to sail?

In the 1970s someone made a leather boat just like the one St. Brendan would have used and tried to sail it from Ireland to America. He was called Tim Severin, and he and four other sailors sailed from Ireland to Iceland in the summer of 1976, and then from Iceland to Newfoundland in the summer of 1977. They had to sail through some rough seas, and past icebergs but the boat did not sink and they made it successfully!

Below is a photograph of Tim Severin's reconstruction of a boat from Brendan's time. The picture shows the boat just as it reached the coast of Newfoundland.

Scientists think that the climate was probably warmer in the times when Brendan was sailing than it is now. Brendan might not have met such gales and rough seas as Tim Severin did on his voyage.

What do we know about the sort of boat St. Brendan would have used?

The boat Brendan would have used would have been made of specially toughened leather, sewn over a wooden frame. The boat would have used sails on the open sea, and people would have rowed it with oars when it was near the land.

Below is an Irish boat, copied from a carving done on a stone pillar sometime between 700 and 800.

Map 1. The North Atlantic Ocean, where St. Brendan would probably have had to go if he did get to America.

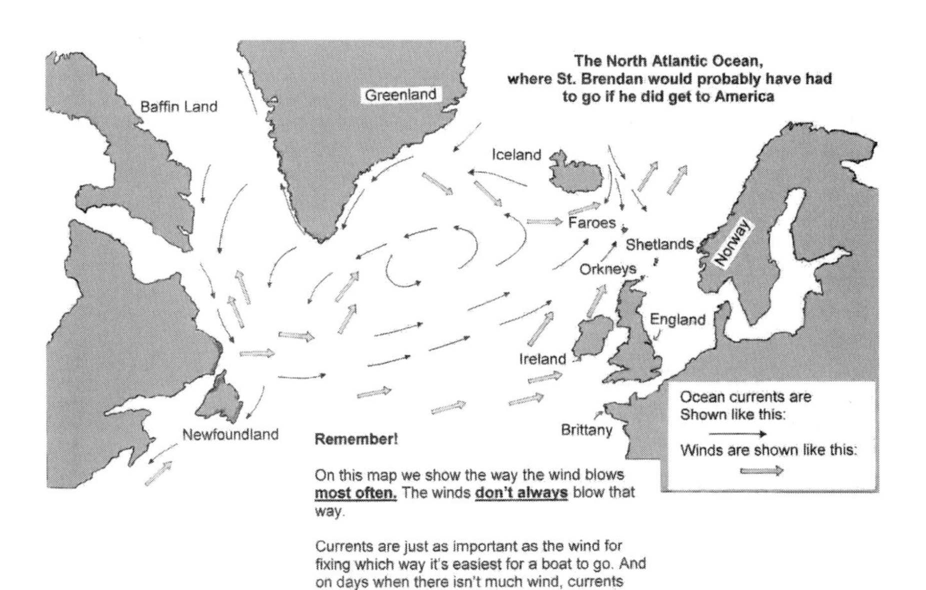

Map 2. Places we think it likely that St. Brendan visited.

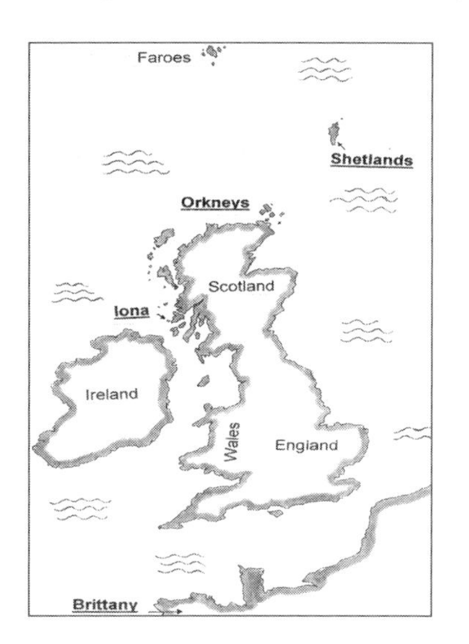

What do we know, or think might be true, about St. Brendan?

- *We know Brendan lived in Ireland between (roughly) 486 and 578.*
- *We know he sailed to Iona, an island several miles off the west coast of Scotland.*
- *We think it is very likely that he sailed to Brittany in France.*
- *We think it is possible he visited the islands beyond the north of Scotland.*
- *We know many Irish monks made voyages in the seas near Ireland at this time.*

Map 1 is especially useful at this juncture since we want to add material to allow students to think about the story in the context of more particular historical knowledge. It is obviously important to check that students have some conception of the size of the Atlantic. But more important, without Map 1, they tend to dismiss the evidence of the sea journeys offered in Map 2 on the grounds that America is so much farther on a direct route that the shorter voyages are irrelevant. Map 1 shows what kind of journey might have taken place. It allows students to see the relationships among the islands that might have broken up Brendan's journey, and how winds and ocean currents would have dictated that he take precisely that kind of route.

Even so, some fourth graders will not see the connections to be made without careful teaching.

Having looked at the further evidence shown above, Shirley (fifth grade) commented, "Yes, it is possible because Tim Severin did it, but you need rations and tools." Students from third grade up can be very suspicious of such a reconstruction, pointing out that Tim Severin knew where he was going, and St. Brendan did not. For third graders, the fact that Tim Severin had a crew of only four represents a crucial difference because they would have eaten less food than a larger crew.

Some students will find it difficult to grasp the idea that because it may have been *possible* for a boat like Brendan's to reach America, this tells us nothing about whether it *did* do so. (Of course, recognizing the possibility makes the question of whether it *did* do so one that may be worth asking.) We can ask students directly: "Tim Severin's voyage proves that a leather boat can sail across the Atlantic. Does that prove that Brendan did make it to America?" Joe, a third grader, *wants* Brendan to have made it, and shifts from a claim about what was possible to a claim about what Brendan actually did:

Joe	This is proof. This is proof of it.
Teacher	What, Tim Severin's copy is the proof?
Joe	Yeah, it . . .
Teacher	What does it prove?
Joe	It proves, like, that he did go from Ireland to America, to the Land of Promise, and if *he* did it, then probably Brendan did it.
Teacher	That *who* did?
Joe	Brendan.
Teacher	It's proof that Brendan *did* go?
Joe	Yeah, it's proof.

The issue of what weight the evidence will bear can be raised at this point: the Severin voyage is strong evidence if our question is whether the voyage was possible, but carries much less weight if the question is whether Brendan actually reached America. This is a difficult idea, but it is accessible to many fourth graders, particularly if something like Cartoon 1 (provided by Phil Suggitt) is used to reinforce the point.

In this example, Charlene, a third grader, doesn't immediately understand what is involved when the teacher asks her to use the idea in another context but then suddenly sees how it works:

Cartoon 1.

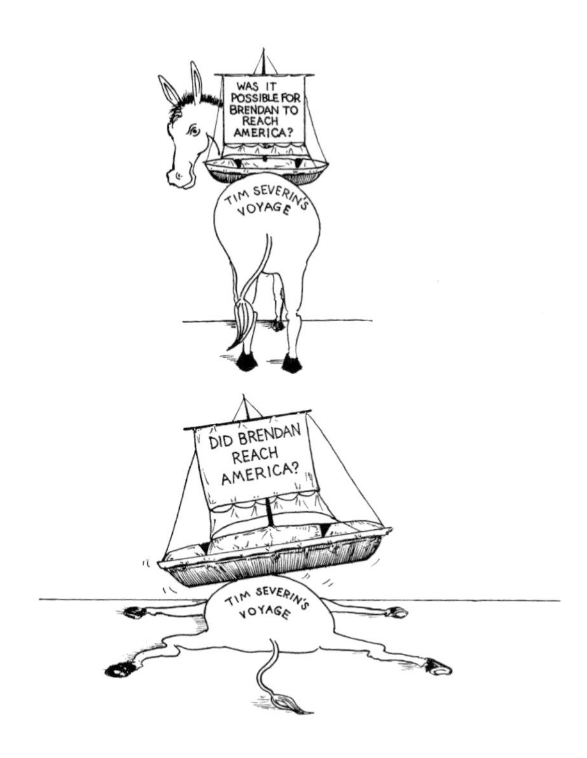

Teacher	Tim Severin's voyage, what did we think it did prove?
Charlene	That Tim Severin got there, but Brendan might've not.

The teacher then asks what questions their exercise books will and will not answer.

Charlene	I don't know what you mean.
Teacher	I'm looking at your exercise book now. What questions *can* I ask that it *will* answer for me?
Joe	It will answer if we are, a nice character—no! If we are messy!
Teacher	And what *won't* it answer?
Charlene	It won't answer, like, if I'm, if I get along with my Mum or my brother, or if I don't.
Teacher	Your exercise book's like the donkey. If we ask it the question about what your writing's like, or what you were doing on a certain day in class, it can carry those questions.

Charlene	Mmm [agrees].
Teacher	If we ask it the question "How do you get on with your Mum?"...
Charlene	It'd collapse!

Once they get used to the idea, students begin to use it themselves, as in this example, also from third grade.

Teacher	Because it's a story about a saint, will it let us say anything about whether Brendan got to America or not? What do you think?
Ricky	I think that story would collapse.
Lenny	I don't think it would collapse for whether he got to America or not, because, um I need to check on the map [hunts for map], Newfoundland, well, that's part of America, isn't it, and he got to Newfoundland.

We can pursue this concept further by asking what difference the evidence about Brendan's *known* seagoing (Map 2 and the factual statements linked to it) makes to the weight Tim Severin's voyage will bear for our big question. Common reactions include the claim that Brendan probably did get *somewhere* (substituting "halfway there" for "possibly got there") and, depending on prior learning, comments about how far Viking or Roman ships managed to sail, with conclusions (positive or negative) about what that meant for Brendan's leather boat.

Thinking About the Story from the Inside

The students have already been thinking about the internal evidence (i.e., the evidence that can be found in the story itself), of course, and some may already have introduced natural explanations for the supernatural events in the story. But we now require a closer and more systematic consideration of the story. Two sets of questions start things off:

> **Make a list of the three things in the story that would best back up the claim that Brendan reached America. How do they back up the claim?**
>
> **What parts of the story make the claim that Brendan reached America a shaky one? Pick the three things that seem to you hardest to accept. How do they make it hard for us to believe that the story shows that Brendan reached America?**

These questions can produce widely varying results. Some students are skeptical from the start, whereas others want Brendan to have succeeded. Both groups find the second question much easier than the first. As an answer to the first question, fruit trees do not amount to much! The only way to see the evidence inside the story as supporting the claim that Brendan reached America is (1) to interpret key events in the story naturalistically, and then (2) to use evidence from outside the story to show how those events fit the route Brendan is most likely to have taken. One powerful line of argument is the difficulty of finding an alternative destination that fits as well as America. If any of the story is to be treated seriously as an actual voyage, what other destination could fit the events better? This kind of understanding appears to be tacit in some youngsters' comments, but to see its importance and be able to articulate it involves sophisticated thinking, generally done spontaneously only by older students.

To bring out the way in which events in the story fit the most likely route, students need to be conscious of alternative ways of seeing some key events. For this purpose, the materials used in this example focus on the crystal column and the "edge of Hell." The first step is to raise the general issue of how we interpret things, using a concrete example—the duck-rabbit and the bird-antelope.

> **Before we take a closer look at bits of the story, we need to think about how we make sense of things we see or things we read. What do these two pictures show? (See Cartoons 2 and 3, provided by Phil Suggitt.)**

Cartoons 2 and 3.

Strictly speaking, because these examples depend on perception and not on how we understand text, they are different from history. There is a danger here. There is no right answer in *any* sense, and nothing turns on which answer is chosen. The danger is that students may think this is true of interpretation in history. It is important to stress that in the case of Brendan, we are trying to decide what happened, and we have something to go on. Students can be reminded that they have already used material from outside the story. If handled carefully, the analogy, despite its defects, is close enough to engage fourth graders, and it creates considerable excitement and amusement among younger students.

The bird-antelope raises questions about the shaded area on its neck. Is this fur or feathers? The answer depends on the interpretation of the whole picture; the details are too ambiguous to settle the issue. We go back and forth between the shading and the overall shape to decide what the animal is. Something analogous applies with Brendan: the way we view the story will help determine how we view particular incidents within it, and vice versa. However, it would not be wise to pursue this point unless the students are already making sense of the basic issue—that some things can be interpreted in more than one way. The next step is to ask the students to look again at the paragraph in the story about the crystal column. Some students will already have seen that the column may have been an iceberg, although many fourth graders do not think of this interpretation at first. If we ask, "Can you think of two different ways this part of the story could be interpreted?" and then provide the pictures below as either a confirmation or a revelation, we can give a concrete example of interpretation, categorizing the pictures as supernatural and natural interpretations. (See Cartoons 4 and 5, provided by Phil Suggitt.)

Cartoons 4 and 5.

This material often provokes exchanges such as the following (fourth grade):

Bill	I think it's a fairy tale, like, a bit like Cinderella and the Fairy Godmother, like . . .
Naomi	Like the birds and spirits and that sort of thing.
Steve	If you reckon it's a fairy tale, you don't see people trying to kill you in fairy tales, do you . . .

Bill	*Some* fairy tales there are—Little Red Riding Hood—the wolf tries to eat you.
Naomi	I think it's a *kind* of fairy tale.
Bill	A fairy tale, 'cos people throwing molten hot rocks, wouldn't they actually burn their hands?
Steve	But it could've been real people, and it could've been a volcano, and the crystal could've been an iceberg, and the fish could've been a whale, and the talking birds [long pause] parrots [triumphantly].
Bill	[Contemptuously] How can you get white parrots? Must be a one-in-a-million chance to see a white parrot.

The "jug" or chalice in the supernatural picture provokes questions and enables us to complicate matters a bit. The fuller version of the story allows the teacher to raise a note of caution about jumping to conclusions.

Before you come to a decision, you ought to look at a fuller version of what the writer actually wrote, not just the summary you've had to work with so far. Here it is.

One day after they had said Mass, they saw a column in the sea. It did not appear to be far away, and yet it took them three days to get near it. When the Man of God came near to it, he couldn't see the top, because it was so high. It was higher than the sky. All around the column was an open-meshed net, with openings so large the boat could pass through the gaps. They didn't know what the net was made of. It was silver in color, but seemed to be harder than marble. The column itself was of clearest crystal. The monks pulled on the meshes of the net to get the boat through it. There was a space about a mile wide between the net and the column. They sailed all day along one side of the column, and could still feel the heat of the sun through its shadow. The Man of God kept measuring, and the side was 700 yards long. It took four days to measure all four sides. On the fourth day they saw an ornamental church plate and jug in a window of the column. They were made of the same material as the column. Saint Brendan took hold of the plate and the jug, and said, "Our Lord Jesus has shown us a miracle, and given me these two gifts so that other people will believe us."

The Mass (which can be explained simply as a religious service) and the title "the Man of God" for St. Brendan both help to emphasize that the story is connected with religious beliefs and is not just a "factual report" of what happened. We can ask, "Has this changed the way you think we should interpret the crystal column, or not? Why?"

We then give the same treatment to the "Hell" passage. The students reread the relevant paragraph of the story, and then we ask, "Is this piece of the story natural or supernatural?" Once again two pictures emphasize the basic point, but this time they are rapidly followed by some new information. It is this information that opens up the possibility of interpreting three major incidents in the voyage, in addition to the iceberg, as indicating just the kinds of things that might have been encountered on a voyage that followed prevailing Atlantic winds and currents. (See Cartoons 6 and 7, provided by Pill Suggitt.)

Cartoons 6 and 7.

Some facts we have good reasons to be sure about

- *The Faroe Islands have had large flocks of sheep on them for a very long time.*
- *Iceland has active volcanoes on it that still erupt even nowadays.*
- *There is very often fog in the area near Newfoundland.*

Some fourth graders will initially deny that that there could be volcanoes in Iceland because volcanoes are hot and Iceland is cold, so it is important not to allow this misconception to make nonsense of the kind of progress we are trying to make. The questions we ask to this end can be straightforward, reinforcing the importance of interpretation: "How should we interpret the visit to the island that Brendan said was Hell? Could the Isle of Sheep have been a real place?" Students quickly appreciate the idea that there may be a case to be made for saying that Brendan passed the Faroes and Iceland, encountered an iceberg somewhere during his journey, and ended up in the fogs close to Newfoundland. For some students, the result is a huge step in understanding. In the following example, Joe, a third grader, begins to see that his earlier ideas were too simple:

Joe	Brendan's gone from Ireland, to the Faroes, named it the Island of Sheep, then went to Iceland, called it [pauses] . . .
Teacher	Called it Hell.
Charlene	Why?
Teacher	Because Hell's supposed to be very hot and smoky and smelling.
Joe	Called it Hell, and saw the people throwing rocks at him which was really a volcano, and then on the way saw the iceberg, which they thought was the crystal column but really it was the iceberg, and then they saw the fog and then they got lost, then came to Newfoundland, and the whole thing is part true, part fiction.
Teacher	Right. But you started by saying it was *all* made up.
Joe	It's not *all* made up. The person going from there to there [points to map] is true. But all

	this [edge of Hell, etc.], all that rubbish is not true.
Teacher	So, why would that be there if it was true that he made that trip? Why would they put it in those other funny ways?
Joe	They put the miracles in because they thought, they would think, that it'd be true.

In the last sentence there are signs that Joe is beginning to see that having miracles in the story might have made sense at the time. This is a big step for a third-grade student.

At this point, we have to be careful that students do not think the matter is sewn up. Rereading the passages about the hymn-singing birds, Jasconius, and the arrow that miraculously lit the lamps is a useful way of reminding students that whatever they say about the story must explain these things as well.

Finding Out What Kind of Story the Brendan Story Is

The problem can now be put to students as follows. If we say this story is just a made-up tale, we have to explain why it appears to make sense as a voyage in the Atlantic Ocean. If we say the story describes a real voyage because we can interpret apparently supernatural events as really being natural, we have to explain the things that do not fit so easily. What this means is that we need to help students consider what kind of story they are dealing with. Doing so raises matters that not all fourth graders can grasp, but it is worth introducing them here even though we will need to return to them in other lessons on other topics. Indeed, none of the ideas dealt with in this material can be assumed to stay with students after just one lesson; all need to be woven into a series of lessons.[14]

The goal here is to help students understand that if we are to know what weight this story can bear as evidence of Brendan's reaching America, we need to know what its writer was trying to accomplish and the conventions of the time (see Box 3-8). If it is a story intended to show what a splendid saint Brendan was, we should expect it to be "embroidered" with supernatural events whether they had a natural basis or not. Just because *we* treat magical events as implausible, we should not expect people *then* to have done the same. Indeed, as a story about a saint, it would be highly implausible without such events. If the students now look at some more evidence, we can ask, "What sort of story is this?"

BOX 3-8 We Can Believe Historical Films When People in Them Behave As We Would

The tendency to assume that people in the past shared our ways of thinking and acting has been found among students in Canada as well as in the United States and the United Kingdom.

Peter Seixas asked Canadian tenth graders to watch selected scenes from two popular films dealing with the relations between Native Americans and whites in the 1860s—*The Searchers* and *Dances with Wolves*.[15] The 10 students were asked to explain the differences between the films and to say which gave a more accurate picture of life for Native Americans and for the whites in the west in the 1860s.

The interpretative framework of *Dances with Wolves* coincided with students' own assumptions: they agreed with its portrayal of Indian and white lives and the picture it gave of relationships between the two groups, and they saw its modern cinematic techniques and the "realistic" portrayal of how people act as making it more believable. Having limited knowledge of the topic, in assessing the film they fell back on their general knowledge of human nature and their sense of a believable narrative. Seixas suggests that, "Ironically, the more a 'historical' film presents life in the past as being similar to life in the present, the more believable it is to these students."

The Searchers, with its dated cinematic conventions and acting, provoked the students into thinking about the status of the film, whereas when they had watched *Dances with Wolves* they had treated it as a window on the past. The conventions of *The Searchers* were dismissed as "the more primitive techniques of an earlier age," but students had more difficulty dealing with its interpretative stance. Seixas emphasizes the importance of confronting students with interpretative stances that differ from their own as a means of challenging and developing ideas about historical films by making the apparent "transparency" of films that accord with our present preconceptions more problematic.

What are writings from those days (500–1000) usually like?

They generally don't give many of the details we might expect (times, dates, or where things happened) and are often vague about exactly what happened. When they give details, they often say different things about the same event.

Often people who wrote in these times weren't trying to get the details right. They weren't writing news reports. They might have been trying to show how a good person ought to live, or how God helped good people and punished bad ones. Other times they might be telling the story of a great hero.

A very common sort of Irish story was the "imram," which was a made-up tale about a sea voyage. People liked hearing such stories. But most imrams were probably written later than the time when the story of St. Brendan's voyage was written.

Some people think "The Voyage of St. Brendan" is different from the usual writings of the time. For instance, one lady who is an expert on writings from 500 to 1,000 is puzzled because "The Voyage of St. Brendan" doesn't keep going on about Brendan doing miracles. She says that when writings from this time are about saints, most of them make sure to have the saint doing lots of miracles. (That is because they wanted to show how good a saint he or she was, and how powerful God is.) But in "The Voyage of St. Brendan," Brendan doesn't do miracles himself.

The material demands a good deal of thought, but with some guidance, fourth-grade students can begin to incorporate it into their arguments:

Bill	I wonder what the entire thing comes to? Nine years and 7 years and 40 days and another 40 days and . . .
Teacher	It adds up to a long time, yes, but it's a bit like . . . What about it saying the iceberg reached the sky, the crystal column reached the sky?
Naomi	It means it's *really* tall.
Teacher	So when it says 40 days and 40 nights?
Steve	It means really long.
Teacher	I mean, if they're not *trying* to tell us how long something takes, then maybe it's a mistake for us to say, "Hang on, lets add all these up and see what they come to," because they're not even *trying*. It's a bit like stories about "Long, long ago. . . ."
Bill	They don't actually tell us when it was, do they? So it's a bit like this, *they* don't actually tell us how long the journey was.
Teacher	That's right. That's what it says here in this bit look [pointing to the students' sheet]—What are writings like in those days?—most stories were like that in those days, they didn't give all the exact figures, they didn't *have* to add up.
Bill	Yeah.

We can now introduce the notion of "embroidering" a story as changing the way it is presented to make it more acceptable to its audience and ask, "Why do people embroider stories? Might people at the time this story was written have had different reasons from ours for embroidering?" We should try to avoid introducing such words as "exaggerate" or "distort," and especially such ideas as "making it exciting." These notions would preempt the everyday ways in which students will already be thinking about the audience, exemplified in the following fourth graders' exchange:

Teacher	What *sort* of story do you think it is?
Steve	A legend, or [pauses] . . .
Teacher	Why would somebody have written a story like this?
Steve	To be famous?
Bill	Or he could make a profit on it selling his story.

The issue here is that our embroidering of a story may be done in different ways and for different reasons from those of people at the time the story took its present form. Our questions must help students rethink their assumptions: "Who is the hero of this story? What sort of person is he? What were saints supposed to be like? If you believed in miracles and supernatural events, what would tell you if someone was a saint? What could someone writing this story (more than a thousand years ago) put in it that would show everyone Brendan was a saint?" Finally, we can ask, "Would embroidering a story like this one make it more or less plausible to people living then? Why?"

At this point we are asking students to grasp, albeit in a simple way, first, that people in the past thought differently from us, and second, that to make sense of what we want to use as evidence, we have to understand how they thought. In doing so, we are touching on empathy, and we need to remember what ideas our students are likely to be working with. Many of them will willingly recognize that people then believed in supernatural events, but see this simply as proof that in those days, people were pretty stupid and therefore gullible (see Box 3-9). Such a deficit view of the past (see also Chapter 2) does not necessarily stop third graders from beginning to understand that the Brendan story may be rather different from a modern travel account.

Teacher	What sort of story was he trying to write?
Ricky	It might be one that he thought, like, if it was a volcano that he made it like *people* throwing it, so like volcanoes are natural things, and he changed them to people, and that, Jesus and everything else like that.

BOX 3-9 The Deficit Past

The idea that people in the past could not do what we can and were not as clever as we are is very stubborn, even in the face of strong pressure. It is worth quoting part of a long exchange among fourth graders to show just *how* stubborn.

Teacher	Could we learn anything from the Brendan story that it's not trying to tell us?
Carly	They weren't very clever.
Teacher	Why?
Carly	'Cos they couldn't make oars, to row the boat.
Jeff:	They did use oars, in the picture.
Carly	Oh, did they? [finds picture] Oh yeah!
Teacher	What do you think then, do you think people then were not as clever as us, or about the same, or cleverer, or what?
Jeff	They can't figure out about volcanoes, and icebergs, and that.
Teacher	So they're not as clever as us?
Jeff	No.
Teacher	You all think that then, do you?
Carly	Not as clever.
David	Technology [points to mini-disc recorder] . . .
Teacher	Does that make me cleverer than you?
David	The people who made it.
Teacher	So you can make one of those, can you?
All	No.
Teacher	So you're as stupid as they were, are you?
Carly	[Laughing] No!
David	We know how to use it.
Carly	They didn't know how to use it.

Teacher	Why would he want to do that?
Ricky	So it's more interesting, and something to do about God.
Teacher	Why would he want to make it something about God?

Teacher	So do you think that if I had Brendan here, it'd take more than 5 minutes to teach him how to make it work?
Carly	No, he'd probably get it straight away, but he couldn't [pauses] . . .
Teacher	This man may have got to America. He could write in Latin—can you write in Latin?
All	No.
Teacher	Well, are you stupider than Brendan then?
Carly	No, but he can't write English!
Jeff	Yeah!
Teacher	So not being able to write English or Latin doesn't make you stupid. So why does knowing which buttons to press on one of those make you cleverer than Brendan?
Carly	*We're* making cars, and *they* just had to walk.
Teacher	And that makes them stupid?
Carly	No . . . [Laughs]
Jeff:	Not *as* clever.
Teacher	What do you mean by being "clever" then?
David	Smart.

The connection between willingness to underestimate people in the past and a deficit picture of the past derived from a technological idea of progress is quite apparent here. The students repeatedly accepted that their argument was inadequate, but kept returning to it anyway. This exchange continued for some time, but there was little sign that it did any more than modify the edges of the students' ideas. Deeper changes require specifically targeted tasks and frequent return to the issue in a variety of contexts.

Ricky	'Cos he said he's a Man of God.
Teacher	Why try to find the Land of Promise? Why go to all this trouble?
Lenny	Because monks are normally very, worship God a lot, and the Island of Promise was to do with God too.

Teacher	Why do you think somebody would write this story then? What do you think they were trying to show?
Lenny	They were trying to show that Brendan was a special man.
Teacher	And what sort of special?
Lenny	Well, sort of, holy.

By the seventh grade, many students should be trying to use their understanding of the world in which people lived and the beliefs and values of the people they are studying to *explain* the things these people did, not just dismiss them.

Teacher	What does the story tell us about the person who actually wrote it? Is there anything we can work out?
Trudi	I think the person who wrote this down believed in God quite strongly, because all the time he's referring things back to God, and that may be from mistakes, or what he'd heard, or been told, but I think if they didn't believe it then they wouldn't have written it down quite so much; it seems very likely they were very strong believers in God.
Haley	I think he probably wanted them to think, "Wasn't God great," probably, or something like that, or saying like, "God's really good, look what he's done, they've reached America," and stuff like that. I think he wanted the audience to think about God.
Trudi	He wanted the readers to realize that if you're good and you worship God, then he's going to be there for you, and he'll look after you, but if you don't, then he won't take care of you, because it seems very certain that they thought that and the reason why he found all these places or visited all these places was because God was looking after him.
Jane	I think that, it seems like the sort of story that was meant for, maybe like, village people who were at church or something, instead of having a Bible reading, maybe having this, getting the message across to them that religion was very

important and they should believe in that, rather than just for maybe like a child reading it for a bedtime story or someone reading it as a book.

It is important, however, not to assume that only older students can think like this. After his group had worked through the material with his teacher, Don, a third grader, expressed the understanding he had achieved:

Teacher	So if the story's written like that, for that sort of reason, does that mean it can tell us more, or tell us less, or what?
Jilly	Probably about the same.
Don	It probably makes it like more, because without God doing miracles, people who weren't saints, they would say, Brendan ain't a saint, 'cos God didn't do miracles for him, so without God, being a saint, I reckon it'd be less, but if Brendan's a saint and God does stuff for him, I reckon that story must be *more* [believable].

We are now dealing with matters that are difficult for most fourth graders, so we can give them some help in the form of some possibilities to talk about. "What sort of story are we dealing with here? Have a look at these suggestions, and decide which you agree with and which you don't: (a) It is just a religious story about what a holy man St. Brendan was, showing what wonderful things he did to find the Land of Promise that was special to God. (b) It is a story about a real voyage that St. Brendan made to America. (c) It is a story based on real events, but meant as a religious story about how holy St. Brendan was. (d) It is an 'imram'—just an exciting made-up voyage story." We have to be careful here about the grounds on which students are making their choice. Some fourth graders choose (a) because the sentence gives details of what is in the story, even when they are thinking something more like (c). But once the alternatives have been clarified, students can make some penetrating points. Helen, a fifth grader, wrote:

> *I think it is (c) because he wasn't all that holy [not enough, presumably, for (a)] and for (b) it wasn't all real like the talking birds, but you could make sense out of that. He wasn't being real holy and I just think that it is based on real events and he misinterpreted some things and he thought some things were supernatural sort of things instead of natural things.*

Andy, an eighth grader, chose (c) and explained: "Because I think that this story *could* have happened (the geography at least), but I think that religious influence was then added to show the power of God/St. Brendan."

The task can be ended here with a return to the big question: "Did an Irish monk land in America about 1000 years before Columbus?" But a further step is possible if there is time and the students are sufficiently engaged in the problem.

Possible clues as to whether Brendan reached America—what's been found in Iceland.
Historians know that:

- *Long after Brendan's time (about 870) the Vikings started to settle in Iceland. They found Irish monks there.*

Possible clues as to whether Brendan reached America—what's been found in Greenland.
Historians know that:

- *When the Vikings first reached Greenland in about 982, they found the remains of a skin-covered boat and some stone huts.*
- *The Inuit used skin-covered boats.*
- *The Inuit usually dug homes out of the ground, and didn't use stones to build them.*
- *At the time the Vikings arrived, the Inuit may not have reached southern Greenland.*

Possible clues as to whether Brendan reached America—what's been found in Vinland.
Historians know that:

- *The Vikings reached Vinland (their name for the northeast coast of what we call Canada and America) between 986 and 1000. They met people who told them about strange men who wore white clothes and walked in a procession carrying poles with white cloths fixed to them, yelling loudly. The Vikings assumed they meant Irishmen.*
- *The Vikings called part of Vinland "White Man's Land," and another part "Greater Ireland."*
- *Later one Viking met people speaking a language he didn't understand. He thought it was like Irish.*
- *Carvings have been found on a rock in West Virginia that look similar to ancient Irish writing. One expert in old languages thinks they are ancient Irish writing. He thinks they say, "At the*

time of sunrise the sun's rays just reach the notch on the left side, when it is Christmas Day." (A "notch" in the rock is a line cut in the rock.)

Which clues fit with which?

Timeline Key

Things about Brendan—words underneath line

Things that were also happening—words above line

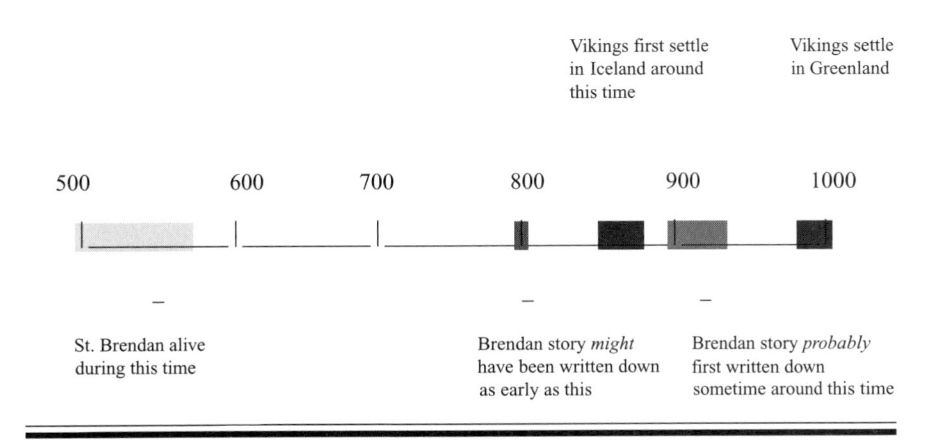

Having made some progress in deciding what kind of story St. Brendan's voyage is, we can go back to looking at other things we know might help in answering our big question. The clues include some quite shaky evidence (we do not have to use all the clues in the example here), and students tell us a great deal about their assumptions as they decide what the evidence shows (see Box 3-10). Students' ideas about the strength of this broader evidence are not easy to predict. They depend on understandings and assumptions about how people behave, how long physical objects survive, the rates at which languages change, and what importance the students attach to "usually" or the views of one "expert." But these are precisely the things we need to bring out at this stage.

A common fourth-grade response is to focus on the content and maintain that the new evidence does not help "because it's all about the Vikings." Insistence on looking carefully at the timeline and thinking about what the

BOX 3-10 The Shrinking Past

Keith Barton's work with young students in history suggests that they shrink the scale of human activities and reduce long-term processes to events or individual actions.[16] The spatial shrinkage is evident in the following example from the Brendan task:

Sonny	I would like, go on a search underwater to look for [Brendan's] boat, it might've sunk.
Charlene	I'd do what Sonny did, but I wouldn't go in a boat, I'd go in a submarine, 'cos you wouldn't sink and die. [third grade]

This is a frequent kind of strategy for finding remains, and despite Charlene's practical solution, the scale of the Atlantic and the task is hugely underestimated.

Teaching the Brendan material also produces signs of temporal shrinkage, even with older students, and sometimes a tendency to reduce a series of events to single occurrences. Some cases are very clear. "I didn't know there were people a thousand years before Columbus," said one eighth grader, "I thought there were just dinosaurs." Some are more subtle:

Anna	Seeing this other evidence I think that they *did* get to America, because the Vikings found Irish monks in Iceland, and they might have stayed on the way to America, they might have stopped and some people stayed there . . . . [seventh grade]

Vikings found can shift students' positions here. But although they can see relevant issues, they do not always find it easy to produce explanations.

Bill	Maybe Brendan got to America on Christmas Day, because it's saying at the time of sunrise a ray grazes the notch on the left side on Christmas Day.
Teacher	Who could have carved it?
Bill	They [the Native Americans] weren't really Christmas Day sort of religious people.
Teacher	How else could it have got carved there then?

It is difficult to see why Anna should think these are Brendan's monks. Why should it be the same group of monks? Is it not more likely that there has been more than one voyage? A teacher using the material comments that (after looking at what the Vikings found in Iceland) her eighth-grade students thought in a similar way with a diametrically opposite conclusion. They "wondered how Irish monks could be at an island 300 years later. They pointed out that there were no women on the island, so how could the community of monks have been continuous since St. Brendan."

Jane (seventh grade) may be making similar—past shrinking—assumptions:

Jane	**It says that the Inuit usually dug homes under the ground and didn't use stones to build them, and when Vikings first reached Greenland in 982 they found the remains of a skin-covered boat and some stone huts, and this probably suggests that it could have been the monks that were there, and the stone huts would have probably survived.**

Bill	Maybe somebody got there before Brendan.
Teacher	What do we need to know?
Bill	We need to know it's definitely Irish writing and it definitely does say that, not . . .
Teacher	And we need to know one other thing as well . . . Think about what you said right at the beginning, that made you suspicious of the story, when you saw the timeline.
Bill	Oh! What time it was.

Seventh graders are usually more skeptical about the Vikings' supposed recognition of the Irish language, often making comments such as "It may not necessarily have been Irish. It could've been any other language." But although they can come up with explanations for the rock carving, they can still find it difficult to envisage alternatives.

Haley	There's some carvings been found on a rock, in erm, Ancient Irish writing, I think that might have something to do with it, if Irishmen were writing on stones then it probably was the monks, who were there, I don't know who else it could be really.
Jane	I agree with Haley, I don't think somebody's going to go to a stone now and write Ancient Irish on it.

The inferences here are fine, provided we rule out more recent fraud or the possibility of simple overinterpretation of marks by people who, like many of the fourth graders, want St. Brendan to have made it to America. If such overinterpretation is a fault, however, it is not one that betrays conceptual weaknesses in connection with understanding evidence, but perhaps an understandable degree of optimism and excitement.

As a final step, we can ask some questions designed to see what more *general* ideas the students are using by the end of the task. "What would you say to someone who said: (a) We can't say anything about this. (b) We weren't there, so anyone can say what they want. (c) We either have to believe the Brendan story or we have to trash it." For fourth graders, we are likely to be quite satisfied if we get responses suggesting that we have had some impact on their everyday ideas. If we can effect a shift such as that evident in the responses of these fourth graders between the beginning of the task and the end, our students will have made valuable progress.

Ideas at the beginning of the topic:

David	You can't get it right because none of us know.
Teacher	Why do none of us know?
David	Well, like everyone's guessed.
Teacher	And why are we guessing?
David	Because we don't know what he really did.
Teacher	And why don't we know?
Jeff	Because we weren't there at that time.

Ideas toward the end of the topic:

Jeff	[If we interpret it naturally] half of it makes sense.
Teacher	So if we can't say, "It's impossible that Brendan reached America," what can we safely say?
Jeff	Inconclusive.
Teacher	Supposing someone said, "If no one left us the true story, we can't know?" Do you agree with that, or disagree with it?
David	Disagree.
Jeff	No, 'cos there's lots of evidence.

(Note that Jeff had not used "inconclusive" before this point, and the word had not been taught.) In response to the final questions, the students take a similar position, and Jeff's last comment in this excerpt could almost sum up our teaching goals for the whole unit:

Teacher	What would you say now, after working through this, to someone who said, "We can't say anything about this?"
Carly	We *could* find out about it.
Teacher	OK, what about the second thing, "We weren't there, so anyone can say what they want?"
David	Nonsense! 'Cos there's evidence, so you can, say . . .
Teacher	So you can't say just what you want? You have to say . . .
David	The truth, what you found out.
Teacher	Has the evidence shown you the *truth*, or . . .?
David	It *helps* you.
Teacher	OK, what about the last one, "We either have to believe the Brendan story or we have to trash it?" What about that one? Is that right or not?
David	No.
Jeff	In the story, there are some things that make sense, you don't have to trash it, you just have to make sense.

Research and experience suggest that understandings such as those displayed by students in the fourth-grade study of St. Brendan's voyage are likely to transfer to higher grades and to different topics.[17] Students who have such learning experiences will be better prepared for the study of the Pilgrims in a later grade. Developing students understanding of core, second-order concepts in history will be more effective if that development is planned across the years. In fact, our most important conclusion is that successfully achieving an effective integration of conceptual (second-order) understanding and content coverage, as emphasized in *How People Learn*, can best be achieved with planning of history teaching across grades 4 through 12. Individual teachers can achieve important shifts in student thinking, as we see in the lessons described above. But student progress and teacher effectiveness will be far greater if those who determine the agenda for history teaching across the school years do so with careful attention to the progression in student understanding of both second-order concepts and content coverage. An illustration of how such planning might be accomplished is provided in Appendix 3A.

APPENDIX 3A IMPLICATIONS FOR PLANNING

Student learning in history will best be supported if instructional planning across the school years includes both second-order concepts and content coverage. Planning for progression in students' mastery of the two, however, differs in several critical respects. The sequence of substantive topics that we plan to address may be ordered by reference to chronology, theme, and scale. We offer an example across 4 years for illustrative purposes:

Grade 4:	The First Americans: Origins and Achievements
	Worlds Apart: Europe, Africa, and Asia before the Voyages of Exploration
Grade 5:	The Great Civilizations of Pre-Columbian America
	The Voyages of Exploration: First Contacts among Native Americans, Europeans, and Africans
Grade 6:	Spanish and Portuguese Conquests
	Early English Colonization: The Pilgrim Fathers
Grade 7:	Government and Liberty in the Early American Colonies
	The American Revolution

Such a plan dictates *what* is to be addressed; *when* the teacher is to do so; and, within limits, *how long* it should take. A topic such as the Pilgrim Fathers, for example, will be taught once and once only at the elementary level or in junior high school. It is likely to be taught to all students in a given grade. And, after a given period of time, all students will move on to a new topic without reference to how much they have or have not learned about the Pilgrim Fathers.

Planning for progression in second-order concepts is different. It is informed not by our selection of particular passages of the past for study, but by models of progression based on systematic research and on classroom experience of the kind illustrated in the discussion of the Pilgrim Fathers and St. Brendan's topics. These models are hierarchical and describe significant stages in the development of students' thinking over time. A model of progression for the second-order concept of *evidence* is given in Box 3A-1.

We should remember that what is presented in Box 3A-1 is *a* model and not *the* model. There is no such thing as a definitive model for evidence or for any other second-order concept, although all research-based models are—or should be—compatible. They may vary, however, in the number of levels they include and in the emphasis given to different aspects of students' thinking. Nor do these models prescribe or describe the ways in which the ideas of any individual student should or will develop. They are generalizations applicable to the majority of students that appear to be sustainable across generations and nationalities. They may be compared with footpaths across a mountainside: these footpaths exist because most walkers have elected to follow a given route across the mountainside; not all walkers will have done so, and more than one trail may lead to the desired destination.

A teacher who leads a school party may *plan* to take students along a chosen path rather than to allow each to find his or her own way across the mountain. Most would find this to be a wise decision even if some students are disposed to seek out the more boggy areas and others to head for sheer rock faces. This analogy breaks down in one crucial respect, however: while it is possible to march students along a mountain trail in reasonably good order, students will move through the levels of a model of progression at very different speeds. For example, they may jump one level altogether, moving straight from level 3 to level 5. Indeed, by tenth grade some students will have moved beyond level 6 of the model in Box 3A-1, while others will remain at level 2. It follows that levels of conceptual understanding cannot be attached to grades or to topics, and that some students will have to repeat work at quite similar levels of conceptual challenge when they change topics, while others will be able to move on to tackle new and more demanding conceptual problems.

This point is illustrated by a comparison of the responses of the sixth-grade (Pilgrim Fathers) and fourth-grade (St. Brendan) students presented

BOX 3A-1 Model of Progression in Ideas About Evidence

1. Pictures of the past

The past is treated as if it is the present; students treat potential evidence as if it offers direct access to the past. Questions about the basis for statements about the past do not arise. Stories are just stories.

2. Information

The past is treated as fixed and known by some authority; students treat potential evidence as information. Given statements to test against evidence, students match information or count sources to solve the problem. Questions arise about whether the information offered is correct or incorrect, but no methodology is attributed to the study of history for answering such questions beyond an appeal to books, diaries, or what has been dug up. These sources, although sometimes seen as being connected with the past, provide transparent information that is either correct or incorrect.

3. Testimony

The past is reported to us either well or badly, by people living at the time. Questions regarding how we know about the past are regarded as sensible; students begin to understand that history has a methodology for testing statements about the past. Conflicts in potential evidence are thought appropriately to be settled by deciding which report is best. Notions of bias, exaggeration, and loss of information in transmission supplement the simple dichotomy between truth telling and lies. Reports are often treated as if the authors are more or less direct eyewitnesses—the more direct, the better.

above. On the whole, the sixth-grade students operate at a higher conceptual level than those in the fourth grade, but the conceptual understanding of *some* fourth-grade students is more advanced (relative to the model of progression in Box 3A-1) than that of *some* sixth-grade students. This observation may appear to argue against the wisdom, or even the practicability, of planning for the progression of understanding with respect to second-order

4. Cut and paste

The past can be probed even if no individual reporter has told us truthfully or accurately what happened. We can piece together a version by picking out the true statements from different reports and combining them. In one student's words, "You take the true bits out of this one, and the best bits out of that one, and when you've got it up, you've got a picture." Notions of bias or lies are supplemented by questions about whether the reporter is in a position to know.

5. Evidence in isolation

Statements about the past can be inferred from pieces of evidence. We can ask questions of sources that they were not designed to answer, so that evidence will bear questions for which it could not be testimony. There are many sources of evidence that are not reports of anything (nineteenth-century rail timetables, for example, were not constructed for the benefit of historians). This means historians may be able to work out historical facts even if no testimony has survived. Evidence may be defective without involving bias or lies. Reliability is not a fixed property of a source, and the weight we can place on any piece of evidence depends on what questions we ask of it.

6. Evidence in context

Evidence can be used successfully only if it is understood in its historical context: we must know what it was intended to be and how it relates to the society that produced it. Making this determination involves the suspension of certain lines of questioning and a provisional acceptance of much historical work as established fact (a known context). We cannot question everything at once. Contexts vary with place and time (a sense of period begins to be important).

concepts. If students cannot be kept together, why not allow them to make their own way across the conceptual mountainside?

There are several answers to this question. First, all students may be expected to make more rapid progress if we plan to take them along a given trail rather than leaving them to find their own way. Second, if trails are made explicit, students may grasp (and, it may be hoped, become metacognitively aware) that they are expected to walk across the mountains rather than play in the foothills and watch the clouds drift by. After all, this is what paths are for—for walking from here to there. If we plan to achieve progress in students' ideas about evidence, change, and so on, students may become aware that their understandings must develop irrespective of changes in the factual scenery as one topic succeeds another. Third, if we plan to achieve progress in students' conceptual understanding in particular ways, it is easier to anticipate the preconceptions and misconceptions that students may bring to any topic. Doing so makes it easier for us to identify, to exploit, and to remediate the ideas students use to make sense of the work at hand. To return to the previous analogy, if we notice that we have lost a few students, that they are no longer with us, it is easier to check back on or near the trail along which we planned to take them than to scour the entire mountain.

If these arguments are accepted, it remains to illustrate what planning in conformity with the second key finding of *How People Learn* might look like. Although planning should address the totality of history education from fourth to twelfth grade and *all* relevant second-order concepts, a more modest illustration may suffice.

As already indicated, history teaching at the fourth-grade level may cover such topics as The First Americans: Origins and Achievements and Worlds Apart: The Americas, Africa, Asia, and Europe before the Voyages of Exploration. These topics are likely to be broken down into a number of units of work intended to occupy 4-8 hours of teaching. The Worlds Apart topic, for instance, might include the following units:

Unit 1: Filling the World with People
Unit 2: People Go Their Separate Ways
Unit 3: First Contacts: Did St. Brendan Sail from Ireland to America?
Unit 4: First Contacts: Why Didn't the Norse Stay in America?

The topic aims to develop students' understanding of a particular period in history, that of the Voyages of Discovery. Students may be relied upon to forget much of what they are taught; thus it is necessary to identify the dates—usually for the key generalizations and understandings, rather than for the details—that we wish them to retain. Teaching tasks and assessments can then be focused on the transmission and development of these key generalizations and understandings. What these are or should be is negotiable. The Worlds Apart topic may focus narrowly, for example, on the independent evolution of new and old world civilizations to provide the students with descriptions and explanations of cultural misunderstandings and clashes in the sixteenth and seventeenth centuries. An alternative approach would aim to give students an understanding of the "one world" revolution that began with the exploration, colonization, and commercial exploration of the Americas and elsewhere, which may be seen as the start of the process we now call "globalization."

What may be less familiar is a stage of planning that goes beyond the identification of key generalizations and, in accordance with the second principle of *How People Learn*, also identifies key ideas about the second-order concepts associated with *evidence* and *accounts*, *change* and *development*, and *empathetic* and *causal explanation* that students use to make sense of the those generalizations. For the units of work listed under the Worlds Apart topic, teaching what we want students to learn with respect to generalizations about the past may be combined with developing their understanding of second-order concepts along the following lines.

Unit 1: Filling the World with People

Target Generalizations About the Past	**Target Ideas About Change**
• Long ago there were only a few people in the whole world. They all lived in a small part of East Africa. The rest of the world was empty—no people. • Very slowly these East Africans increased their numbers and spread all over the world—to the rest of Africa, Asia, Australia, Europe, and the Americas. • We may look different and speak different languages, but we are all descended from the same small groups of East Africans. • *Some* Native Americans are descended from the first groups of people to reach North and then South America.	• Things were not always as they are now—they were different in the past. • All bits of the past were not the same. Some bits of the past were more different from each other than from the present. • Not all differences matter, and some are far more important than others. • When there are significant differences between two bits of the past, we say that things have *changed.* • When things are different in ways that don't matter much, we say that there is *continuity with the past.*

It should be noted, first, that attempts to refine students' understanding of change, as of any other second-order concept, should not displace teaching about the past, but will certainly affect the ways in which such teaching takes place. The discussion of the Pilgrim Fathers' and Voyage of St. Brendan tasks illustrates the nature of this impact. It is not practical to address all second-order concepts within a single unit of work. For this reason, the conceptual focus of a set of units is likely to vary, as indicated below.

Unit 2: People Go Their Separate Ways

Target Generalizations About the Past

- People forgot where their ancestors had come from and knew only about other groups of people who lived nearby. People who lived in Africa, Asia, and Europe knew nothing about the first Americans. People who lived in America knew nothing about those living in Africa, Asia, and Europe. They also knew nothing about most other groups of Americans.
- Most groups of people had little contact with each other, so languages and ways of life became more and more different.
- Over long periods of time, great but very different civilizations developed in Africa, Asia, the Americas, and Europe.

Target Ideas About Empathetic Explanation

- People in the past saw things differently from the way we see them today. (For example, their maps of the world do not look like ours.)
- People in the past had to be very clever to achieve what they did. (For example, we would find it very difficult to make such good maps and charts using the same tools as our predecessors.)
- People in the past thought and behaved differently from us because they had to solve different problems. (For example, a Portolan chart was of more use to a medieval sailor in the Mediterranean than a modern atlas would have been.)

Unit 3: First Contacts:
Did St. Brendan Sail from Ireland to America?

Target Generalizations About the Past	**Target Ideas About Evidence and Accounts**
• In the past, many stories were told about people sailing to what could have been America. One of these stories is about an Irish monk, St. Brendan. • We cannot be sure whether St. Brendan really did sail to America. • We *do* know that even if St. Brendan did sail to America, no one followed him or knew how to repeat his voyage.	• We can work out what happened in the past from what is left. • Some things left from the past weren't meant to tell us anything, but we can still use them to find things out. • The weight we can put on the evidence depends on the questions we ask. • Often we can't be certain about the past, but we can produce stronger or weaker arguments about what it makes most sense to say.

The target ideas in these units are informed by the model of progression for evidence outlined earlier and, as previously argued, cover the range of learning outcomes accessible to the majority of fourth-grade students. Some students will still struggle to master these ideas in seventh and eighth grades, whereas the understanding of others will have moved far beyond even the most difficult of these ideas.

A final set of examples deals with the concept of causal explanation—provided in Unit 4 on page 172.

In the examples given for the Worlds Apart topic, each second-order concept is addressed once and once only. If two topics are taught at each grade, it follows that each second-order concept will be revisited at least once each year and that planning for systematic progression across grades is possible.

The examples provided here are, of course, only an illustration of the start of the planning process. Detailed planning with reference to content, materials, and activities must flesh out the key generalizations and ideas exemplified above. At the same time, our planning should also take account of the other key findings of *How People Learn*. The planning grid presented in Box 3A-2 shows how all three key findings might figure in planning to develop students' understanding of the concept of evidence, using the St. Brendan and Pilgrims' tasks as examples.

Unit 4: First Contacts: Why Didn't the Norse Colonists Stay in America?

Target Generalizations About the Past

- The first *definite* contacts between Native Americans and non-American peoples occurred when Norse sailors and colonists landed and attempted to settle in North America.
- The Norse were trying to do what they had done before—to find and to settle in empty land.
- But America was *not* empty. It was already full of people about whom the Norse knew nothing. The Native Americans fought the Norse and threw them out of the country.

Target Ideas About Causal Explanation

- Some things happen because people want and have the power to make them happen (e.g., the colonization of Iceland and Greenland).
- Other things happen that people don't want and try to prevent (e.g., the Norse eviction from North America and the later destruction of the Greenland colonies).
- Explanations of why people do things are not always the same as explanations of why things happen.
- To explain why things happen, we sometimes refer to causes that people can't or don't know how to control (e.g., climate changes, differences in population size and density).

The first column in the planning grid shows the content to be covered and the key questions that organize that content. The key questions are designed to allow us to bring together the content and the relevant second-order understandings. Although there are two different topics—St. Brendan and the Pilgrims—the questions for both the fourth- and sixth-grade work are concerned with the same key question: "How do we know?" Teaching will therefore need to focus on the concept of historical evidence. But decisions will need to be made to ensure that the teaching is appropriate for the age and ability of the students.

Before more precise teaching goals can be written into plans of this kind, some consideration must be given to the first key finding of *How People Learn*—that "students come to the classroom with preconceptions." In accordance with this finding, the planning examples for fourth and sixth grades include in the second column of the grid likely *preconceptions to be checked out.* These are planning reminders of the preconceptions about evidence that research suggests students are likely to hold. At the same time, we must keep in mind the range of ideas we are likely to encounter at any age. The point is not that all students will think the same things, but that we might expect to find ideas such as these among most fourth- or sixth-grade students, depending on what has been taught before. So if our sixth graders have already done the St. Brendan task, as well as similar work designed to develop their understanding of evidence in the context of other topics, we would expect that many of them already understand the preconceptions listed as needing to be considered in the Pilgrim Fathers' task. If the students have done no such work, we would be safer to anticipate their still holding some of the preconceptions listed under the Brendan task when the time comes to tackle the Pilgrims' task.

The preconceptions listed in Box 3A-2 for both grade 4 (ideas about sources as information or as testimony) and grade 6 (ideas about sources as evidence in isolation) relate to the progression model for evidence (Box 3A-1). That model also provides a framework for thinking about teaching targets; in Box 3A-2, the third column for both grades 4 and 6 sets forth the key conceptual understandings to be taught, in line with the second finding of *How People Learn*. These understandings build the preconceptions listed in the previous column, and are intended to ensure that our teaching enables students to consolidate or extend their previous learning. Thus, whereas the St. Brendan task targets some rather broad principles about the use of evidence that make history possible, the Pilgrims' task concentrates on important ideas about how inferences can be drawn from testimony, ideas that allow students to consolidate their understanding of evidence. The Pilgrims' task also sets a planning target for extending students' understanding by introducing ideas about situating evidence in the broader context of the society from which it comes.

If the St. Brendan grid and the Pilgrims' grid are examined together, the relationship between the preconceptions to be checked out and the key conceptual understandings to be taught becomes evident. It is this relationship that is crucial for ensuring that progression in students' understanding takes place. The evidence progression model (Box 3A-1) provides an aid to planning here. For example, it is important for a sixth-grade teacher to know not just what content has been taught to students in previous grades, but also what conceptual understandings have been gained. If colleagues are guided by common planning, such knowledge of students' understanding is likely to be a more realistic goal.

The key point here is that when students move from one topic to another, they should also be given the opportunity to move forward conceptually. It is important for teachers to have a sense of the possible progression for students. In addition to supporting the kind of planning that ensures students are given work appropriate to their abilities, this kind of knowledge can help in dealing with the range of abilities that are likely to exist within

BOX 3A-2 Planning for Progression in Ideas About Evidence

Key questions and content	Key Finding #1 Preconceptions to be checked out	Key Finding #2 Key conceptual understandings to be taught	Key Finding #3 Metacognitive questions
Grade 4 (St. Brendan task)			
How do we know?	**Sources as information**	**Sources as evidence in isolation**	
St. Brendan: Did an Irish monk reach America 1000 years before Columbus? **Substantive content** • Irish voyages • Viking voyages	• The past is given. • We can't know about the past because we weren't there. **Sources as testimony** • We can find out something about the past from reports that have survived. • If no one told the truth about what happened, we can't find anything out.	• We can work out what happened in the past from what is left. • Some things left from the past weren't meant to tell us anything, but we can still use them to find things out. • The weight we can put on the evidence depends on the questions we ask. • Often we can't be certain about the past, but we can produce stronger or weaker arguments as to what it makes most sense to say.	• Am I clear what question I'm asking? • Do I know what kind of thing this is? • Do I know what the writer is trying to do? • Does my argument work for the hard bits as well as the easy bits?

Grade 6 (Pilgrim Fathers' task)

How do we know?

How do we know about the arrival of the Pilgrims in America?

Substantive content

- Separatism
- Early English colonization
- The Pilgrim Fathers
- The Plymouth Settlement
- The Wampanoags

Sources as evidence in isolation

- We can work out what happened in the past from what is left.
- Some things left from the past weren't meant to tell us anything, but we can still use them to find things out.
- The weight we can put on the evidence depends on the questions we ask.
- Often we can't be certain about the past, but we can produce stronger or weaker arguments as to what it makes most sense to say.

Sources as evidence in isolation

- To use testimony as evidence, we need to take into account the circumstances in which it was produced.
- Testimony can unintentionally reflect the ideas and beliefs of those who produced it and still be valuable as evidence for historians.
- People can produce representations of past events that are not necessarily intended as reconstructions.

Sources as evidence in context

- Inferences from sources must take account of their cultural assumptions.

- Are my questions the same as other people's?
- How do the differences in our questions affect the way the sources can be used?
- Can the sources answer my questions? What other kinds of sources will I need?
- Do I know the circumstances in which this source was produced?
- Do I understand what beliefs or values might make the writer see things in the way he or she does?
- How do those beliefs and values affect the way I can use this as evidence?

any one class. If the fourth-grade teacher understands the learning plans of the sixth-grade teacher, it becomes possible to introduce some ideas earlier for students who may benefit. It may also be important for the sixth-grade teacher to be able to reinforce understandings that have been taught earlier but are shaky for some students.

The third key finding of *How People Learn*—that "a metacognitive approach to instruction can help students learn to take control of their own learning by defining learning goals and monitoring their progress in achieving them"—is also an important aspect of the planning process. The last column on the planning grids in Box 3A-2 lists the metacognitive questions adopted for these units of work. It is clear that these questions are closely related to the kinds of understandings we are trying to develop in students and can help raise their consciousness of what is at issue when using evidence. Questions of this kind increase students' awareness of the knowledge and understanding they have, and enable them to see that some answers to questions actually solve problems while other answers do not. This kind of awareness helps students recognize that answers provided by other students are relevant to the problems they themselves faced in their attempts at answers. Planning of the kind exemplified here that links questions to key second-order concepts can help teachers develop these questions into full-fledged metacognitive strategies. Moreover, metacognitive questions have additional advantages. Students' use of such questions allows their teachers to gain insight into their understanding and their misconceptions and thereby take advantage of learning opportunities that arise in the classroom, and to think about the kinds of adjustments that will be necessary in day-to-day planning to support individual learning needs, as well as longer-term goals.

The planning principles discussed here for fourth and sixth grades with respect to evidence would, of course, need to be extended to other second-order concepts and to other grades to enable the formulation of a long-term plan for a school history curriculum. These principles provide a structure for systematically revisiting ideas that inform all the history we want our students to learn, regardless of the topic. Such ideas are at the heart of history. They introduce students to the possibility of treating accounts of particular passages of the past as better or worse, more or less valid, in a rational way. History such as this does not succumb to vicious relativism on the one hand or to fundamentalism on the other. Rather, it exemplifies the central values of an open society.

NOTES

1. Examples of research in history education confirming this principle include Shemilt (1980) and Lee and Ashby (2000, 2001). Experience with a series of curriculum changes (the Schools History Project, the Cambridge History Project, and, more recently, the National Curriculum for History) and public assessment of students' work in the United Kingdom have provided additional confirmatory evidence.
2. Lee and Ashby, 2000.
3. We would like to thank the students and teachers in schools in Essex and Kent in England, and in Oakland (California) in the United States who took part in trials of the two tasks presented in this chapter. All names in the text are pseudonyms, and U.K. "year groups" have been converted into U.S. "grade" equivalents; for example, U.K. year 7 pupils are given as grade 6. While this is only an approximate equivalence, research (e.g. Barton, 1996; VanSledright, 2002, pp. 59-66) offers examples of ideas very similar to those found in the United Kingdom, and responses to the second task in the two countries suggest that differences between education systems do not invalidate the approximation.
4. For research on student ideas about evidence, see Shemilt (1980, 1987) and Lee et al. (1996).
5. Todd and Curtis, 1982.
6. Jordan et al., 1985.
7. Wineburg, 2001.
8. Dickinson and Lee, 1984; Ashby and Lee, 1987.
9. Shemilt, 1978.
10. Shemilt, 1980, 1987; Lee et al., 1996.
11. VanSledright, 2002.
12. Leinhardt, 1994.
13. The teaching material was inspired by and is indebted to Tim Severin's book describing his "Brendan Voyage."
14. Leinhardt, 1994.
15. Seixas, 1993, 1994.
16. Barton, 1996.
17. Shemilt, 1980.

REFERENCES

Ashby, R, and Lee, P.J. (1987). Children's concepts of empathy and understanding in history. In C. Portal (Ed.), *The history curriculum for teachers* (pp. 62-88). London, England: Falmer Press.

Barton, K.C. (1996). Narrative simplifications in elementary students' historical thinking. In J. Brophy (Ed.), *Advances in research on teaching vol. 6: Teaching and learning history* (p. 67). Greenwich, CT: JAI Press.

Dickinson, A.K., and Lee, P.J. (1984). Making sense of history. In A.K. Dickinson, P.J. Lee, and P.J. Rogers (Eds.), *Learning history* (pp. 117-153). London, England: Heinemann.

Jordan, W.D., Greenblatt, M., and Bowes, J.S. (1985). *The Americans: The history of a people and a nation.* Evanston, IL: McDougal, Littell.

Lee, P.J., and Ashby, R. (2000). Progression in historical understanding among students ages 7 to 14. In P. Seixas, P. Stearns, and S. Wineburg (Eds.), *Knowing, teaching and learning history: National and international perspectives* (pp. 192-222). New York: University Press.

Lee, P.J., and Ashby, R. (2001). Empathy, perspective taking and rational understanding. In O.L. Davis Jr., S. Foster, and E. Yaeger (Eds.), *Historical empathy and perspective taking in the social studies.* Boulder, CO: Rowman and Littlefield.

Lee, P.J., Ashby, R., and Dickinson, A.R. (1996). Progression in children's ideas about history. In M. Hughes (Ed.), *Progression in learning.* Bristol, PA: Multilingual Matters.

Leinhardt, G. (1994). History: A time to be mindful. In G. Leinhardt, I.L. Beck, and C. Stainton (Eds.), *Teaching and learning in history.* Mahwah, NJ: Lawrence Erlbaum Associates.

Seixas, P. (1993). Popular film and young people's understanding of the history of native-white relations. *The History Teacher, 26,* 3.

Seixas, P. (1994). Confronting the moral frames of popular film: Young people respond to historical revisionism. *American Journal of Education,* 102.

Severin, T. (1996). *The Brendan voyage.* London, England: Abacus.

Shemilt, D. (1978). *History 13-16 evaluation study.* Unpublished evaluation report submitted to the Schools Council, London, England.

Shemilt, D. (1980). *History 13-16 evaluation study.* Edinburgh, Scotland: Holmes McDougall.

Shemilt, D. (1987). Adolescent ideas about evidence and methodology in history. In C. Portal (Ed.), *The history curriculum for teachers.* London, England: Falmer Press.

Todd, L.P., and Curtis, M.(1982). *The rise of the American nation.* Orlando FL: Harcourt Brace Jovanovitch.

VanSledright, B. (2002). *In search of America's past* (pp. 59-66). New York: Teachers College Press.

Wineburg, S. (2001). *Historical thinking and other unnatural acts.* Philadelphia, PA: Temple University Press.

4

"They Thought the World Was Flat?" Applying the Principles of How People Learn in Teaching High School History

Robert B. Bain

For at least a century, educational critics and school reformers have pointed to high school history teaching as the model for poor and ineffective pedagogy. Consider, for example, the introduction to a series of nineteenth-century books on teaching written by psychologist G. Stanley Hall:

> History was chosen for the subject of the first volume of this educational library because, after much observation in the schoolrooms of many of the larger cities in the eastern part of our country, the editor . . . is convinced that no subject so widely taught is, on the whole, taught so poorly, almost sure to create a distaste for historical study—perhaps forever.[1]

History education, Hall observed, involved generally unprepared teachers who used ineffective methods to turn history into the driest of school subjects. "The high educational value of history is too great," Hall explained, "to be left to teachers who merely hear recitations, keeping the finger on the place in the text-book, and only asking the questions conveniently printed for them in the margin or the back of the book."[2] In a call to instructional arms, Hall and other late-nineteenth-century reformers urged teachers to move beyond lecture, recitation, and textbooks, asking them to "saturate" history teaching with more active historical pedagogy.

Most subsequent educational critics have shared Hall's concerns about the quality of history instruction and embraced the recommendation that teachers reform history teaching to make it more effective and engaging. However, critics have disagreed vigorously about the goals and features of an improved pedagogy. The language of reform reflects these disagreements, often urging history teachers to choose either student-centered or teacher-centered pedagogies, an emphasis on facts or concepts, hands-on learning or lecture, textbooks or primary sources, depth or breadth, inquiry or direct instruction.

History teachers know that the choices are neither so dichotomous nor so simple. Framing the instructional situation as a set of either-or choices, such as abandoning textbooks in favor of primary sources or substituting student inquiry projects for teachers' lectures, ignores the perennial challenges that history students and, consequently, history teachers face in trying to learn history and develop historical understanding. History is a vast and constantly expanding storehouse of information about people and events in the past. For students, learning history leads to encounters with thousands of unfamiliar and distant names, dates, people, places, events, and stories. Working with such content is a complex enterprise not easily reduced to choices between learning facts and mastering historical thinking processes. Indeed, attention to one is necessary to foster the other. As *How People Learn* suggests, storing information in memory in a way that allows it to be retrieved effectively depends on the thoughtful organization of content, while core historical concepts "such as stability and change" require familiarity with the sequence of events to give them meaning. Moreover, learning history entails teaching students to think quite differently than their "natural" inclinations. As Wineburg[3] suggests, historical thinking may often be an "unnatural" act, requiring us to think outside familiar and comfortable assumptions and world views. Such work, then, requires both substantial knowledge and skill on the part of the teacher to help students learn historical content while expanding their capacities to use evidence, assess interpretations, and analyze change over time.

This chapter addresses the challenges high school history teachers confront every day when, facing large classes, predefined course goals, and the required use of textbooks, they try to engage students in the intellectual work of learning and "doing" history. Given the demands on history teachers and the intellectual challenges students face while learning history, how might high school history teachers use the ideas found in *How People Learn* to construct history-specific instructional environments that support students as they work toward deeper historical understanding? As a veteran high school history teacher with over 25 years of experience, I begin by showing how I cast traditional history topics and curricular objectives as historical problems for my students to study. Reformers have long argued that historical inquiry ought to be part of history teaching, but often teachers see it as something either on the margins of instruction or as a replacement for traditional teaching. This chapter takes a different approach by building upon traditional curricular mandates and pedagogy to place inquiry at the heart of instruction. Using a case study developed around my students' studies of Columbus, exploration, and the concept of the "flat earth," I focus on ways teachers can restructure familiar curricular objectives into historiographic problems that engage students in historical thinking. Formulating such historical problems is a critical first step in history teaching.

But it is not sufficient simply to add problem formulation to the extant history curriculum and pedagogy. This chapter goes beyond problem formulation to suggest ways teachers might design history-specific "tools" to help students do history throughout the curriculum. These modest cognitive tools—"mindtools" as David Jonassen[4] calls them—provide useful ways to help students grapple with sophisticated historical content while performing complex historical thinking and acquiring substantive knowledge. Again drawing on my experiences with my students, this chapter makes a case for transforming lectures and textbooks from mere accounts of events into supports that help students grapple with historical problems as they learn historical content and construct historical meaning.

WHERE TO BEGIN? TRANSFORMING TOPICS AND OBJECTIVES INTO HISTORICAL PROBLEMS

History begins with—and often ends with—questions, problems, puzzles, curiosities, and mysteries. Historians frame and build their historical research around problems emerging from a complex mix of personal and professional interests, unexamined and underexamined questions, gaps in established literature and knowledge, and recurring puzzles and issues. Like detectives working intently on solving the mystery at hand, historians face questions and puzzles that direct their scholarship, giving it meaning and providing coherence.[5] Seeking the answers to perplexing questions does more than simply make history an engaging activity for historians; working with problems also helps historians select, organize, and structure their historical facts. It is no surprise, therefore, that most attempts to reform history education urge teachers to begin with "big" questions. If historians are driven to learn content by their questions, so, too, might students find history engaging, relevant, and meaningful if they understood the fundamental puzzles involved. Students, like historians, can use historical problems to organize data and direct their inquiries and studies. Therefore, creating and using good questions is as crucial for the teacher as it is for the researcher.

However, much as high school history teachers might wish to frame their instruction around the historical problems arising from compelling interests, gaps, puzzles, or mysteries, they must deal with a different set of constraints from those faced by historians. History teachers are charged with teaching their students a history that others have already written; thus they typically begin with course outcomes in hand, determined by curricular mandates (i.e., district or state) or the imperatives of external testing (i.e., state exams, Advanced Placement or International Baccalaureate tests). Using the normative discourse of curriculum and standards documents, history is cast into discrete behavioral objectives and measurable student outcomes, readily used by the bureaucracies of schooling, such as testing and textbooks. Although the authors of those outcomes often started with compelling questions, central ideas, and enduring problems, the bigger issues gradually fall away as the curricula are written, reshaped, vetted, voted upon, and adopted. History, then, arrives at the classroom door as lists of things students must learn and, thus, teachers must teach—missing the problems and questions that make the content coherent, significant, and even fascinating.

Of course, beginning with measurable outcomes helps teachers establish targets for teaching and learning. However, curricular objectives rarely connect outcomes to their intellectual roots, that is, to the historical problems and questions that generated such understanding in the first place. Whatever their value for conducting assessments, lists of curricular objectives do not (nor are they intended to) provide the disciplinary connections, patterns, or relationships that enable teachers and students to construct coherent pictures of the history they study. Lists of instructional outcomes rarely frame history as an unfinished mystery that invites students to join the investigation or points teachers toward historiographic questions that might begin and sustain instruction. Nor do curricular lists help teachers anticipate students' preinstructional understandings, develop a reasonable and educationally sound trajectory of lessons, or build connections across content objectives. Yet the knowledge base summarized in *How People Learn* suggests that these are critical to effective teaching and learning. Given the form of most standards documents, history teachers must offer the intellectual and historical context necessary to provide meaning and coherence across discrete objectives.

One way teachers can build instructional cohesion, as suggested in *How People Learn,* is to organize the curriculum around history's key concepts, big ideas, and central questions.[6] Teachers can provide instructional substance by grounding the abstractions found in standards and curriculum documents in meaningful historical problems. But how do we move from lists of loosely connected objectives to central historiographic questions? How do we transform inert historical topics into historical problems?

In a sense, history teachers in the United States must play a form of instructional *Jeopardy* by inventing the big questions to fit the curricular answers. Like historians working backward from given events to the questions that precipitated them,[7] history teachers work backward from given objectives to the big historical questions. Unlike historians, however, who work only along historical lines of thinking, teachers must be bifocal by pursuing both *historical* and *instructional* lines of thinking. History teachers must go beyond merely doing history or thinking historically themselves;

they must be able to help others learn history and learn to think historically. Therefore, history teachers have to employ an instructional as well as historical logic when designing history problems, moving beyond historiographic issues to consider their students and the context within which their students learn history.

What does this mean in practice? First, teachers should try to design historiographic problems that provide links across objectives to connect the multiple scales of instructional time that teachers and students share: activities, lessons, units, and courses. Ideally, each scale is clearly nested within and connected to others, so students can see how activities become lessons forming coherent units that combine for unified courses. Unfortunately, students rarely experience such coherence in their history courses, as reflected in their belief that history comprises lists of facts, packaged in chronological containers—such as textbook chapters—that have little discernable connection to each other. Unifying problems, if well designed and historically interesting, can provide a larger frame to help students develop meaningful connections across activities, lessons, units, and courses.

Second, in creating instructional problems, teachers also must pay attention to the multiple facets of historical knowledge—history's facts, concepts, and disciplinary patterns of thinking. Aiming for instructional coherence does not mean that teachers will sacrifice the substance and rigor of the discipline in crafting problems to study. Good problems look to both the contours and details of historical stories, asking, for example, "How has democracy in the United States changed over time? What explains differences in mobility or technology over time?" Working with such problems requires students to grapple with important historical details while extending their understanding of and skill in using key historical concepts, such as significance, cause and effect, change and continuity, evidence, and historical accounts.

Further, in creating instructional problems, teachers must carefully consider the hidden challenges their students face when studying history and employing historical thinking. For example, extraordinary knowledge and skill are required to "put oneself in another's shoes," for the world views of previous generations of people were profoundly different from our own. Ninth graders can "imagine" what it felt like to be a European explorer or Native American, but their natural inclination will be to presume more similarity than difference across time. Students find it difficult to imagine a world not yet shaped by science or the Industrial Revolution, a world in which there were no social services and running water, a world in which U.S. citizens did not take democracy for granted. Students' historical present—recognized or not—shapes their understanding of the past—another dimension for teachers to consider in designing historical problems for students to study.[8]

Thus, in constructing problems or questions, high school history teachers must work on multiple instructional and historiographic levels, crafting historical problems that are transportable across scales of instructional time—activities, lessons, units, and courses—while capturing the factual, conceptual, and cognitive processes central to generating historical understanding and challenging students' assumptions. In framing these problems, history teachers must ask, "What historical questions will connect the course activities and provoke my students to learn content as they extend their capacity for historical thinking?" The following case study embodies this question by first describing the complex historical problems I used to organize my high school course and then creating a related problem for a unit within that course.

"Problematizing" Historical Accounts to Raise Year-Long Historical Questions

Creating central questions or problems challenges teachers to work at the intersection of two separate junctures—what is historically significant and what is instructive for and interesting to students. In my high school history courses, I often met this challenge by "problematizing" historical accounts—history's stories, interpretations, narratives, and representations. Focusing on historical accounts gave me material to create a robust set of problems that stimulated, organized, and guided instruction over an entire course.

What do I mean by problematizing historical accounts? At the unit level—instruction ranging from about a week to a month—it means raising questions about particular historical stories, narratives, or interpretations. At the level of the whole course, however, it means raising questions that are fundamental to historical understanding:

> **What is the difference between historical accounts and the "past"? How do events that occurred in the past and the accounts that people create about the past differ? If the past is fleeting, happening only once and then disappearing, how is it possible for people living in the present to create accounts of the past? How do historians move from evidence of the past to construct historical explanations and interpretations? How do historians use evidence, determine significance, structure turning points, and explain continuity and change within their accounts? Are some historical accounts "better" than others? Why? By what standards do historians assess historical accounts? Why do accounts of the same event differ and change**

over time? Does it make a difference which version of the past we accept?

Such questions touch upon every facet of the discipline of history, constituting the foundational problems historians confront when doing history.

Though it might appear obvious, focusing on historical accounts would already represent a major break from traditional history instruction. The accounts that historians write and adults read—such as the currently popular biography of John Adams or the groundbreaking *Cheese and the Worms*[9]—are typically too rich and deep, too complex and time-consuming, to find their way into textbooks. Students do not read about John Adams' life, his relationship with his wife, his travels to Europe, his passions and enthusiasms, but rather read that he was President, that he held certain positions, and that he died on the same day as Thomas Jefferson. Only these discrete bits of information, the traces of historical accounts, make their way into textbooks or into curricular objectives.

Raising questions about accounts helps students see the water in which they are swimming. Historical accounts—or rather, the vestigial remains of historical accounts—are ubiquitous in high school history courses. Textbooks, media, handouts, lectures, classroom materials, technology, and teachers surround history students with fragments of historical narratives and interpretations, yet rarely do students see the nature and structure of these interpretations. Much of high school history finds students exploring vast evidenceless and authorless expanses of curriculum that promote, as historian David Lowenthal[10] asserts, a "credulous allegiance" to some version of the past:

> Historical faith is instilled in school. "Youngsters have been taught history as they were taught math as a finite subject with definite right or wrong answers," frets a museum director. Most history texts are "written as if their authors did not exist. . . ." High marks depend on giving the "correct" gloss to regurgitated facts. Textbook certitude makes it hard for teachers to deal with doubt and controversy; saying "I don't know" violates the authoritative norm and threatens classroom control.

Problematizing historical accounts, then, makes visible what is obscured, hidden, or simply absent in many history classrooms. It helps move school history beyond reproducing others' conclusions to understanding how people produced those conclusions, while considering the limitations and strengths of various interpretations. By making historical accounts our essential historical problem, we can help students develop familiarity with historical writing; identify ways in which people have interpreted past events; recognize, compare, and analyze different and competing interpretations of events; examine reasons for shifts in interpretations over time; study the ways people use evidence to reason historically; and consider interpretations in relationship to various historical periods. Indeed, all of the familiar features of history classrooms—textbooks, lectures, primary sources, maps, time lines, and even worksheets—take on new meaning for students when viewed as historical accounts.

This approach does not preclude using themes, such as changes in migration, ideas, or political culture, but rather forces teachers to anchor their themes in the issues of historical representation and interpretation. Nor does a focus on interpretation favor process at the expense of facts. In looking carefully at historical accounts, we must teach historical facts; more important however, we must also raise questions about why we should (or whether we should) consider particular sets of facts important. The study of interpretations demands that students look carefully at the ways people use facts to form and support historical accounts. Indeed, factual understanding becomes even more significant as students grapple with how people use facts in representing the past.

Moreover, a focus on multiple, shifting accounts does not mean students will hold all accounts to be equally compelling or plausible; rather, like historians, students must develop tools to evaluate and access competing stories of the past, considering evidence and argument while learning to judge what constitutes sound historical reasoning. In systematically questioning historical interpretations over the course of a school year, we can help students understand that accounts differ, and that those differences lie in the questions authors ask, the criteria they use to select evidence, and the spatial and temporal backdrop people use to tell their stories.

Therefore, I placed the fundamental questions about historical understanding cited earlier at the heart of our study for the year.

> In creating historical stories or interpretations, what questions were the historians trying to answer? How did the historians, typically not present at the events they were studying, use evidence from the past to answer their questions and construct explanations or interpretations? Within their accounts, how did the historians determine significance, structure turning points, and explain continuity/change over time? Why do accounts of the same events differ, shift in interpretation, or come into and out of fashion? Are some historical accounts "better" than others? Why? By what standards are we assessing historical accounts? Does it make a difference which version of the past we accept?

Teachers will need to explicitly introduce and help students frame central problems and concepts at the outset of a course and use them regularly, even before the students fully understand them. That is what I did, using the distinctions between "the past" and "history" to introduce students to the problems involved in creating and using historical accounts. On the surface, the difference between the past and history appears to be an easy one for students to perceive and understand. But high school teachers know how long it takes for students to fully understand and employ such distinctions in their thinking.

There are many ways to introduce these ideas, but a particularly powerful one is to have students write a short history of an event they all shared and then compare their respective histories. For example, an activity I often used was to have students write a history of the first day of school that they would read aloud on the second day. The great variance in students' choice of facts, details, stories, and perspectives revealed differences between the event under study (i.e., the first day of school) and the accounts of that event. This simple activity helped reveal the distinctions between events and historical accounts because students experienced the differences when writing about and comparing their shared pasts.

The most significant instructional goal and feature of the activity involved our naming these distinctions by creating two new and key terms—"H(ev)" and "H(ac)"—standing for "history-as-event" and "history-as-account." Why make up such new historical terms? Students typically enter history class with established conceptions and assumptions about history. They use the word "history" in two very different ways: (1) history as a past occurrence ("Well, that happened in history.") or (2) history as an account of a past occurrence ("I wrote that in my history.") Their everyday and commonsense uses of the word "history" blur the distinction between the past and accounts of the past and reinforce typical conceptions that history is but a mirror of the past. A crucial instructional move, therefore, involves creating a language to help students break out of their ordinary, customary use of "history" to make fundamental disciplinary distinctions.

Once defined, the phrases "history-as-event" and "history-as-account" or the invented terms H(ev) and H(ac) were used almost daily by students to name and frame materials commonly encountered, including textbooks, films, and class lectures. This simple linguistic device helped them situate accounts, regardless of how authoritative, in relationship to the events described by those accounts. This, in turn, heightened students' sensitivity to and awareness of when we were discussing an interpretation and when we were discussing an event. In exploring the distinction between history-as-event and history-as-account, students generated questions they used to consider the relationship between events and the accounts that describe them. For example, one class produced these questions:

> **How do accounts relate to the event they describe? Do the accounts capture the full event? Is it possible for accounts to fully capture events? How and why do accounts of the same event differ? Do they use different facts? Different sources? Different pictures? Different language? Do the accounts identify different turning points or significant events in the game?**

> **Are the accounts connected to each together? Are there other possible accounts of the event? Do accounts serve different purposes? What explains the fact that people studying the same event create differing accounts? Can one account be better than another? How can we assess competing truth claims? Does it matter which version of an event we accept as true? What makes one account more compelling than another? How does an account use evidence to make its claims?**

These questions, initially discussed in relationship to students' history of the first day of class, formed a valuable backdrop for each successive unit. Initial distinctions, introduced and then used regularly, helped students demystify historical accounts by constantly reminding them that historical texts are products of human thought involving investigation, selection, evaluation, and interpretation.

Establishing these initial distinctions provided students with the beginnings of a new conceptual map for the discipline of history, a map we used regularly to locate their position in historical territory. "So, were we just now working with events or accounts of those events? Who constructed the account? What evidence did they use in building the narrative or interpretation?"

No one should think that merely pointing out conceptual distinctions through a classroom activity equips students to make consistent, regular, and independent use of these distinctions. Established habits of thinking that history and the past are the same do not disappear overnight. Merely generating questions about historical accounts did not mean that my students developed the knowledge and skill needed to answer those questions, or even to raise those questions on their own. In making conceptual distinctions between the past and accounts of the past, it did not follow automatically that students developed the intellectual skills to analyze, evaluate, or construct historical accounts. Indeed, students did not even fully grasp the distinctions represented in the new linguistic conventions they were using, such as history-as-event/H(ev) and history-as-account/H(ac). Still, while not lulled into thinking that introducing concepts meant students had mastered those concepts, I expected students to use these terms regularly. In subsequent activities, the terms served as intellectual "mindtools" to guide student thinking, helping and, at times, forcing students to analyze their everyday uses of the word "history." Thus in building on students' nascent historical thinking, I tried to push them to develop more refined and nuanced historical knowledge and skill while framing a historical problem large enough to inform our entire course.

Accounting for the "Flat Earth": Building a Unit-Level Problem

How might we create a problem for a unit of study that would engage students, assist in posing the larger disciplinary questions about accounts noted above, and meet curricular objectives such as those that characterize the traditional topic of European exploration of the Americas? Early in the school year, I asked a class of ninth-grade history students, "What do you know about Columbus sailing the ocean blue in 1492? And what do you know about the people of Europe on the eve of Columbus' voyages? What were they like? What did they believe and think?"

Ben	Well, people of Europe didn't know anything about the United States or Canada, because people had not been there yet. They wanted to get to China to trade, but most people were scared to sail across the Atlantic.
Teacher	Why? What were their fears?
Ben	The world was flat and you could fall off it . . .
Amanda	People would not give him money for his ships because they figured he would fail. But Columbus proved them wrong. . . .
Ellen	Not really. Columbus never really went all the way around the earth.
Teacher	So?
Ellen	Well, people could still believe the earth was flat, just that there was another land before you got to the end of the earth.
Teacher	Oh, then, people would have to really wait until someone sailed all the way around the world before they changed their ideas?
Ellen	Yeah.
Teacher	Well, for how long did this idea exist?
Bill	All the way back to earliest times. Everyone always thought the world was flat.
Ellen	Except some scientists, right?

With some gentle questioning on my part, the students collectively told the standard and widely accepted story of Columbus, an Italian sailor who received funds from the king and queen of Spain to go to the east by sailing west. Europeans thought this was "crazy" because people had thought—forever—that the world was flat. Columbus, motivated by his search for gold, did land in the New World, but thought he had arrived in China and the Indies, which is why he named the people there "Indians" before conquering them.

For about 10 to 15 minutes, I probed students' ideas about Columbus and fifteenth-century Europe, capturing key points of agreement and disagreement on the chalkboard. I then encouraged students to think about the source of their understanding, expanding our discussion by asking, "How do you know that the flat-earth story is true? Where did you learn about it? What evidence do you have?" After a few minutes of comments ranging from "everyone knows" to "our elementary teacher told us," it was clear that students could not point to a specific account that supported their understanding of the event.

Because historical accounts were the focus for both the course and the unit, I gave the students several excerpts from the writing of nineteenth-century historians, excerpts I selected to substantiate the common view that Europeans at the time of Columbus typically believed the earth was flat (see Box 4-1). I used these nineteenth-century historical accounts simply to support students' preinstructional thinking about the flat earth, intending to return to analyze the accounts later in the unit.[11] I asked the students to read the accounts and to look for places where the accounts supported, extended, or contested their thinking about Columbus and Europeans.

In general, these accounts typify the story about Europe and Columbus that emerged in historical writing in the nineteenth century, a story that, as the students' discussion revealed, continues to hold sway with most students (and adults). The excerpts tell of Columbus' attempt to sail west to China and the challenges posed by other Europeans and their beliefs about the flat world. They reveal how the irrational beliefs of European sailors, clergy, and nobility hindered Columbus, who knew, heroically, that the world was round. They show how, in trying to achieve his dream, Columbus encountered European sailors who were afraid he and his crew would fall off the edge of the earth, clergy who were horrified by his heretical neglect of the Church and the Scripture, and elites who were shocked by Columbus' disregard for established geographic knowledge. According to these accounts, Columbus was different from other Europeans of his age: daring, courageous, and blessed with the humanist's faith that people were capable of great things if they learned enough and tried hard enough.

By design, little in these accounts surprised the students, confirming much of what they knew already about Columbus and the era in which he lived.

Carlos	He [Columbus] proved everyone wrong because he guessed the world was round.
Ellen	I think I knew that others wouldn't fund him

	because they thought the world was flat and he would fall off the edge. How could that be a good investment?
Jim	Well, he didn't know much geography because he thought he was going to India, that's why he called people Indians, right?

The only hint of surprise for students was that no account mentioned the "discovery" of a people and a new land. Mark brought up this point, telling us, "Columbus thought he discovered America, but there were natives living there." Concerning the story of the flat earth, students were confident that the flat-earth belief was a real obstacle to Columbus and other explorers.

However, most contemporary historians no longer regard this to be the case. This story of the pre-Columbian belief in the flat earth therefore provides a wonderful opportunity to explore both the details of life in fifteenth-century Europe and larger issues concerning the relationship between historical accounts and the events they attempt to represent. Columbus, most historians today argue, was hardly alone in believing the world was round; indeed, according to recent historical accounts, most educated or even partially educated Europeans believed the world was round.[12] The elite, for example, did not resist Columbus because they thought he would fall off the earth's edge; rather, they thought he had underestimated the size of the earth and would never be able to sail so far in open water (a quite reasonable concern had there not been an unanticipated land mass upon which Columbus could stumble).

Yet my students believed with unquestioning certitude that people prior to Columbus thought the earth was flat. Schooled by their culture and entering the history classroom filled with specific stories about historical events we were studying, they were hardly historical blank slates. The flat-earth story is a part of the national, collective memory. Adults regularly use it as metaphor to describe the ignorance or superstitions of the masses. "Belief in the flat earth" is shorthand for any idea that blinds people to seeking and seeing the truth. My high school students understood and could use this flat-earth metaphor. And like most people, they did not see that this story of the fifteenth-century belief in a flat earth was simply an account of the past and not the past itself. For them, the flat-earth belief was an undisputed feature of the event. Whatever distinctions students had made in our earlier lessons between events and accounts, they had not yet realized that those distinctions were relevant to their own beliefs about the flat-earth story. When faced with a story of the past that they themselves held, students returned to their presumptions that the past is a given, an unwavering set of facts that historians unearth, dust off, and then display.

BOX 4-1 Accounts of Columbian Voyages

1. "Columbus was one of the comparatively few people who at that time believed the earth to be round. The general belief was that it was flat, and that if one should sail too far west on the ocean, he would come to the edge of the world, and fall off."

SOURCE: Eggleston (1904, p. 12).

2. "'But, if the world is round,' said Columbus, 'it is not hell that lies beyond the stormy sea. Over there *must* lie the eastern strand of Asia, the Cathay of Marco Polo, the land of the Kubla Khan, and Cipango, the great island beyond it.' 'Nonsense!' said the neighbors; 'the world isn't round—can't you *see* it is flat? And Cosmas Indicopleustes [a famous geographer] who lived hundreds of years before you were born, says it is flat; and he got it from the Bible. . . '"

SOURCE: Russell (1997, pp. 5-6).

3. "Columbus met with members of the Clergy and Spanish elite at Salamanca, who told him: 'You think the earth is round, and inhabited on the other side? Are you not aware that the holy fathers of the church have condemned this belief? . . . Will you contradict the fathers? The Holy Scriptures, too, tell us expressly that the heavens are spread out like a tent, and how can that be true if the earth is not flat like the ground the tent stands on? This theory of yours looks heretical.'"

SOURCE: Russell (1997, pp. 5-6).

4. "Many a bold navigator, who was quite ready to brave pirates and tempests, trembled at the thought of tumbling with his ship into one of the openings into hell which a widespread belief placed in the Atlantic at some unknown distance from Europe. This terror among sailors was one of the main obstacles in the great voyage of Columbus."

SOURCE: White (1896, p. 97).

Two critical features of teaching history are displayed here. The first involves probing students' thinking about the historical problem they are studying and making their thinking visible for all to see. History education entails helping students learn to think historically. Students' thinking resides at the instructional center; therefore, teachers must regularly take stock of it

5. "At Council of Salamanca, one of the 'learned' men asked Columbus: 'Is there any one so foolish . . . as to believe that there are antipodes with their feet opposite to ours: people who walk with their heels upward, and their heads hanging down? That there is a part of the world in which all things are topsy-turvy; where the trees grow with their braches downward, and where it rains, hails, and snows upward? The idea of the roundness of the earth . . . was the cause of the inventing of this fable. . . .'"

SOURCE: Irving (1830, p. 63).

6. "There appeared at this time a remarkable man—Christopher Columbus. . . . He began to astonish his country men with strange notions about the world. He boldly asserted that it was round, instead of flat; that it went around the sun instead of the sun going around it; and moreover, that day and night were caused by its revolution on its axis. These doctrines the priests denounced as contrary to those of the church. When he ventured to assert that by sailing west, he could reach the East Indies, they questioned not only the soundness of his theory, but that of his intellect."

SOURCE: Patton and Lord (1903, p. 12).

7. "Now, the sailors terror-stricken, became mutinous, and clamored to return. They thought they had sinned in venturing so far from land. . . . Columbus alone was calm and hopeful; in the midst of these difficulties, he preserved the courage and noble self-control. . . . His confidence in the success of his enterprise, was not the ideal dream of a mere enthusiast; it was founded in reason, it was based on science. His courage was the courage of one, who, in the earnest pursuit of truth, loses sight of every personal consideration."

SOURCE: Patton and Lord (1903, pp. 13-14).

and make it visible. The above class discussion is an example of a formative assessment whereby I tried to probe the thinking of the whole class. I asked students to weigh in on the problem, had them spend time documenting their thinking by writing about it in their journals, and then collected their thinking on the board.

Gathering student thinking is but a first step. History teachers do not take stock of student thinking merely to stimulate interest—though it certainly can have that important effect—but also to hold it up for critical examination. This observation leads to the second key feature of history teaching demonstrated here: asking students to explain how they know what they know about the historical event. Merely asking students to retell a historical story or narrate an event is insufficient for high school history students; rather, teachers must press students to document their understanding, and to explain the evidence they are using to draw conclusions or to accept one historical account over another. Like a historian querying a text, I prodded my students by asking for evidence and support. And like a historian who uses sources to extend understanding, I asked the students how each new piece of evidence or account supported, extended, or contested their historical thinking. Here again, language used regularly—"support," "extend," or "contest"—helped novice historians analyze critically the relationship between new sources and their own understanding.

In this case, my students could not point to the specific source of their knowledge about the flat earth, and so I provided them with historical accounts to support their ideas. Then to challenge their thinking and to draw the distinction between the story they knew and the event under study, I provided students with two sources of evidence that contested their assumptions and ideas: the first, a picture of a classical statue of Atlas holding up a celestial globe, created between 150 and 73 B.C.E.; and the second, an explanation by Carl Sagan of how the classical scholar Eratosthenes determined the circumference of the world in the third century B.C.E. (see Box 4-2). In groups of three, students discussed how these sources supported, extended, and/or contested their thinking about Columbus and the flat-earth idea. We then began our class discussion by asking, "If, as you and other historians have explained, people prior to 1492 generally believed that the earth was flat, then how do we explain the classical story of Atlas holding up a round earth or of Eratosthenes figuring out the earth's circumference over 2,000 years ago?"

The pictures of Atlas resonated with stories the students knew or pictures they had seen before. The story of Eratosthenes—though not explicitly remembered from earlier courses—connected with students' ideas that some ancient "scientists" were capable of unusually progressive thinking, such as building the pyramids or planning great inventions. In other words, these stories were familiar to the students, yet they made no connection between these stories and that of the flat earth. They had compartmentalized their understandings and did not see that they possessed ideas relevant to the question at hand. Use of the pictures of Atlas or stories of pre-Columbian geographers called upon features of students' background knowledge to provoke them to reconsider the certitude with which they held the flat-earth story:

Andrew	Those other stories [accounts we read before] made it sound as if Columbus was the scientist who discovered the earth was round. But I think other scientists had figured out the world was round, like Galileo. I mean, didn't he?
Teacher	I think, I mean, wasn't Galileo born in the sixteenth century, after the Columbian voyages?
Andrew	Ok, but what I mean is that I don't really think that Columbus was the first to prove the world was round. I mean, he didn't exactly prove it. These others had thought it was round and he just proved you wouldn't fall off the edge of the earth. They thought it. He proved it.
Sarena	Now, I sort of remember that many educated people believed the earth was round. Seems odd, that everyone believed the earth was flat but Columbus, doesn't it?

As I orchestrated the class discussion, I intentionally prodded students to consider the story of the flat earth as a specific historical account that may or may not be supported by evidence and, like all historical accounts, one that emerged at a particular time and place:

So, did fifteenth-century people believe that the earth was flat? What evidence do you have? What evidence do other accounts provide? Was it possible that people at one time, say during the Classical era, had such knowledge of the world, only to forget it later? Why might the flat-earth story emerge? What purpose would it serve? Does it make a difference which version of the story people believe? Could it be that the view adopted throughout our culture is unsupported by evidence? When did it develop and become popular? Why?

The conversation in the class turned to the discrepant information students confronted, the discrepancies that resided at the juncture of their assumed ideas about the past and the presented evidence. The discussion about this specific case also began to call into question what the students generally believed about people in the past. "If people at the time of Columbus believed in a flat earth," I asked, "what might explain how people at least 1,500 years before Columbus crafted globes or created (and resolved) problems about the earth's circumference? Is it possible that at one time people had knowledge of a round earth that was 'lost'?"

BOX 4-2 Ancient Views of Earth Flat or Round?

The Atlas Farnese

In 1575, this marble figure of Atlas holding a celestial globe was found in Rome. It is called the Atlas Farnese, as Farnese was the name of the collection it entered. It was created by sculptor Crates. The exact date of the sculpture is not known. However, scholars assume that it was made sometime after 150 A.D. because of the representation of the vernal equinox on the globe, which is similar to that in Ptolemy's Almagest. To give you an idea of the size, the sphere has a diameter of about 25 1/2 inches.

THE STORY OF ERATOSTHENES AND THE EARTH'S CIRCUMFERENCE

'The discovery that the Earth is a little world was made, as so many important human discoveries were, in the ancient Near East, in a time some humans call the third century BC, in the greatest metropolis of the age, the Egyptian city of Alexandria. Here there lived a man named Eratosthenes.

. . . He was an astronomer, historian, geographer, philosopher, poet, theater critic and mathematician. . . . He was also the director of the great library of Alexandria, where one day he read in a papyrus book that in the southern frontier outpost of Syene . . . at noon on June 21 vertical sticks cast no shadows. On the summer solstice, the longest day of the year, the shadows of temple columns grew shorter. At noon, they were gone. The sun was directly overhead.

It was an observation that someone else might easily have ignored. Sticks, shadows, reflections in wells, the position of the Sun—

of what possible importance could such simple everyday matters be? But Eratosthenes was a scientist, and his musings on these commonplaces changed the world; in a way, they made the world. Eratosthenes had the presence of mind to do an experiment, actually to observe whether in Alexandria vertical sticks cast shadows near noon on June 21. And, he discovered, sticks do.

Eratosthenes asked himself how, at the same moment, a stick in Syene could cast no shadow and a stick in Alexandria, far to the north, could cast a pronounced shadow. Consider a map of ancient Egypt with two vertical sticks of equal length, one stuck in Alexandria, the other in Syene. Suppose that, at a certain moment, each stick casts no shadow at all. This is perfectly easy to understand—provided the Earth is flat. The Sun would then be directly overhead. If the two sticks cast shadows of equal length, that also would make sense of a flat Earth: the Sun's rays would then be inclined at the same angle to the two sticks. But how could it be that at the same instant there was no shadow at Syene and a substantial shadow at Alexandria?

The only possible answer, he saw, was that the surface of the Earth is curved. Not only that: the greater the curvature, the greater the difference in the shadow lengths. The Sun is so far away that its rays are parallel when they reach the Earth. Sticks placed at different angles to the Sun's rays cast shadows of different lengths. For the observed difference in the shadow lengths, the distance between Alexandria and Syene had to be about seven degrees along the surface of the Earth; that is, if you imagine the sticks extending down to the center of the Earth, they would there intersect at an angle of seven degrees. Seven degrees is something like one-fiftieth of three hundred and sixty degrees, the full circumference of the Earth. Eratosthenes knew that the distance between Alexandria and Syene was approximately 800 kilometers, because he hired a man to pace it out. Eight hundred kilometers times 50 is 40,000 kilometers: so that must be the circumference of the Earth.

This is the right answer. Eratosthenes' only tools were sticks, eyes, feet and brains, plus a taste for experiment. With them he deduced the circumference of the Earth with an error of only a few percent, a remarkable achievement for 2,200 years ago. He was the first person to accurately measure the size of the planet.'

SOURCE: Sagan (1985, pp. 5-7).

To help students frame this problem more sharply—as well as to begin revealing the core historiographic debate—students read selections from the work of two contemporary scholars, Daniel Boorstin and Stephen Jay Gould (see Box 4-3). In one excerpt, Boorstin argues that the Middle Ages was a "great interruption" in the intellectual progress begun in Classical times, describing this interruption as an era when people were "more concerned with faith than facts."[13] On the other hand, Gould rejects the idea of a great interruption in European geographic knowledge, pointing to a story of continuity rather than discontinuity of ideas.

I used these excerpts strategically, for I wanted to provoke an in-class discussion and move the class toward framing an instructional/historical problem that would guide our study of European discovery: "Did people in 1492 generally believe in the flat earth? If not, when did the story of the flat earth arise? Who promoted that account? Why would people tell stories about the flat earth if the stories were not supported by evidence? What historical accounts explain European exploration of the Americas? How have historians changed those accounts over time?"

In thus problematizing the Columbian account and framing these questions, I sharpened the larger historiographic questions we were using to structure the entire course and the specific curricular objectives for the unit under study. In investigating these questions and analyzing the shifting and competing interpretations of exploration and explorers, high school history students also worked toward mastering the key content objectives for this unit of history. For example, while grappling with issues related to the nature of historical interpretation and knowledge, students had to study the context for and impact of European exploration from a number of perspectives. Historical knowledge—facts, concepts, and processes—shaped almost every feature of the unit, from the framing of the problem through the questions we employed during discussions. Students learned historical facts in the context of these large historical questions, and once they understood the questions, they saw they could not answer them without factual knowledge. The old and false distinction between facts and interpretations or between content and process collapses here. How can students learn about the accounts of the past—the growth of the flat-earth story, for example—without studying the knowledge and ideas of fourteenth- and fifteenth-century Europeans, the features of the waning Middle Ages, the emerging renaissance, tensions between the orthodoxy of the church and new scientific ideas, or the new mercantile impulses that promulgated reasonable risks in the name of profit? As students studied the development of the flat-earth story, an idea of the late eighteenth/early nineteenth century, they also worked with facts about early American national growth, conflicts with Britain and France, and Protestant concerns about Irish immigration. In trying to understand how this account of the past developed and became popular, students used specific factual detail to make their cases.

Learning historical content, though, was not the only factor that shaped the instruction. In helping students frame a historiographic problem, we publicly took stock of students' background knowledge and of their historical conceptions and misconceptions. Simply revealing students' thinking does not help them achieve higher levels of understanding. But by making visible what students thought, I was able to use their ideas to design subsequent instruction and thus encourage them to use historical evidence to question or support their ideas. The activities discussed above asked students to juxtapose their understanding against historical evidence or established historical accounts. The pedagogical moves were specifically historical; that is, in probing students' knowledge about a historical event, we went beyond just surveying what students knew or what they wanted to learn, a popular technique that begins many lessons (e.g., "Know-Want to know-Learned" charts). Rather, like historians, we used new evidence and other historical accounts to support, extend, or contest students' understanding. In establishing the unit problem, we created a place for students to consider the relationship among their own historical interpretations of the events, those of other historians, and historical evidence. Again, the three verbs I consistently asked students to use—"support," "extend," and "contest"—helped them situate historical interpretations and sources in relationship to their understanding.

Unit-level historical and instructional problems, then, emerged at the intersection of the essential course problems, the unit's specific curricular objectives, and students' understanding. Having formed historical problems and with sources now in hand, we might say that the students were doing history. However, we are cautioned by *How People Learn* and by scholarship on the challenges novices face in employing expert thinking to look beyond the trappings of the activity and consider the supports students may need to use the problems and resources effectively as they study history.

DESIGNING A "HISTORY-CONSIDERATE" LEARNING ENVIRONMENT: TOOLS FOR HISTORICAL THINKING

A central feature of learning, as *How People Learn* points out, involves students "engag[ing] in active processes as represented by the phrase 'to do.'"[14] The students in this case study were engaged in the active processes of history as they raised historiographic problems about accounts in general and the case of Columbus in particular, and in the subsequent use of historical sources to investigate those problems. In emphasizing the need to en-

BOX 4-3 Was There a Great Interruption in European Geographic Knowledge?

'Christian Europe did not carry on the work of [ancient thinkers such as] Ptolemy. Instead the leaders of orthodox Christendom built a grand barrier against the progress of knowledge about the earth. Christian geographers in the Middle Ages spent their energies embroidering a neat, theologically appealing picture of what was already known, or what was supposed to be known. . . .

It is easier to recount what happened than to explain satisfactorily how it happened or why. After the death of Ptolemy, Christianity conquered the Roman Empire and most of Europe. Then we observe a Europe-wide phenomenon of scholarly amnesia, which afflicted the continent from A.D. 300 to at least 1400. During those centuries Christian faith and dogma suppressed the useful image of the world that had been so slowly, so painfully, and so scrupulously drawn by ancient geographers. . . .

We have no lack of evidence of what the medieval Christian geographers thought. More than six hundred mappae mundi, maps of the world, survive from the Middle Ages. . . .

What was surprising was the Great Interruption. All people have wanted to believe themselves at the center. But after the accumulated advances of classical geography, it required amnesiac effort to ignore the growing mass of knowledge and retreat into a world of faith and caricature. . . . The Great Interruption of geography we are about to describe was a . . . remarkable act of retreat.'

Christian geography had become a cosmic enterprise, more interested in everyplace than in anyplace, more concerned with faith than with facts. Cosmos-makers confirmed Scripture with their graphics, but these were no use to a sea captain delivering a cargo of olive oil from Naples to Alexandria. . . .

SOURCE: Boorstin (1990, pp. 100, 102, 146).

gage students in the practices of the discipline, it is tempting to conclude that simply doing something that resembles a disciplinary activity is by itself educative and transformative. There is a danger, however, if teachers uncritically accept the historian's practices as their own and confuse doing history with doing history teaching.

History teachers, curriculum designers, and assessment architects need to be cautious when attempting to transplant activities from a community of history experts to a body of student novices. Historical tasks embedded

Dramatic to be sure, but entirely fictitious. There never was a period of "flat earth darkness" among scholars (regardless of how many uneducated people may have conceptualized our planet both then and now). Greek knowledge of sphericity never faded, and all major medieval scholars accepted the earth's roundness as an established fact of cosmology. Ferdinand and Isabella did refer Columbus's plans to a royal commission headed by Hernando de Talavera, Isabella's confessor and, following defeat of the Moors, Archbishop of Granada. This commission, composed of both clerical and lay advisers, did meet, at Salamanca among other places. They did pose some sharp intellectual objections to Columbus, but all assumed the earth's roundness. As a major critique, they argued that Columbus could not reach the Indies in his own allotted time, because the earth's circumference was too great. . . .

Virtually all major medieval scholars affirmed the earth's roundness. . . . The twelfth-century translations into Latin of many Greek and Arabic works greatly expanded general appreciation of natural sciences, particularly astronomy, among scholars, and convictions about the earth's sphericity both spread and strengthened. Roger Bacon (1220-1292) and Thomas Aquinas (1225-1274) affirmed roundness via Aristotle and his Arabic commentators, as did the greatest scientists of later medieval times, including John Buriden (1300-1358) and Nicholas Oresme (1320-1382).

SOURCE: Gould (1995, p. 42).

within an expert community draw meaning from the group's frames, scripts, and schemas. Experts differ from novices, as *How People Learn* explains, and this is an important point for history teachers to bear in mind. Students learning history do not yet share historians' assumptions. They think differently about text, sources, argument, significance, and the structure of historical knowledge.[15] The frames of meaning that sustained the disciplinary task within the community of historians will rarely exist within the classroom. Initially, students typically resist the transplanted activity, or the culture of the classroom assimilates the "authentic" activity, using it to sustain novices' naive or scholastic views. Engaging students in some legitimate disciplinary activity without restructuring the social interaction or challenging students' presuppositions will yield only ritualistic understanding. The problem for teachers is to design activities that will engage students in historical cognition without yielding to the assumption that disciplinary tasks mechanically develop students' higher functions.

As a classroom teacher, I was often caught in this paradox of trying to have my students work actively with history at the same time that I was trying to help them acquire the "unnatural" dispositions and habits of mind necessary to engage in history's intellectual work. Take, for example, the reading of primary sources—an intellectual activity that now appears to be synonymous with historical thinking in U.S. classrooms and on standardized exams. Using primary sources as historians do involves more than just finding information in sources; it requires that students pay attention to features within and outside of the text, such as who wrote the source, when was it created, in what circumstances and context, with what language, and for what reasons. Working with these questions in mind is challenging for high school students, a challenge not met merely by giving them the chance to use primary sources in grappling with a historical question.[16] Indeed, the opening activities discussed above demonstrated this point to me clearly, as only 2 of 55 asked for information about the authors in the authorless handouts I provided to frame the flat-earth problem. Though the students and I had established a good historiographic problem using competing sources, the students still needed support in doing more sophisticated reading and thinking.

The key word above is "support." As a history teacher, I wanted my students to engage in more complicated work than they could perform on their own. Believing, as Bruner [17] argues, that teachers can teach any subject to anybody at any age in some form that is honest, I found, even as a veteran history teacher, that putting historical work into honest and appropriate form for my students was an ongoing challenge. This was particularly true in classes where the learners developed history's cognitive skills at varying rates and to varying degrees—a characteristic of every class I ever taught, regardless of how small or how homogeneous. History teachers regularly face the dilemma of reducing the challenge of the historical tasks they ask students to tackle or simply moving on, leaving behind or frustrating a number of students. Instead of making such a choice, teachers can keep the intellectual work challenging for all their students by paying careful attention to the design and use of history-specific cognitive tools to help students work beyond their level of competence. The underlying idea is that with history-specific social assistance, history students can exhibit many more competencies than they could independently, and through history-specific social assistance, history's higher-order analytic approaches emerge and are subsequently internalized. Tharp and Gallimore[18] remind us that "until internalization occurs, *performance must be assisted.*" By attending to students' thinking and by embedding historians' disciplinary thinking into classroom artifacts and interactions, we can transform a class of novices into a community with shared, disciplinary expertise. Participating in such a community opens up opportunities for students to internalize the discipline's higher functions.

What do I mean by history-specific tools and social assistance? Here I refer to visual prompts, linguistic devices, discourse, and conceptual strategies that help students learn content, analyze sources, frame historical problems, corroborate evidence, determine significance, or build historical arguments. In short, these cognitive tools help students engage in sophisticated historical thinking. I demonstrated an example of a history-specific cognitive tool earlier in this chapter in my discussion of opening activities that helped students distinguish between history-as-event and history-as-account. In framing these distinctions as they emerged from students' experiences, we transcended these experiences by creating linguistic devices—H(ev) and H(ac)—that students used to explore the historical landscape. With guidance, students' experiences in the first few days of school produced a set of tools in the form of terms that they subsequently used to analyze historical events and sources. Later work on the flat-earth question revealed that students did not fully understand and were not regularly applying these distinctions on their own. In other words, they had not internalized these differences. However, the linguistic supports and my repeated reminders continued to help students use these distinctions in their studies. The special terms helped sharpen students' thinking in ways that the common use of the word "history" did not. With continued use, students began to employ the differences between the past and stories about the past more effectively and without prompting. Eventually, our need to refer to the constructed terms, H(ev) and H(ac), declined. Typically by the end of the first semester, though still regularly using the ideas behind the terms, we were using the terms only occasionally.

Reading of primary sources was another area in which specially created history-specific tools helped students engage in more sophisticated thinking. Here I established a group reading procedure to assist students in analyzing, contextualizing, sourcing, and corroborating historical material.[19] To create history-specific metacognitive tools, I tried to embed such thinking within our classroom interactions around reading primary and secondary sources. By modifying reciprocal teaching procedures[20] to reflect the strategies historians use when reading primary sources, I established reading procedures that enabled a group of students to read and question sources together in ways they did not on their own.[21]

The key here was a discipline-specific division of labor whereby I assigned each student or pair of students to "become" a particular type of historical question or questioner. For example, some students were assigned to ask "What other sources support or contest this source?" and thus became "corroborators"; others were assigned to ask about the creator of a source and thus became "sourcers." Within specific roles, students questioned classmates about the documents we were reading together, and so the discussion unfolded. Some students posed questions reflected in general reading strategies and asked classmates to identify confusing language, define difficult words, or summarize key points. However, the remaining roles/questions—e.g., corroborator, sourcer, contextualizer—were specific to the discipline of history, encouraging students to pose questions expert historians might ask. Using historians' strategies—such as corroborating, contextualizing, and sourcing—students asked their classmates questions about who created the source, its intended audience, the story line, what else they knew that supported what was in the source, and what else they knew that challenged what was in the source.

Thus, having equipped each student with a particular set of questions to ask classmates, we reread the accounts of Columbus and the flat earth (Box 4-1):

Teacher	Does anyone have any questions for their classmates about these sources? Let's begin with maybe a question about vocabulary or summaries, ok? Who wants to begin?
Chris	I guess I will. How would you summarize these stories?
Teacher	Do you want someone to summarize all the stories, all the excerpts? Or, maybe an aspect of the stories?
Chris	Ok, I guess just an aspect. What do you think these say about Columbus? Ellen?
Ellen	He is smart.
Chris	Anything else?
Ellen	Brave?
Aeysha	Chris' question has got me thinking about my questions. What do all of these stories say about the kind of person Columbus was? Do they have [some] agreement . . . with each other about him?
Teacher	Let's stop and think about this question and use our journals to write a "2-minute" essay

about what these tell us about the kind of person Columbus was.

The journal writing gave students time to work out an answer informally on paper before publicly talking about their ideas. After a few minutes of writing time, the students had worked out more-detailed pictures of Columbus as represented in the accounts. For example, Ellen wrote:

> *In these stories, Columbus appears to be smart. He is a real individual and pretty brave. Everyone else was just following the ideas of the day and he was a protester, a rebel against everyone else. These glorify him.*

After reading a few students' journal entries aloud, I asked whether anyone else had some questions to ask classmates about the sources:

Sarena	I do. Does anyone notice the years that these were written? About how old are these accounts? Andrew?
Andrew	They were written in 1889 and 1836. So some of them are about 112 years old and others are about 165 years old.
Teacher	Why did you ask, Sarena?
Sarena	I'm supposed to ask questions about when the source was written and who wrote it. So, I'm just doing my job.
Andrew	Actually, I was wondering if something was happening then that made Columbus and this story popular. Did historians discover something new about Columbus in the 1800s?
Rita	How do you know they were historians who wrote these?
Andrew	Because the title says "Historian's Accounts."
Rita	Yeah, but Washington Irving wrote about the headless horseman. Was he a historian? And he wrote stories for kids. Were these taken from books for young kids? Maybe that is why they tell such stories about Columbus, like he was some big hero?

As they asked questions, classmates returned to the documents, made journal entries, and discussed their answers. Thus, in this structured manner, the class raised multiple questions that guided everyone's reading and discussion of text. And students raised a number of questions that could not be answered from the sources in front of them. They offered conjectures and speculations that we would explore through later resources, including primary sources, secondary sources, textbooks, and lectures.

This reading activity was initially awkward and time-consuming with its role assignments, complex questioning, journaling, and discussion. It differed from cooperative activities whereby a group divides a historical topic, such as European exploration, and then researches a particular component of the topic, such as Spanish explorers or English explorers or natives' responses to exploration, before reporting to classmates what they have learned about their piece of the content. In this example, the division of labor occurred along the lines of thinking needed to read and analyze a historical text. The facets of the complex historical thinking—not merely the topical features—then defined and divided the students' intellectual work. By using these roles to read and then question each other, the students avoided their habit of treating historical text as they would other text, merely as a place to find "authoritative" information.

I used this structured reading and discussion activity because I did not initially expect individual students to be capable of performing a complete, complex historical analysis of a document or a document set. Paradoxically, however, from the beginning students needed to do such analysis to work on the historical and instructional tasks I assigned. Rather than lower disciplinary standards or allow novices merely to mimic experts, we used this reading strategy to enable students—as a group—to participate in this complex, disciplinary activity. Initially, the designed cognitive tools (e.g., group reading procedure) and the teacher carried most of the intellectual load that enabled students to participate in the activity.[22]

As *How People Learn* explains, history teachers need to design student-, content-, and assessment-centered learning environments to support students' historical study. In a sense, teachers work to build a history-specific culture that, through its patterns of interactions, instructional tasks, and artifacts, assists students in thinking historically (for more examples see Bain, 2000). In designing this environment, teachers try to make the key features of expert historical thought accessible for students to use as needed—during class discussion or while working in groups, at home, or on exams. "You're giving your students crutches," some teachers have told me, "and you should not let students use crutches." However, I like the analogy because I know few people who will use crutches unless they need them. Once able to get around without them, people cast the crutches aside. So it has been with the history-specific tools in my classroom. Once students have internalized the distinctions between "past" and "history" or the multiple strategies designed to help them read sources with more power, they find that our classroom supports slow them down or get in their way. When that happens, students stop using them. On the other hand, the supports remain available when students need assistance.

In such an environment, the lecture and textbook acquire new meaning. Given our focus on historical accounts, students start to use and see lectures and textbooks as examples of historical accounts. Students can apply the same sets of questions to the textbook and to my lectures that they do to other historical accounts and sources. For example, "How does this lecture support, expand, or contest what I already understand? What else corroborates this account? What shaped it?"

Also, we can reconsider texts and lectures as possible suports—history-specific cognitive tools—to help students think historically, and not just as vehicles to transmit information. Teachers can design and use lectures and textbooks strategically to help students frame or reframe historiographic problems; situate their work in larger contexts; see interpretations that might support, extend, or contest their emerging views; work more efficiently with contradictions within and among sources; and encounter explanations and sources that, because of time, availability, or skill, students would not be able to use. With help, students can learn to actively "read" lectures and textbooks, and then use both critically and effectively in their historical study.

For example, consider again the problem my students confronted once they began to allow the possibility that fifteenth-century Europeans might not have thought the earth was flat or that people had not always told that historical story. The students raised deep, rich, and complex historical questions:

> **Have the stories about Columbus changed since 1492? If so, in what ways did they change? What factors explain the shifting views about Columbus? Why did the story change? Does it matter which view or interpretation people hold about the story?**

The pride and excitement I derived from their questions was tempered by a recognition of how limited were our time and resources. Realistically, where would my students go to flesh out the contours of this historical problem and find the details to give it meaning? Would their textbook give the evidence needed to move forward? Had the primary sources I provided given students the material necessary to paint the larger historical picture, resolve their confusions, or answer their questions? The students needed help organizing their ideas, putting sources and evidence within a larger temporal context, understanding discrepant sources, and expanding both the facts and interpretations at hand. If my students were going to do more than ask powerful questions, they needed some assistance. In the midst of their historical inquiries appeared to be a perfect "time for telling."[23]

Therefore, I designed a lecture specifically to help students consider temporal shifts in the way people have regarded the Columbian story, questions that emerged after students had encountered discrepant accounts of the story. I saw this as a chance to revisit the unit's central problem and bring forward facts, concepts, ideas, and interpretations that might help students further their inquiries and develop their explanations. I began the lecture by asking students to write five dates in their journals—1592, 1692, 1792, 1892, and 1992—and then to predict how people living in the colonies and later in the United States marked the 100th, 200th, 300th, 400th, and 500th anniversary of the Columbian voyages. After the students had written their predictions in their journals and spent a few minutes talking about what they expected and why, I provided them with historical information about the changing and shifting nature of the Columbian story over the past 500 years.

For example, in 1592 and 1692, the European colonists and Native Americans made almost no acknowledgment of the centennial and bicentennial of the Columbian voyages. Indeed, there was little acknowledgment of Columbus as the "founder" of America. By 1792, however, the situation had changed, and a growing Columbian "sect" had emerged among former colonists and new citizens of the United States. People in the United States began to celebrate Columbus as the man who had "discovered" the new world. Columbia as a symbol took shape during this era, and people across the continent used one form of Columbus or another to name new cities and capitals. By 1892, the celebration of Columbianism was in full swing. King's College had changed its name to Columbia, and the U.S. Congress had funded the Columbian Exposition for the 1892 World's Fair. It was in the period between the third and fourth centennials that the flat earth became a key feature of the story, popularized in no small part by Washington Irving's 1830 biography of Columbus.[24]

Things had changed quite significantly by 1992. For example, in its exhibition to remember ("celebrate" and "commemorate" were contested words by 1992) the 500th anniversary of the Columbian voyages, the Smithsonian museum made no mention of "discovery," preferring to call its exhibit the "Columbian Exchange." Moreover, Columbus no longer held sway as an unquestioned hero, and many communities chose to focus on conquest and invasion in marking October 12, 1992. For example, the city council in Cleveland, Ohio, changed the name of Columbus Day to Indigenous People's Day. In crafting this lecture, I also selected supporting documents and texts as handouts. For example, I gave students longer sections from Washington Irving's *The Life and Voyages of Christopher Columbus*[25] or Kirkpatrick Sales' critical *Conquest of Paradise*[26] as examples of the different perspectives historians took in the nineteenth and twentieth centuries.

We treated the lecture as a secondary source, as a historical account constructed by the history teacher that other historians—i.e., history students—could use to investigate a historical problem. Consequently, at key points during the lecture, we stopped to employ our tools for thinking about historical accounts, asking, for example, "What are you hearing that supports, contests, or expands your thinking abut this issue?" The lecture did not answer exhaustively the larger questions concerning why certain accounts came into and out of fashion or why historians "changed their minds." But going well beyond the standard view of the lecture as a way to transmit information, this lecture provided needed intellectual support at a critical juncture to help students extend their historical understanding.

CONCLUSION

When my high school students began to study history, they tended to view the subject as a fixed entity, a body of facts that historians retrieved and placed in textbooks (or in the minds of history teachers) for students to memorize. The purpose of history, if it had one, was to somehow inoculate students from repeating past errors. The process of learning history was straightforward and, while not always exciting, relatively simple. Ironically, when I first entered a school to become a history teacher over 30 years ago, I held a similar view, often supported by my education and history courses—that teaching history was relatively straightforward and, while not always exciting, relatively simple. I no longer hold such innocent and naive views of learning or teaching history, and I try to disabuse my students of these views as well. Indeed, our experiences in my history classrooms have taught us that, to paraphrase Yogi Berra, it's not what we don't know that's the issue, it's what we know for sure that just isn't so. As this chapter has shown, learning and teaching history demands complex thinking by both teachers and students. It centers around interesting, generative, and organizing problems; critical weighing of evidence and accounts; suspension of our views to understand those of others; use of facts, concepts, and interpretations to make judgments; development of warrants for those judgments; and later, if the evidence persuades, changes in our views and judgments.

Helping students develop such historical literacy requires that history teachers expand their understanding of history learning, a task supported by the ideas found in *How People Learn* and the emerging scholarship on historical thinking. Such research paints a complex picture of learning that helps teachers rethink the connections among students' preinstructional ideas, curricular content, historical expertise, and pedagogy. This view of learning avoids the false dichotomies that have defined and hindered so many past attempts to improve history instruction. It helps teachers go beyond facile either–or choices to show that traditional methods, such as lectures, can be vital and engaging ways of helping students use historical facts and ideas and that, despite the enthusiasm hands-on activities generate, they do not automatically foster historical thinking. More important, this scholarship suggests ways teachers may transform both traditional and newer pedagogical methods to help deepen students' historical understanding. To borrow language from my case study, *How People Learn* expands and challenges our thinking about learning history, and thus assists teachers in marshaling the effort and understanding needed to enact a more sophisticated and effective historical pedagogy.

We should harbor no illusions about the challenges awaiting teachers and students engaged in such history instruction. Teaching the stories of the past while also teaching students how to read, criticize, and evaluate these stories is a complex task. It is difficult to help students recognize that all historical accounts, including those we hold, have a history. While encouraging students to recognize that all history involves interpretation, teachers must simultaneously challenge the easy conclusion that all interpretations are therefore equally compelling. Rather, historical literacy demands that students learn to evaluate arguments and decide which positions, given the evidence, are more or less plausible, better or worse. Historical study asks students to consider what they know, how they know it, and how confidently or tentatively they are "entitled" to hold their views.

It is equally important to remember the pleasures that such historical study can provide both teachers and students. Through history, teachers can fill the class with enduring human dramas and dilemmas, fascinating mysteries, and an amazing cast of historical characters involved in events that exemplify the best and worst of human experience. In what other field of study can students experience such a range of possibilities and get to know so many people and places? Where else would my students have the chance to encounter fifteenth-century Europeans and Native Americans, people from Christopher Columbus to Montezuma, and life in so many different societies and cultures?

Even this brief description of the difficulties and joys involved in learning history reveals why the study of history is so crucial and, therefore, worth our efforts. "History," historian Peter Stearns has written, "should be studied because it is essential to individuals and to society, and because it harbors beauty".[27] A disciplined study of history promotes exactly the type of reasoned thought our students deserve to have and democratic societies so desperately need.

ACKNOWLEDGMENTS

I want to thank Suzanne Wilson, Sam Wineburg, Jeff Mirel, Suzanne Donovan, John Bransford, and Kieran Egan for their thoughtful reading of this chapter. I benefited greatly from their generous support and valuable comments. Suzanne Wilson, in particular, provided me with timely and important criticism throughout the project. Greg Deegan and Bonnie Morosi also provided important help at an early stage in this work.

NOTES

1. Hall, 1883, p. vii.
2. Ibid, p. viii.
3. Wineburg, 2001.
4. Jonassen, 2000. Jonassen uses the word "mindtools" in relationship to computers and technological learning environments, seeing these as "intellectual partners with the learner in order to engage and facilitate critical thinking and higher learning." The tools I discuss in this chapter, while not electronic, serve as supports to help students engage in historical thinking, and thus fit the spirit of Jonassen's description.
5. Winks, 1969.
6. National Research Council, 1999, pp. 29-30; Levstik and Barton, 1997.
7. Collingwood, 1944.
8. Wineburg, 2001; Davis et al., 2001; Lowenthal, 1985; Shemilt, 1984.
9. McCullough, 2001; Ginzburg et al., 1980.
10. Lowenthal 1996, p. 116.
11. Initially, I gave these accounts to students without references to reinforce the need for attention to the content presented in the source. If no student asked for reference information, I provided it later. However, if a student requested this information, I gave that student the fully referenced handout shown in Box 4-1. When I taught this lesson recently, only 2 of 55 students asked about who had produced the accounts.
12. Bushman, 1992; Crosby, 1987; Russell, 1991; Sales, 1990; Schlereth, 1992.
13. Boorstin, 1990, p. 146.
14. National Research Council, 1999, p. 120.
15. Wineburg, 2001; Lee and Ashby, 2000; Leinhardt, 2000; Levstik, 2000; Barton, 1997; Seixas, 1994.
16. Wineburg, 2001.
17. Bruner, 1977.
18. Tharp and Gallimore, 1998, p. 20.
19. Wineburg, 2001.
20. Palinscar and Brown, 1984.
21. National Research Council, 1999, p. 55; Wineburg, 2001; Bain, 2000.
22. Cole, 1996.
23. Schwartz and Bransford, 1998.
24. Bushman, 1992; Crosby, 1987; Russell, 1991; Schlereth, 1992.
25. Irving, 1830.
26. Sales, 1990.
27. Stearns, 1998.

REFERENCES

Bain, R.B. (2000). Into the breach: Using research and theory to shape history instruction. In P. Seixas, P. Stearns, and S. Wineburg (Eds.), *Knowing, teaching and learning history: National and international perspectives* (pp. 331-353). New York: University Press.

Barton, K. (1997). "I just kinda know": Elementary students' ideas about historical evidence. *Theory and Research in Social Education, 25*(4), 407-430.

Boorstin, D.J. (1990). *The discoverers: A history of man's search to know his world and himself.* Birmingham, AL: Gryphon Editions.

Bruner, J. (1977). *The process of education.* Cambridge, MA: Harvard University Press.

Bushman, C.L. (1992). *America discovers Columbus: How an Italian explorer became an American hero.* Hanover, NH: University Press of New England.

Cole, M. (1996). *Cultural psychology: A once and future discipline.* Cambridge, MA: Belknap Press of Harvard University Press.

Collingwood, R.G. (1944). *An autobiography.* New York: Penguin Books.

Crosby, A.W. (1987). *The Columbian voyages, the Columbian exchange and their historians.* Washington, DC: American Historical Association.

Davis, O.L., Yeager, E.A. and Foster, S.J. (Eds.). (2001). *Historical empathy and perspective: Taking in the social studies.* Lanham, MD: Rowman & Littlefield.

Eggleston, E. (1904). *The new century history of the United States.* New York: American Book.

Ginzburg, C., Tedeschi, J.A., and Tedeschi, A. (1980). *The cheese and the worms: The cosmos of a sixteenth-century miller.* Baltimore: Johns Hopkins University Press.

Gould, S.J. (1995). *Dinosaur in a haystack: Reflections in natural history.* New York: Harmony Books.

Hall, G.S. (1883). Introduction. In G.S. Hall (Ed.), *Methods of teaching history* (pp. v-xii). Boston, MA: D.C. Heath.

Irving, W. (1830). *The life and voyages of Christopher Columbus.* New York: Burt.

Jonassen, D.H. (2000). *Computers as mindtools for schools: Engaging critical thinking,* 2nd ed. Upper Saddle River, NJ: Merrill.

Lee, P.J., and Ashby, R. (2000). Progression in historical understanding among students ages 7-14. In P. Seixas, P. Stearns, and S. Wineburg (Eds.), *Knowing, teaching and learning history: National and international perspectives* (pp. 199-222). New York: University Press.

Leinhardt, G. (2000). Lessons on teaching and learning history from Paul's pen. In P. Seixas, P. Stearns, and S. Wineburg (Eds.), *Knowing, teaching and learning history: National and international perspectives* (pp. 223-245). New York: University Press.

Levstik, L.S. (2000). Articulating the silences: Teachers' and adolescents' conceptions of historical significance. In P. Seixas, P. Stearns, and S. Wineburg (Eds.), *Knowing, teaching and learning history: National and international perspectives.* (pp. 284-305). New York: University Press.

Levstik, L.S., and Barton, K.C. (1997). *Doing history: Investigating with children in elementary and middle schools.* Mahwah, NJ: Lawrence Erlbaum Associates.

Lowenthal, D. (1985). *The past is a foreign country.* Cambridge, England: Cambridge University Press.

Lowenthal, D. (1996). *Possessed by the past: The heritage crusade and the spoils of history.* New York: Free Press.

McCullough, D.G. (2001). *John Adams.* New York: Simon and Schuster.

National Center for History in the Schools. (1996). *National standards for history.* C.A. Crabtree and G.B. Nash (Eds.). Los Angeles, CA: Author, University of California.

National Research Council. (1999). *How people learn: Brain, mind, experience, and school.* Committee on Developments in the Science of Learning. J.D. Bransford, A.L. Brown, and R.R. Cocking (Eds.). Commission on Behavioral and Social Sciences and Education. Washington, DC: National Academy Press.

Palinscar, A.S., and Brown, A.L. (1984). Reciprocal teaching of comprehension monitoring activities. *Cognition and Instruction, 1,* 117-175.

Patton, J.H., and Lord, J. (1903). The history and government of the United States. New York: The University Society.

Russell, J.B. (1997). *Inventing the flat earth: Columbus and modern historians.* New York: Praeger. (Original work in J. Johonnot [1887]. *Ten great events in history* [pp. 123-130]. New York: Appleton.)

Sagan, C. (1985). *Cosmos.* New York: Ballantine Books.

Sales, K. (1990). *The conquest of paradise: Christopher Columbus and the Columbian legacy.* New York: Knopf.

Schlereth, T.J. (1992). Columbia, Columbus, and Columbianism. *Journal of American History, 79*(3), 937-968.

Schwartz, D.L., and Bransford, J.D. (1998). A time for telling. *Cognition and Instruction, 16*(4), 475-522.

Seixas, P. (1994). Students' understanding of historical significance. *Theory and Research in Social Education, 22,* 281-304.

Shemilt, D. (1984). Beauty and the philosopher: Empathy in history and classroom. In A.K. Dickinson, P.J. Lee, and P.J. Rogers (Eds.), *Learning history* (pp. 39-84). London, England: Heinemann.

Stearns, P.N. (1998). *Why study history?* Available: http://www.theaha.org/pubs/stearns.htm [Accessed February 3, 2003].

Stearns, P.N., Seixas, P., and Wineburg, S. (Eds.). (2000). *Knowing, teaching and learning history: National and international perspectives.* New York: University Press.

Tharp, R.G., and Gallimore, R. (1998). *Rousing minds to life: Teaching, learning, and schooling in social context.* Cambridge, England: Cambridge University Press.

White, A.D. (1896). *A history of the warfare of science with theology in Christendom.* New York: Appleton.

Wineburg, S.S. (2001). *Historical thinking and other unnatural acts: Charting the future of teaching the past.* Philadelphia: Temple University Press.

Winks, R.W. (1969). *The historian as detective: Essays on evidence.* New York: Harper & Row.

A FINAL SYNTHESIS:
REVISITING THE THREE LEARNING PRINCIPLES

Pages 215-566 are not printed in this volume.
They are on the CD attached to the back cover.

13

Pulling Threads

M. Suzanne Donovan and John D. Bransford

What ties the chapters of this volume together are the three principles from *How People Learn* (set forth in Chapter 1) that each chapter takes as its point of departure. The collection of chapters in a sense serves as a demonstration of the second principle: that a solid foundation of detailed knowledge and clarity about the core concepts around which that knowledge is organized are both required to support effective learning. The three principles themselves are the core organizing concepts, and the chapter discussions that place them in information-rich contexts give those concepts greater meaning. After visiting multiple topics in history, math, and science, we are now poised to use those discussions to explore further the three principles of learning.

ENGAGING RESILIENT PRECONCEPTIONS

All of the chapters in this volume address common preconceptions that students bring to the topic of focus. Principle one from *How People Learn* suggests that those preconceptions must be engaged in the learning process, and the chapters suggest strategies for doing so. Those strategies can be grouped into three approaches that are likely to be applicable across a broad range of topics.

1. ***Draw on knowledge and experiences that students commonly bring to the classroom but are generally not activated with regard to the topic of study.***

This technique is employed by Lee, for example, in dealing with students' common conception that historical change happens as an *event.* He points out that students bring to history class the everyday experience of "nothing much happening" until an event changes things. Historians, on the other hand, generally think of change in terms of the *state of affairs.* Change in this sense may include, but is not equivalent to, the occurrence of events. Yet students have many experiences in which things change gradually—experiences in which "nothing happening" is, upon reflection, a mischaracterization. Lee suggests, as an example, students might be asked to "consider the change from a state of affairs in which a class does not trust a teacher to one in which it does. There may be no event that could be singled out as marking the change, just a long and gradual process."

There are many such experiences on which a teacher could draw, such as shifting alliances among friends or a gradual change in a sports team's status with an improvement in performance. Each of these experiences has characteristics that support the desired conception of history. Events are certainly not irrelevant. A teacher may do particular things that encourage trust, such as going to bat for a student who is in a difficult situation or postponing a quiz because students have two other tests on the same day. Similarly, there may be an incident in a group that changes the dynamic, such as a less popular member winning a valued prize or taking the blame for an incident to prevent the whole group from being punished. But in these contexts students can see, perhaps with some guided discussion, that single events are rarely the sole explanation for the state of affairs.

It is often the case that students have experiences that can support the conceptions we intend to teach, but instructional guidance is required to bring these experiences to the fore. These might be thought of as "recessive" experiences. In learning about rational number, for example, it is clear that whole-number reasoning—the subject of study in earlier grades—is dominant for most students (see Chapter 7). Yet students typically have experience with thinking about percents in the context of sale items in stores, grades in school, or loading of programs on a computer. Moss's approach to teaching rational number as described in Chapter 7 uses that knowledge of percents to which most students have easy access as an alternative path to learning rational number. She brings students' recessive understanding of proportion in the context of reasoning about percents to the fore and strengthens their knowledge and skill by creating multiple contexts in which proportional reasoning is employed (pipes and tubes, beakers, strings). As with events in history, students do later work with fractions, and that work at times presents them with problems that involve dividing a pizza or a pie into discrete parts—a problem in which whole-number reasoning often dominates. Because a facility with proportional reasoning is brought to bear, however, the division of a pie no longer leads students so easily into whole-number traps.

Moss reinforces proportional reasoning by having students play games in which fractions (such as $^1/_4$) must be lined up in order of size with decimals (such as .33) and percents (such as 40 percent). A theme that runs throughout the chapters of this volume, in fact, is that students need many opportunities to work with a new or recessive concept, especially when doing so requires that powerful preconceptions be overturned or modified.

Bain, for example, writes about students' tendency to see "history" and "the past" as the same thing: "No one should think that merely pointing out conceptual distinctions through a classroom activity equips students to make consistent, regular, and independent use of these distinctions. Students' habits of seeing history and the past as the same do not disappear overnight." Bain's equivalent of repeated comparisons of fractions, decimals, and percents is the ever-present question regarding descriptions and materials: is this "history-as-event"—the description of a past occurrence—or "history-as-account"—an explanation of a past occurrence. Supporting conceptual change in students requires repeated efforts to strengthen the new conception so that it becomes dominant.

2. Provide opportunities for students to experience discrepant events that allow them to come to terms with the shortcomings in their everyday models.

Relying on students' existing knowledge and experiences can be difficult in some instances because everyday experiences provide little if any opportunity to become familiar with the phenomenon of interest. This is often true in science, for example, where the subject of study may require specialized tools or controlled environmental conditions that students do not commonly encounter.

In the study of gravity, for example, students do not come to the classroom with experiences that easily support conceptual change because gravity is a constant in their world. Moreover, experiences they have with other forces often support misconceptions about gravity. For example, students can experience variation in friction because most have opportunities to walk or run an object over such surfaces as ice, polished wood, carpeting, and gravel. Likewise, movement in water or heavy winds provide experiences with resistance that many students can easily access. Minstrell found his students believed that these forces with which they had experience explained why they did not float off into space (see Chapter 11). Ideas about buoyancy and air pressure, generally not covered in units on gravity, influenced these students' thinking about gravity. Television images of astronauts floating in space reinforced for the students the idea that, without air to hold things down, they would simply float off.

Minstrell posed to his students a question that would draw out their thinking. He showed them a large frame from which a spring scale hung and placed an object on the scale that weighed 10 pounds. He then asked the students to consider a situation in which a large glass dome would be placed over the scale and all the air forced out with a vacuum pump. He asked the students to predict (imprecisely) what would happen to the scale reading. Half of Minstrell's students predicted that the scale reading would drop to zero without air; about a third thought there would be no effect at all on the scale reading; and the remainder thought there would be a small change. That students made a prediction and the predictions differed stimulated engagement. When the experiment was carried out, the ideas of many students were directly challenged by the results they observed.

In teaching evolution, Stewart and colleagues found that students' everyday observations led them to underestimate the amount of variation in common species. In such cases, student observations are not so much "wrong" as they are insufficiently refined. Scientists are more aware of variation because they engage in careful measurement and attend to differences at a level of detail not commonly noticed by the lay person. Stewart and colleagues had students count and sort sunflower seeds by their number of stripes as an easy route to a discrepant event of sorts. The students discovered there is far more variation among seeds than they had noticed. Unless students understand this point, it will be difficult for them to grasp that natural selection working on natural variation can support evolutionary change.

While discrepant events are perhaps used most commonly in science, Bain suggests they can be used productively in history as well (see Chapter 4). To dislodge the common belief that history is simply factual accounts of events, Bain asked students to predict how people living in the colonies (and later in the United States) would have marked the anniversary of Columbus's voyage 100 years after his landing in 1492 and then each hundred years after that through 1992. Students wrote their predictions in journals and were then given historical information about the changing Columbian story over the 500-year period. That information suggests that the first two anniversaries were not really marked at all, that the view of Columbus's "discovery of the new world" as important had emerged by 1792 among former colonists and new citizens of the United States, and that by 1992 the Smithsonian museum was making no mention of "discovery" but referred to its exhibit as the "Columbian Exchange." If students regard history as the reporting of facts, the question posed by Bain will lead them to think about *how* people might have celebrated Columbus's important discovery, and not *whether* people would have considered the voyage a cause for celebration at all. The discrepancy between students' expectation regarding the answer to the question and the historical accounts they are given in the classroom lecture cannot help but jar the conception that history books simply report events as they occurred in the past.

3. Provide students with narrative accounts of the discovery of (targeted) knowledge or the development of (targeted) tools.

What we teach in schools draws on our cultural heritage—a heritage of scientific discovery, mathematical invention, and historical reconstruction. Narrative accounts of how this work was done provide a window into change that can serve as a ready source of support for students who are being asked to undergo that very change themselves. How is it that the earth was discovered to be round when nothing we casually observe tells us that it is? What is place value anyway? Is it, like the round earth, a natural phenomenon that was discovered? Is it truth, like $e = mc^2$, to be unlocked? There was a time, of course, when everyday notions prevailed, or everyday problems required a solution. If students can witness major changes through narrative, they will be provided an opportunity to undergo conceptual change as well.

Stewart and colleagues describe the use of such an approach in teaching about evolution (see Chapter 12). Darwin's theory of natural selection operating on random variation can be difficult for students to grasp. The beliefs that all change represents an advance toward greater complexity and sophistication and that changes happen in response to use (the giraffe's neck stretching because it reaches for high leaves, for example) are widespread and resilient. And the scientific theory of evolution is challenged today, as it was in Darwin's time, by those who believe in intelligent design—that all organisms were made perfectly for their function by an intelligent creator. To allow students to differentiate among these views and understand why Darwin's theory is the one that is accepted scientifically, students work with three opposing theories as they were developed, supported, and argued in Darwin's day: William Paley's model of intelligent design, Jean Baptiste de Lamarck's model of acquired characteristics based on use, and Darwin's theory of natural selection. Students' own preconceptions are generally represented somewhere in the three theories. By considering in some depth the arguments made for each theory, the evidence that each theorist relied upon to support his argument, and finally the course of events that led to the scientific community's eventually embracing Darwin's theory, students have an opportunity to see their own ideas argued, challenged, and subjected to tests of evidence.

Every scientific theory has a history that can be used to the same end. And every scientific theory was formulated by particular people in particular circumstances. These people had hopes, fears, and passions that drove their work. Sometimes students can understand theories more readily if they learn about them in the context of those hopes, fears, and passions. A narrative that places theory in its human context need not sacrifice any of the technical material to be learned, but can make that material more engaging and meaningful for students.

The principle, of course, does not apply only to science and is not restricted to discovery. In mathematics, for example, while some patterns and relationships were discovered, conventions that form our system of counting were *invented.* As the mathematics chapters suggest, the use of mathematics with understanding—the engagement with problem solving and strategy use displayed by the best mathematics students—is undermined when students think of math as a rigid application of given algorithms to problems and look for surface hints as to which algorithm applies. If students can see the nature of the problems that mathematical conventions were designed to solve, their conceptions of what mathematics is can be influenced productively.

Historical accounts of the development of mathematical conventions may not always be available. For purposes of supporting conceptual change, however, fictional story telling may do just as well as history. In *Teaching as Story Telling,* Egan[1] relates a tale that can support students' understanding of place value:

A king wanted to count his army. He had five clueless counselors and one ingenious counselor. Each of the clueless five tried to work out a way of counting the soldiers, but came up with methods that were hopeless. One, for example, tried using tally sticks to make a count, but the soldiers kept moving around, and the count was confused. The ingenious counselor told the king to have the clueless counselors pick up ten pebbles each. He then had them stand behind a table that was set up where the army was to march past. In front of each clueless counselor a bowl was placed. The army then began to march past the end of the table.

As each soldier went by, the first counselor put one pebble into his bowl. Once he had put all ten pebbles into the bowl, he scooped them up and then continued to put one pebble down for each soldier marching by the table. He had a very busy afternoon, putting down his pebbles one by one and then scooping them up when all were in the bowl. Each time he scooped up the ten pebbles, the clueless counselor to his left put one pebble into her bowl [gender equity]. When her ten pebbles were in her bowl, she too scooped them out again, and continued to put one back into the bowl each time the clueless counselor to her right picked his up.

The clueless counselor to her left had to watch her through the afternoon, and he put one pebble into his bowl each time she picked

hers up. And so on for the remaining counselors. At the end of the afternoon, the counselor on the far left had only one pebble in his bowl, the next counselor had two, the next had seven, the next had six and the counselor at the other end of the table, where the soldiers had marched by, had three pebbles in his bowl. So we know that the army had 12,763 soldiers. The king was delighted that his ingenious counselor had counted the whole army with just fifty pebbles.[2]

When this story is used in elementary school classrooms, Egan encourages the teacher to follow up by having the students count the class or some other, more numerous objects using this method.

The story illustrates nicely for students how the place-value system allows the complex problem of counting large numbers to be made simpler. Place value is portrayed not as a truth but as an invention. Students can then change the base from 10 to other numbers to appreciate that base 10 is not a "truth" but a "choice." This activity supports students in understanding that what they are learning is designed to make number problems raised in the course of human activity manageable.

That imaginative stories can, if effectively designed, support conceptual change as well as historical accounts is worth noting for another reason: the fact that an historical account is an *account* might be viewed as cause for excluding it from a curriculum in which the nature of the account is not the subject of study. Historical accounts of Galileo, Newton, or Darwin written for elementary and secondary students can be contested. One would hope that students who study history will come to understand these as accounts, and that they will be presented to students as such. But the purpose of the accounts, in this case, is to allow students to experience a time when ideas that they themselves may hold were challenged and changed, and that purpose can be served even if the accounts are somewhat simplified and their contested aspects not treated fully.

ORGANIZING KNOWLEDGE AROUND CORE CONCEPTS

In the *Fish Is Fish* story discussed in Chapter 1, we understand quite easily that when the description of a human generates an image of an upright fish wearing clothing, there are some key missing concepts: adaptation, warm-blooded versus cold-blooded species, and the difference in mobility challenges in and out of water. How do we know which concepts are "core?" Is it always obvious?

The work of the chapter authors, as well as the committee/author discussions that supported the volume's development, provides numerous insights about the identification of core concepts. The first is observed most explicitly in the work of Peter Lee (see Chapter 2): that two distinct types of core concepts must be brought to the fore simultaneously. These are concepts about the nature of the discipline (what it means to engage in doing history, math, or science) and concepts that are central to the understanding of the subject matter (exploration of the new world, mathematical functions, or gravity). Lee refers to these as first-order (the discipline) and second-order (the subject) concepts. And he demonstrates very persuasively in his work that students bring preconceptions about the discipline that are just as powerful and difficult to change as those they bring about the specific subject matter.

For teachers, knowing the core concepts of the discipline itself—the standards of evidence, what constitutes proof and disproof, and modes of reasoning and engaging in inquiry—is clearly required. This requirement is undoubtedly at the root of arguments in support of teachers' course work in the discipline in which they will teach. But that course work will be a blunt instrument if it focuses only on second-order knowledge (of subject) but not on first-order knowledge (of the discipline). Clarity about the core concepts of the discipline is required if students are to grasp what the discipline—history, math, or science—is about.

For identifying both first- and second-order concepts, the obvious place to turn initially is to those with deep expertise in the discipline. The concepts that organize experts' knowledge, structure what they see, and guide their problem solving are clearly core. But in many cases, exploring expert knowledge directly will not be sufficient. Often experts have such facility with a concept that it does not even enter their consciousness. These "expert blind spots" require that "knowledge packages"[3]—sets of related concepts and skills that support expert knowledge—become a matter for study.

A striking example can be found in Chapter 7 on elementary mathematics. For those with expertise in mathematics, there may appear to be no "core concept" in whole-number counting because it is done so automatically. How one first masters that ability may not be accessible to those who did so long ago. Building on the work of numerous researchers on how children come to acquire whole-number knowledge, Griffin and Case's[4] research conducted over many years suggests a core conceptual structure that supports the development of the critical concept of *quantity*. Similar work has been done by Moss and Case[5] (on the core conceptual structure for rational number) and by Kalchman, Moss, and Case[6] (on the core conceptual structure for functions). The work of Case and his colleagues suggests the important role cognitive and developmental psychologists can play in extending understanding of the network of concepts that are "core" and might be framed in less detail by mathematicians (and other disciplinary experts).

The work of Stewart and his colleagues described in Chapter 12 is another case in which observations of student efforts to learn help reshape understanding of the package of related core concepts. The critical role of natural selection in understanding evolution would certainly be identified as a core concept by any expert in biology. But in the course of teaching about natural selection, these researchers' realization that students underestimated the variation in populations led them to recognize the importance of this concept that they had not previously identified as core. Again, experts in evolutionary biology may not identify population variation as an important concept because they understand and use the concept routinely—perhaps without conscious attention to it. Knowledge gleaned from classroom teaching, then, can be critical in defining the connected concepts that help support core understandings.

But just as concepts defined by disciplinary experts can be incomplete without the study of student thinking and learning, so, too, the concepts as defined by teachers can fall short if the mastery of disciplinary concepts is shallow. Liping Ma's study of teachers' understanding of the mathematics of subtraction with regrouping provides a compelling example. Some teachers had little conceptual understanding, emphasizing procedure only. But as Box 13-1 suggests, others attempted to provide conceptual understanding without adequate mastery of the core concepts themselves. Ma's work provides many examples (in the teaching of multidigit multiplication, division of fractions, and calculation of perimeter and area) in which efforts to teach for understanding without a solid grasp of disciplinary concepts falls short.

SUPPORTING METACOGNITION

A prominent feature of all of the chapters in this volume is the extent to which the teaching described emphasizes the development of metacognitive skills in students. Strengthening metacognitive skills, as discussed in Chapter 1, improves the performance of all students, but has a particularly large impact on students who are lower-achieving.[7]

Perhaps the most striking consistency in pedagogical approach across the chapters is the ample use of classroom discussion. At times students discuss in small groups and at times as a whole class; at times the teacher leads the discussion; and at times the students take responsibility for questioning. A primary goal of classroom discussion is that by observing and engaging in questioning, students become better at monitoring and questioning their own thinking.

In Chapter 5 by Fuson, Kalchman, and Bransford, for example, students solve problems on the board and then discuss alternative approaches to solving the same problem. The classroom dialogue, reproduced in Box 13-2, supports the kind of careful thinking about why a particular problem-solv-

BOX 13-1 Conceptual Explanation Without Conceptual Understanding

Liping Ma explored approaches to teaching subtraction with regrouping (problems like 52 – 25, in which subtraction of the 5 ones from the 2 ones requires that the number be regrouped). She found that some teachers took a very procedural approach that emphasized the order of the steps, while others emphasized the concept of composing a number (in this case into 5 tens and 2 ones) and decomposing a number (into 4 tens and 12 ones). Between these two approaches, however, were those of teachers whose intentions were to go beyond procedural teaching, but who did not themselves fully grasp the concepts at issue. Ma[8] describes one such teacher as follows:

> *Tr. Barry, another experienced teacher in the procedurally directed group, mentioned using manipulatives to get across the idea that "you need to borrow something." He said he would bring in quarters and let students change a quarter into two dimes and one nickel: "a good idea might be coins, using money because kids like money. . . . The idea of taking a quarter even, and changing it to two dimes and a nickel so you can borrow a dime, getting across that idea that you need to borrow something."*
>
> *There are two difficulties with this idea. First of all, the mathematical problem in Tr. Barry's representation was 25 – 10, which is not a subtraction with regrouping. Second, Tr. Barry confused borrowing in everyday life—borrowing a dime from a person who has a quarter—with the "borrowing" process in subtraction with regrouping—to regroup the minuend by rearranging within place values. In fact, Tr. Barry's manipulative would not convey any conceptual understanding of the mathematical topic he was supposed to teach.*

Another teacher who grasps the core concept comments on the idea of "borrowing" as follows:[9]

> *Some of my students may have learned from their parents that you "borrow one unit form the tens and regard it as 10 ones". . . . I will explain to them that we are not borrowing a 10, but decomposing a 10. "Borrowing" can't explain why you can take a 10 to the ones place. But "decomposing" can. When you say decomposing, it implies that the digits in higher places are actually composed of those at lower places. They are exchangeable . . . borrowing one unit and turning it into 10 sounds arbitrary. My students may ask me how can we borrow from the tens? If we borrow something, we should return it later on.*

ing strategy does or does not work, as well as the relative benefits of different strategies, that can support skilled mathematics performance.

Similarly, in the science chapters students typically work in groups, and the groups question each other and explain their reasoning. Box 13-3 reproduces a dialogue at the high school level that is a more sophisticated version of that among young mathematics students just described. One group of students explains to another not only what they concluded about the evolutionary purpose of different coloration, but also the thinking that led them to that conclusion and the background knowledge from an earlier example that supported their thinking. The practice of bringing other knowledge to bear in the reasoning process is at the heart of effective problem solving, but can be difficult to teach directly. It involves a search through one's mental files for what is relevant. If teachers simply give students the knowledge to incorporate, the practice and skill development of doing one's own mental search is shortchanged. Group work and discussions encourage students to engage actively in the mental search; they also provide examples from other students' thinking of different searches and search results. The monitoring of consistency between explanation and theory that we see in this group discussion (e.g., even if the male dies, the genes have already been passed along) is preparation for the kind of self-monitoring that biologists do routinely.

Having emphasized the benefits of classroom discussion, however, we offer two cautionary notes. First, the discussion cited in the chapters is *guided* by teachers to achieve the desired learning. Using classroom discussion well places a substantial burden on the teacher to support skilled discussion, respond flexibly to the direction the discussion is taking, and steer it productively. Guiding discussion can be a challenging instructional task. Not all questions are good ones, and the art of questioning requires learning on the part of both students and teachers.[10] Even at the high school level, Bain (see Chapter 4) notes the challenge a teacher faces in supporting good student questioning:

Sarena	Does anyone notice the years that these were written? About how old are these accounts? Andrew?
Andrew	They were written in 1889 and 1836. So some of them are about 112 years old and others are about 165 years old.
Teacher	Why did you ask, Sarena?
Sarena	I'm supposed to ask questions about when the source was written and who wrote it. So, I'm just doing my job.

BOX 13-2 Supporting Skilled Questioning and Explaining in Mathematics Problem Solving

In the dialogue below, young children are learning to explain their thinking and to ask questions of each other—skills that help students guide their own learning when those skills are eventually internalized as self-questioning and self-explaining.

Teacher	Maria, can you please explain to your friends in the class how you solved the problem?
Maria	Six is bigger than 4, so I can't subtract here [pointing] in the ones. So I have to get more ones. But I have to be fair when I get more ones, so I add ten to both my numbers. I add a ten here in the top [pointing] to change the 4 to a 14, and I add a ten here in the bottom in the tens place, so I write another ten by my 5. So now I count up from 6 to 14, and I get 8 ones (demonstrating by counting "6, 7, 8, 9, 10, 11, 12, 13, 14" while raising a finger for each word from 7 to 14). And I know my doubles, so 6 plus 6 is 12, so I have 6 tens left. [She thought, "1 + 5 = 6 and 6 + ? = 12 tens. Oh, I know 6 + 6 = 12, so my answer is 6 tens."]
Jorge	I don't see the other 6 in your tens. I only see one 6 in your answer.
Maria	The other 6 is from adding my 1 ten to the 5 tens to get 6 tens. I didn't write it down.
Andy	But you're changing the problem. How do you get the right answer?
Maria	If I make both numbers bigger by the same amount, the difference will stay the same. Remember we looked at that on drawings last week and on the meter stick.
Michelle	Why did you count up?

Palincsar[11] has documented the progress of students as they move beyond early, unskilled efforts at questioning. Initially, students often parrot the questions of a teacher regardless of their appropriateness or develop questions from a written text that repeat a line of the text verbatim, leaving a blank to be filled in. With experience, however, students become productive questioners, learning to attend to content and ask genuine questions.

Maria	Counting down is too hard, and my mother taught me to count up to subtract in first grade.
Teacher	How many of you remember how confused we were when we first saw Maria's method last week? Some of us could not figure out what she was doing even though Elena and Juan and Elba did it the same way. What did we do?
Rafael	We made drawings with our ten-sticks and dots to see what those numbers meant. And we figured out they were both tens. Even though the 5 looked like a 15, it was really just 6. And we went home to see if any of our parents could explain it to us, but we had to figure it out ourselves and it took us 2 days.
Teacher	Yes, I was asking other teachers, too. We worked on other methods too, but we kept trying to understand what this method was and why it worked. And Elena and Juan decided it was clearer if they crossed out the 5 and wrote a 6, but Elba and Maria liked to do it the way they learned at home. Any other questions or comments for Maria? No? Ok, Peter, can you explain your method?
Peter	Yes, I like to ungroup my top number when I don't have enough to subtract everywhere. So here I ungrouped 1 ten and gave it to the 4 ones to make 14 ones, so I had 1 ten left here. So 6 up to 10 is 4 and 4 more up to 14 is 8, so 14 minus 6 is 8 ones. And 5 tens up to 11 tens is 6 tens. So my answer is 68.
Carmen	How did you know it was 11 tens?
Peter	Because it is 1 hundred and 1 ten and that is 11 tens.

Similarly, students' answers often cannot serve the purpose of clarifying their thinking for classmates, teachers, or themselves without substantial support from teachers. The dialogue in Box 13-4 provides an example of a student becoming clearer about the meaning of what he observed as the teacher helped structure the articulation.

BOX 13-3 Questioning and Explaining in High School Science

The teacher passes out eight pages of case materials and asks the students to get to work. Each group receives a file folder containing the task description and information about the natural history of the ring-necked pheasant. There are color pictures that show adult males, adult females, and young. Some of the pages contain information about predators, mating behavior, and mating success. The three students spend the remainder of the period looking over and discussing various aspects of the case. By the middle of the period on Tuesday, this group is just finalizing their explanation when Casey, a member of another group, asks if she can talk to them.

Casey	**What have you guys come up with? Our group was wondering if we could talk over our ideas with you.**
Grace	**Sure, come over and we can each read our explanations.**

These two groups have very different explanations. Hillary's group is thinking that the males' bright coloration distracts predators from the nest, while Casey's group has decided that the bright coloration confers an advantage on the males by helping them attract more mates. A lively discussion ensues.

Ed	**But wait, I don't understand. How can dying be a good thing?**
Jerome	**Well, you have to think beyond just survival of the male himself. We think that the key is the survival of the kids. If the male can protect his**

Group work and group or classroom discussions have another potential pitfall that requires teacher attention: some students may dominate the discussion and the group decisions, while others may participate little if at all. Having a classmate take charge is no more effective at promoting metacognitive development—or supporting conceptual change—than having a teacher take charge. In either case, active engagement becomes unnecessary. One approach to tackling this problem is to have students rate their group effort in terms not only of their product, but also of their group dy-

	young and give them a better chance of surviving then he has an advantage.
Claire	Even if he dies doing it?
Grace	Yeah, because he will have already passed on his genes and stuff to his kids before he dies.
Casey	How did you come up with this? Did you see something in the packets that we didn't see?
Grace	One reason we thought of it had to do with the last case with the monarchs and viceroy.
Hillary	Yeah, we were thinking that the advantage isn't always obvious and sometimes what is good for the whole group might not seem like it is good for one bird or butterfly or whatever.
Jerome	We also looked at the data in our packets on the number of offspring fathered by brighter versus duller males. We saw that the brighter males had a longer bar.
Grace	See, look on page 5, right here.
Jerome	So they had more kids, right?
Casey	We saw that table too, but we thought that it could back up our idea that the brighter males were able to attract more females as mates.

The groups agree to disagree on their interpretation of this piece of data and continue to compare their explanations on other points. While it may take the involvement of a teacher to consider further merits of each explanation given the data, the students' group work and dialogue provide the opportunity for constructing, articulating, and questioning a scientific hypothesis.

namics.[12] Another approach, suggested by Bain (Chapter 4), is to have students pause during class discussion to think and write individually. As students discussed the kind of person Columbus was, Bain asked them to write a 2-minute essay before discussing further. Such an exercise ensures that students who do not engage in the public discussion nonetheless formulate their ideas.

Group work is certainly not the only approach to supporting the development of metacognitive skills. And given the potential hazard of group

BOX 13-4 Guiding Student Observation and Articulation

In an elementary classroom in which students were studying the behavior of light, one group of students observed that light could be both reflected and transmitted by a single object. But students needed considerable support from teachers to be able to articulate this observation in a way that was meaningful to them and to others in the class:

Ms. Lacey	I'm wondering. I know you have a lot of see-through things, a lot of reflect things. I'm wondering how you knew it was see-through.
Kevin	It would shine just, straight through it.
Ms. Lacey	What did you see happening?
Kevin	We saw light going through the . . .
Derek	Like if we put light . . .
Kevin	Wherever we tried the flashlight, like right here, it would show on the board.
Derek	And then I looked at the screen [in front of and to the side of the object], and then it showed a light on the screen. Then he said, come here, and look at the back. And I saw the back, and it had another [spot].
Ms. Lacey	Did you see anything else happening at the material?
Kevin	We saw sort of a little reflection, but we, it had mostly just see-through.
Derek	We put, on our paper we put reflect, but we had to decide which one to put it in. Because it had more of this than more of that.
Ms. Lacey	Oh. So you're saying that some materials . . .
Derek	Had more than others . . .

dynamics, using some individual approaches to supporting self-monitoring and evaluation may be important. For example, in two experiments with students using a cognitive tutor, Aleven and Koedinger[13] asked one group to explain the problem-solving steps to themselves as they worked. They found that students who were asked to self-explain outperformed those who spent the same amount of time on task but did not engage in self-explanation on transfer problems. This was true even though the common time limitation meant that the self-explainers solved fewer problems.

Ms. Lacey	. . . are doing, could be in two different categories.
Derek	Yeah, because some through were really reflection and see-through together, but we had to decide which.
	[Intervening discussion takes place about other data presented by this group that had to do with seeing light reflected or transmitted as a particular color, and how that color compared with the color of the object.]
	[at the end of this group's reporting, and after the students had been encouraged to identify several claims that their data supported among those that had been presented previously by other groups of students]
Ms. Lacey	There was something else I was kinda convinced of. And that was that light can do two different things. Didn't you tell me it went both see-through and reflected?
Kevin & Derek	Yeah. Mm-hmm.
Ms. Lacey	So do you think you might have another claim there?
Derek	Yeah.
Kevin	Light can do two things with one object.
Ms. Lacey	More than one thing?
Kevin	Yeah.
Ms. Lacey	Okay. What did you say?
Kevin & Derek	Light can do two things with one object.

See Chapter 10 for the context of this dialogue.

Another individual approach to supporting metacognition is suggested by Stewart (Chapter 12). Students record their thinking early in the treatment of a new topic and refer back to it at the unit's end to see how it has changed. This brings conscious attention to the change in a student's own thinking. Similarly, the reflective assessment aspect of the ThinkerTools curriculum described in Chapter 1 shifts students from group inquiry work to evaluating their group's inquiry individually. The results in the ThinkerTools case suggest that the combination of group work and individual reflective assessment is more powerful that the group work alone (see Box 9-5 in Chapter 9).

PRINCIPLES OF LEARNING AND CLASSROOM ENVIRONMENTS

The principles that shaped these chapters are based on efforts by researchers to uncover the rules of the learning game. Those rules as we understand them today do not tell us how to play the best instructional game. They can, however, point to the strengths and weakness of instructional strategies and the classroom environments that support those strategies. In Chapter 1, we describe effective classroom environments as learner-centered, knowledge-centered, assessment-centered, and community-centered. Each of these characteristics suggests a somewhat different focus. But at the same time they are interrelated, and the balance among them will help determine the effectiveness of instruction.

A community-centered classroom that relies extensively on classroom discussion, for example, can facilitate learning for several reasons (in addition to supporting metacognition as discussed above):

- It allows students' thinking to be made transparent—an outcome that is critical to a learner-centered classroom. Teachers can become familiar with student ideas—for example, the idea in Chapter 7 that two-thirds of a pie is about the same as three-fourths of a pie because both are missing one piece. Teachers can also monitor the change in those ideas with learning opportunities, the pace at which students are prepared to move, and the ideas that require further work—key features of an assessment-centered classroom.
- It requires that students explain their thinking to others. In the course of explanation, students develop a disposition toward productive interchange with others (community-centered) and develop their thinking more fully (learner-centered). In many of the examples of student discussion throughout this volume—for example, the discussion in Chapter 2 of students examining the role of Hitler in World War II—one sees individual students becoming clearer about their own thinking as the discussion develops.
- Conceptual change can be supported when students' thinking is challenged, as when one group points out a phenomenon that another group's model cannot explain (knowledge-centered). This happens, for example, in a dialogue in Chapter 12 when Delia explains to Scott that a flap might prevent more detergent from pouring out, but cannot explain why the amount of detergent would always be the same.

At the same time, emphasizing the benefits of classroom discussion in supporting effective learning does not imply that lectures cannot be excellent pedagogical devices. Who among us have not been witness to a lecture from which we have come away having learned something new and important? The Feynman lectures on introductory physics mentioned in Chapter 1, for example, are well designed to support learning. That design incorporates a strategy for accomplishing the learning goals described throughout this volume.[14] Feynman anticipates and addresses the points at which students' preconceptions may be a problem. Knowing that students will likely have had no experiences that support grasping the size of an atom, he spends time on this issue, using familiar references for relative size that allow students to envision just how tiny an atom is.

But to achieve effective learning by means of lectures alone places a major burden on the teacher to anticipate student thinking and address problems effectively. To be applied well, this approach is likely to require both a great deal of insight and much experience on the part of the teacher. Without such insight and experience, it will be difficult for teachers to anticipate the full range of conceptions students bring and the points at which they may stumble.[15] While one can see that Feynman made deliberate efforts to anticipate student misconceptions, he himself commented that the major difficulty in the lecture series was the lack of opportunity for student questions and discussion, so that he had no way of really knowing how effective the lectures were. In a learner-centered classroom, discussion is a powerful tool for eliciting and monitoring student thinking and learning.

In a knowledge-centered classroom, however, lectures can be an important accompaniment to classroom discussion—an efficient means of consolidating learning or presenting a set of concepts coherently. In Chapter 4, for example, Bain describes how, once students have spent some time working on competing accounts of the significance of Columbus's voyage and struggled with the question of how the anniversaries of the voyage were celebrated, he delivers a lecture that presents students with a description of current thinking on the topic among historians. At the point at which this lecture is delivered, student conceptions have already been elicited and explored. Because lectures can play an important role in instruction, we stress once again that the emphasis in this volume on the use of discussion to elicit students' thinking, monitor understanding, and support metacognitive development—all critical elements of effective teaching—should not be mistaken for a pedagogical recommendation of a single approach to instruction. Indeed, inquiry-based learning may fall short of its target of providing students with deep conceptual understanding if the teacher places the full burden of learning on the activities. As Box 1-3 in Chapter 1 suggests, a lecture that consolidates the lessons of an activity and places the activity in the conceptual framework of the discipline explicitly can play a critical role in supporting student understanding.

How the balance is struck in creating a classroom that functions as a learning community attentive to the learners' needs, the knowledge to be mastered, and assessments that support and guide instruction will certain vary from one teacher and classroom to the next. Our hope for this volume, then, is that its presentations of instructional approaches to addressing the key principles from *How People Learn* will support the efforts of teachers to play their own instructional game well. This volume is a first effort to elaborate those findings with regard to specific topics, but we hope it is the first of many such efforts. As teachers and researchers become more familiar with some common aspects of student thinking about a topic, their attention may begin to shift to other aspects that have previously attracted little notice. And as insights about one topic become commonplace, they may be applied to new topics.

Beyond extending the reach of the treatment of the learning principles of *How People Learn* within and across topics, we hope that efforts to incorporate those principles into teaching and learning will help strengthen and reshape our understanding of the rules of the learning game. With physics as his topic of concern, Feynman[16] talks about just such a process: "For a long time we will have a rule that works excellently in an overall way, even when we cannot follow the details, and then some time we may discover a *new rule*. From the point of view of basic physics, the most interesting phenomena are of course in the *new* places, the places where the rules do not work—not the places where they *do* work! That is the way in which we discover new rules."

We look forward to the opportunities created for the evolution of the science of learning and the professional practice of teaching as the principles of learning on which this volume focuses are incorporated into classroom teaching.

NOTES

1. Egan, 1986.
2. Story summarized by Kieran Egan, personal communication, March 7, 2003.
3. Liping Ma's work, described in Chapter 1, refers to the set of core concepts and the connected concepts and knowledge that support them as "knowledge packages."
4. Griffin and Case, 1995.
5. Moss and Case, 1999.
6. Kalchman et al., 2001.
7. Palincsar, 1986; White and Fredrickson, 1998.
8. Ma, 1999, p. 5.
9. Ma, 1999, p. 9.

10. Palincsar, 1986.
11. Palincsar, 1986.
12. National Research Council, 2005 (Stewart et al., 2005, Chapter 12).
13. Aleven and Koedinger, 2002.
14. For example, he highlights core concepts conspicuously. In his first lecture, he asks, "If, in some cataclysm, all of scientific knowledge were to be destroyed, and only one sentence passed on to the next generation of creatures, what statement would contain the most information in the fewest words? I believe it is the atomic hypothesis that all things are made of atoms—little particles that move around in perpetual motion, attracting each other when they are a little distance apart, but repelling upon being squeezed into one another.
15. Even with experience, the thinking of individual students may be unanticipated by the teacher.
16. Feynman, 1995, p. 25.

REFERENCES

Aleven, V., and Koedinger, K. (2002). An effective metacognitive strategy: Learning by doing and explaining with a computer-based cognitive tutor. *Cognitive Science, 26*, 147-179.

Egan, K. (1986). *Teaching as story telling: An alternative approach to teaching and curriculum in the elementary school* (vol. iii). Chicago, IL: University of Chicago Press.

Feynman, R.P. (1995). *Six easy pieces: Essentials of physics explained by its most brilliant teacher.* Reading, MA: Perseus Books.

Griffin, S., and Case, R. (1995). Re-thinking the primary school math curriculum: An approach based on cognitive science. *Issues in Education, 3*(1), 1-49.

Kalchman, M., Moss, J., and Case, R. (2001). Psychological models for the development of mathematical understanding: Rational numbers and functions. In S. Carver and D. Klahr (Eds.), *Cognition and instruction: Twenty-five years of progress* (pp. 1-38). Mahwah, NJ: Lawrence Erlbaum Associates.

Ma, L. (1999). *Knowing and teaching elementary mathematics.* Mahwah, NJ: Lawrence Erlbaum Associates.

Moss, J., and Case, R. (1999). Developing children's understanding of rational numbers: A new model and experimental curriculum. *Journal for Research in Mathematics Education, 30*(2).

Palincsar, A.S. (1986). *Reciprocal teaching: Teaching reading as thinking.* Oak Brook, IL: North Central Regional Educational Laboratory.

Stewart, J., Cartier, J.L., and Passmore, C.M. (2005). Developing understanding through model-based inquiry. In National Research Council, *How students learn: History, mathematics, and science in the classroom.* Committee on How People Learn, A Targeted Report for Teachers, M.S. Donovan and J.D. Bransford (Eds.). Division of Behavioral and Social Sciences and Education. Washington, DC: The National Academies Press.

White, B., and Fredrickson, J. (1998). Inquiry, modeling and metacognition: Making science accessible to all students. *Cognition and Instruction,* 6(1), 3-117.

OTHER RESOURCES

National Academy of Sciences. (1998). *Teaching about evolution and the nature of science.* Working Group on Teaching Evolution. Washington, DC: National Academy Press: Available: http://books.nap.edu/catalog/5787.html.

National Academy of Sciences. (2004). *Evolution in Hawaii: A supplement to teaching about evolution and the nature of science* by Steve Olson. Washington, DC: The National Academies Press. Available: http://www.nap.edu/books/0309089913/html/.

Biographical Sketches of Committee Members and Contributors

Rosalyn Ashby is a lecturer in education in the History in Education Unit in the School of Arts and Humanities in the University of London Institute of Education. Her work focuses on designing history curricula, assessment systems, and support materials for teachers. She now leads a history teacher-training course. Prior to becoming a university lecturer, Ashby taught history, politics and economics, and then worked as a history adviser with primary and secondary teachers. She has published numerous articles and book chapters, including many coauthored with Peter Lee regarding children's ideas about history. She is an editor of the *International Review of History Education*. She has a degree in American history and government from the University of Essex.

Robert B. Bain is assistant professor in the school of education at the University of Michigan. He teaches social studies education and investigates history education, the intersection between the disciplines and social studies instruction, and professional development. Previously, he spent more than 25 years as a high school history teacher. Among other publications, he has coauthored an article on professional development of elementary school teachers.

John D. Bransford (*Chair*) is James W. Mifflin university professor and professor of education at the University of Washington in Seattle. Previously, he was centennial professor of psychology and education and codirector of the Learning Technology Center at Vanderbilt University. Early work by Bransford and his colleagues in the 1970s included research in the areas of human learning and memory and problem solving; this research helped shape the "cognitive revolution" in psychology. An author of seven books and hundreds of articles and presentations, Bransford's work focuses on the areas of cognition and technology. He served as cochair of the National Research Council (NRC) committee that authored *How People Learn: Brain, Mind, Experience, and School.* He received a Ph.D. in cognitive psychology from the University of Minnesota.

Susan Carey is a professor of psychology at Harvard University. Carey's research concerns the evolutionary and ontogenetic origins of human knowledge in a variety of domains, including number, lexical semantics, physical reasoning, and reasoning about intentional states. She studies conceptual change involving older children, and focuses on three domains of knowledge: number, intuitive biology, and intuitive physics. She received a Ph.D. from Harvard University.

Jennifer L. Cartier is an assistant professor in the Department of Instruction and Learning at the University of Pittsburgh. Her research interests include student learning in classrooms where modeling is a focus and teacher education—particularly the ways in which hands-on curriculum materials can be implemented to engage elementary school students in realistic scientific practices. She has published articles describing students' reasoning in genetics in *Science and Education* and *BioQUEST Notes* and she has coauthored a book chapter describing the use of black-box activities to introduce students to aspects of scientific argumentation.

M. Suzanne Donovan (*Study Director*) is also director of the NRC's Strategic Education Research Partnership (SERP) and coeditor of the project's two reports, *Strategic Education Research Partnership* and *Learning and Instruction: A SERP Research Agenda.* At the NRC, she served as director of the previous study that produced *How People Learn: Bridging Research and Practice,* and she was coeditor for the NRC reports *Minority Students in Special and Gifted Education* and *Eager to Learn: Educating Our Preschoolers.* Previously, she was on the faculty of Columbia University. She has a Ph.D. in public policy from the University of California at Berkeley.

Kieran Egan is a professor in the Faculty of Education at Simon Fraser University in Burnaby, Canada. Dr. Egan was the 1991 winner of the Grawemeyer Award in Education for his analyses of children's imaginations. His recent books include *The Educated Mind: How Cognitive Tools Shape Our Understanding* (University of Chicago Press) and *Getting It Wrong from the Beginning: Our Progressivist Inheritance from Herbert Spencer, John Dewey, and Jean Piaget* (Yale University Press).

Karen C. Fuson is a professor emeritus in the School of Education and Social Policy and in the Psychology Department at Northwestern University. After teaching high school mathematics to Chicago inner-city African-American students for 3 years, she began research to ascertain how to help all students enter high school with more knowledge of mathematics. She has conducted extensive research regarding children's learning of mathematical concepts from ages 2 through 12, focusing in on the development of effective teaching and learning materials, including the "Children's Math World's K through 5" curriculum, supporting effective learning for children from various backgrounds, and ambitious accessible learning paths through school mathematics. Fuson was a member of the NRC committee that authored *Adding It Up: Helping Children Learn Mathematics.*

Sharon Griffin is an associate professor of education and an adjunct associate professor of psychology at Clark University. She is coauthor of "Number Worlds," a research-based mathematics program for young children, coauthor of *What Develops in Emotional Development?* (Plenum), and author of several articles on cognitive development and mathematics education. For the past 10 years, she has sought to improve mathematics learning and achievement for young children by developing and evaluating programs to "provide the central conceptual prerequisites for success in school math to children at risk for school failure." Griffin is currently participating in an advisory capacity on national projects, in Canada and the United States, to enhance the cognitive, mathematical, and language development of "high-need" preschool children, from birth to 5 years.

Mindy Kalchman is an assistant professor in the School of Education at DePaul University. Her research interests include children's learning of mathematics, theory-based curriculum design, and the effect of discoveries from the field of developmental cognitive psychology on classroom practice. She has coauthored numerous articles regarding mathematics education and curriculum and has conducted workshops on how to teach functions. Kalchman also served as a consulting content editor for the development of the Ontario mathematics curriculum for grades 9–12. She received her Ph.D. from the Ontario Institute for Studies in Education, University of Toronto.

Kenneth R. Koedinger is an associate professor in the Human Computer Interaction Institute and Psychology Department at Carnegie Mellon University. His research interests include cognitive modeling, problem solving and learning, intelligent tutoring systems, and educational technology. Earlier in his career, Koedinger was a teacher in an urban high school. He has developed computer simulations of student thinking that are used to guide the construction of educational materials and are the core of intelligent software systems that provide students with individualized interactive learning assistance. He has developed such "cognitive tutors" for mathematics that are now in use in over 1700 schools.

Pamela Kraus is a research scientist and cofounder of FACET Innovations. She is currently working on the Diagnoser projects and related professional development projects and she is helping conduct the research and organize the facet clusters in the physical sciences. In addition, Kraus works closely with the resource teachers from across the state as they produce assessment tools. She received a Ph.D. from the University of Washington.

Peter J. Lee is a senior lecturer in education in the History Education Unit of the School of Arts and Humanities at the Institute of Education of The University of London. Previously, he taught history in primary and secondary schools. Lee has directed several research and curriculum development projects (the latter with Denis Shemilt). He has edited five books on history education, and published numerous chapters and articles exploring children's ideas about history, many of them coauthored with Rosalyn Ashby. He is an editor of the *International Review of History Education.* He received a history degree at Oxford University.

Shirley J. Magnusson is the Cotchett Professor of Science and Mathematics Teacher Education at the California Polytechnic State University. She has taught science to students at the elementary, middle school, high school, and college levels since 1980. She joined the faculty at the University of Michigan in 1991 as a science teacher educator, specializing in learning and instruction in science at the elementary school level. She collaborated with Annemarie Palincsar on a program of research that has sought to define and study the outcomes from an approach to inquiry-based science instruction known as Guided Inquiry supporting Multiple Literacies (GIsML). Publications of Magnusson's work have appeared in the *Journal of the Learning Sciences, Teaching and Teacher Education,* the *Journal of Science Education and Technology,* and *Learning Disabilities Quarterly,* as well as a number of books such as *Science Teacher Knowledge, Cognition and Instruction: Twenty-five Years of Progress,* and *Translating Educational Theory into Practice.*

James Minstrell is cofounder and research scientist at FACET Innovations, LLC. This position followed a lengthy career as a science and mathematics teacher and classroom researcher in the learning of physical science and mathematics. He received the Presidential Award for Excellence in Science and Mathematics Teaching from the National Science Foundation. Minstrell served on the U.S. Department of Education's Expert Panel on Science and

Mathematics Education. He has published numerous articles, with a major focus on understanding of mathematics and physics.

Joan Moss is an assistant professor in the Department of Human Development and Applied Psychology at the Ontario Institute for Studies in Education at the University of Toronto. Previously she worked as a master teacher at the Institute of Child Study Laboratory School. Her research interests include children's development and understanding of rational numbers and proportional reasoning. More recently, Moss has been working on classroom-based studies of children's development of algebraic thinking. Her work in professional development includes preservice training, as well as coordination of learning opportunities with novice elementary school mathematics teachers using a Japanese lesson study approach. She has published widely and is an author of a mathematics textbook series. Moss carried out postdoctoral research at the University of California at Berkeley.

Annemarie Sullivan Palincsar is the Jean and Charles Walgreen professor of reading and literacy at the University of Michigan's School of Education. She has conduced extensive research on peer collaboration in problem-solving activity, instruction to promote self-regulation, acquisition and instruction of literacy with primary students at risk for academic difficulty, and how children use literacy in the context of guided inquiry experiences. She was a member of the NRC committees that produced the reports *How People Learn: Bridging Research and Practice,* and *Preventing Reading Difficulties in young Children*. Palincsar is currently coeditor of *Cognition and Instruction*.

Cynthia M. Passmore is an assistant professor in the School of Education at the University of California, Davis. She specializes in science education and is particularly interested in student learning and reasoning about scientific models. Her research also focuses on preservice and in-service teacher professional development. She teaches the science methods courses for single and multiple subjects credential candidates, as well as graduate courses in science education. Earlier in her career she worked as a high school science teacher in East Africa, Southern California, and Wisconsin.

Denis Shemilt has worked at the University of Leeds for more than 25 years, where he has been evaluator of the Schools History Project 13-16, and codirector of the Cambridge History Project. Until recently, he was head of the School of Education at Trinity and All Saints, a constituent college of the university, devoting time to educational management at the expense of real work. He is now focusing on training history teachers and pursuing a long-postponed interest in the development of students' historical frameworks.

He has published numerous contributions to history education, including the *History 13-16 Evaluation Study* and papers on students' ideas about change, evidence, and empathy in history. He received a degree in education from the University of Manchester.

James Stewart is a professor in the School of Education's Department of Curriculum and Instruction at the University of Wisconsin-Madison. His research interests include student understanding, reasoning, and problem solving in science, particularly in the biological sciences. Stewart's recent publications include articles on student understanding in genetics and evolutionary biology in *Science Education* and the *Journal of Research in Science Teaching* and a book chapter, "Teaching Science in a Multicultural Perspective."

Suzanne M. Wilson is a professor in the Department of Teacher Education and director of the Center for the Scholarship of Teaching at Michigan State University. She was a history and mathematics teacher for 6 years; directed the Teacher Assessment Project at Stanford University; taught third-grade social studies in a professional development school; and has directed several research projects exploring the relationship of teachers' practice to curriculum mandates. Wilson teaches prospective and practicing teachers, as well as prospective teacher educators and researchers.

Samuel S. Wineburg is professor of education at Stanford University, where he directs the Ph.D. program in History Education. His research explores the development of historical thinking among adolescents and the nature of historical consciousness. Wineburg's book, *Historical Thinking and Other Unnatural Acts: Charting the Future and Past,* was awarded the 2002 Frederic W. Ness Prize for the "most important contribution to the understanding and improvement of liberal education" by the Association of American Colleges and Universities. He was a member of the NRC committee that wrote *How People Learn: Brain, Mind, Experience, and School.* He received his Ph.D. from Stanford University.

Index

This index includes the text of the full version of *How Students Learn: History, Mathematics, and Science*, which can be found on the CD attached to the back cover.

A

B

C

D

E

H

J

K

L

N

O

Q

R

S

T

U

V

W

Y

How Students Learn

HISTORY IN THE CLASSROOM

Committee on *How People Learn*, A Targeted Report for Teachers

M. Suzanne Donovan and John D. Bransford, *Editors*

Division of Behavioral and Social Sciences and Education

NATIONAL RESEARCH COUNCIL
OF THE NATIONAL ACADEMIES

THE NATIONAL ACADEMIES PRESS
Washington, D.C.
www.nap.edu

THE NATIONAL ACADEMIES PRESS • 500 Fifth Street, N.W. • Washington, D.C. 20001

NOTICE: The project that is the subject of this report was approved by the Governing Board of the National Research Council, whose members are drawn from the councils of the National Academy of Sciences, the National Academy of Engineering, and the Institute of Medicine. The members of the committee responsible for the report were chosen for their special competences and with regard for appropriate balance.

This study was supported by Award No. R215U990024 between the National Academy of Sciences and the U.S. Department of Education. Any opinions, findings, conclusions, or recommendations expressed in this publication are those of the author(s) and do not necessarily reflect the views of the organizations or agencies that provided support for the project.

Library of Congress Cataloging-in-Publication Data

National Research Council (U.S.). Committee on How People Learn, A Targeted Report for Teachers.
How students learn : history, mathematics, and science in the classroom / Committee on How People Learn, A Targeted Report for Teachers ; M. Suzanne Donovan and John D. Bransford, editors.
p. cm.
"Division of Behavioral and Social Sciences and Education."
Includes bibliographical references and index.
ISBN 0-309-07433-9 (hardcover) — ISBN 0-309-08948-4 (pbk.) — ISBN 0-309-08949-2 (pbk.) — ISBN 0-309-08950-6 (pbk.) 1. Learning. 2. Classroom management. 3. Curriculum planning. I. Donovan, Suzanne. II. Bransford, John. III. Title.
LB1060.N38 2005
370.15′23—dc22

2004026246

Additional copies of this report are available from the National Academies Press, 500 Fifth Street, N.W., Lockbox 285, Washington, DC 20055; (800) 624-6242 or (202) 334-3313 (in the Washington metropolitan area); Internet, http://www.nap.edu

Printed in the United States of America.

Suggested citation: National Research Council. (2005). *How Students Learn: History in the Classroom*. Committee on *How People Learn*, A Targeted Report for Teachers, M.S. Donovan and J.D. Bransford, Editors. Division of Behavioral and Social Sciences and Education. Washington, DC: The National Academies Press.